The ROCK & WATER GARDEN EXPERT

Dr. D.G. Hessayon

First published in Great Britain
by pbi Publications 1993

All Editions & Reprints: 435,000 copies

This Edition published 1996
by Expert Books
a division of Transworld Publishers Ltd

Copyright © Dr.D.G.Hessayon 1993, 1996

The right of Dr.D.G.Hessayon to be identified
as author of this work has been asserted in accordance
with sections 77 and 78 of the Copyright Designs and
Patents Act 1988.

A catalogue record for this book is available from the British Library

TRANSWORLD PUBLISHERS LTD
61–63 Uxbridge Road, London W5 5SA

Distributed in the United States
by Sterling Publishing Co. Inc.,
387 Park Avenue South,
New York, NY 10016–8810

Distributed in Canada by
Cavendish Books Inc.,
Unit 5, 801 West 1st Street,
North Vancouver, B.C. V7P 1A4

EXPERT BOOKS

Contents

Neither the Publishers nor the Author can accept liability for the use of any of the materials or methods recommended in this book or for any consequences arising out of their use, nor can they be held responsible for any errors or omissions that may be found in the text or may occur at a future date as a result of changes in rules, laws or equipment.

Printed and bound in Great Britain by Jarrold & Sons Ltd, Norwich

ISBN 0 903505 38 X © D. G. HESSAYON 1996

CHAPTER 1

LOOKING AT ROCK GARDENS

Both rock and water were old-established garden features before anyone dreamt of having lawns, beds or borders. Thousands of years ago the first Japanese garden was nothing more than an expanse of white stone chippings with a single Cleyera tree at the centre, and the Ancient Persian 'paradise' had a long canal and fountains at its heart.

The attraction is easy to understand — these two elements bring a natural feel to the surroundings. Until fairly recently, however, they were primarily the preserve of the wealthy. Before the latter part of the 19th century rocks were used to create bold structures in large estates and it was not until the middle of the 20th century that pond and fountain construction became simple and economical enough for the ordinary gardener.

It has taken a long time, but both rock and water gardening have at last come of age. There is now enormous popular interest in all aspects of the water garden, and rock garden plants are grown in great numbers and variety these days in both rockeries and rock-free situations. It is interesting that both these natural elements have several features in common. They can extend for a few square feet or more than a quarter of an acre, and both provide the opportunity to grow a range of plants not found in the ordinary garden. The drawbacks they share are that careful planning and preparation are required and an appreciable amount of labour and money is necessary for their creation. The purpose of this book is to introduce the world of rock and water gardening to the ordinary gardener rather than to serve as a text-book for the experienced specialist.

The first section is devoted to the use of rock garden plants, popularly referred to as 'alpines'. There have been three periods in the history of the rock garden and its place in Britain. This history has been surprisingly short.

The first period was a time to show off the rocks and the term **Rockwork** is used in this book to describe such a structure. It began in the middle of the 18th century with the building of the first grottoes, and then in Victorian times there was the grouping of massive rocks in some of our Grand Gardens. The giant millstone grit boulders at Chatsworth are an outstanding example. Apart from some ferns and evergreens there was little planting amongst these stones. By the latter part of the 19th century the age of the large rockwork was over.

In 1772 the second period of this history began — a garden of rubble and Icelandic basaltic lava was created in a greenhouse at Chelsea Physic Garden for the cultivation of plants collected from the Swiss Alps. Here the rocks were used as a home for plants rather than to provide just an ornamental feature, and the term **Rock Garden** is used in this book to describe such a structure. This second period got off to a slow start, although rock gardens were created at various sites in Britain and the idea of laying stones to give the appearance of a natural outcrop was developed. Things changed in the 1860s and the rock garden at last took its place as an important part of the British garden. Rockeries were built at Kew in 1867 and in Edinburgh in 1871, and in 1870 William Robinson's *Alpine Flowers for English Gardens* was published. During this period and into the early 20th century Pulhamite 'Stone' was manufactured in Broxbourne in Hertfordshire and used to create public and private rock gardens throughout the country.

The three decades from 1900 to 1930 were the heyday of the rock garden. Reginald Farrer was the leading figure and his *My Rock Garden* became the first 'bible' on the subject. Plant hunters scoured the mountains of the world for new alpines and the rock garden at Wisley was started in 1911. In the years immediately prior to World War II interest in the rock garden declined, and only recently has there been a resurgence.

During the 1920s and 1930s the idea of growing alpines in non-rock situations took root, and this coupled with the appearance of the garden centre in the second half of the 20th century brought about the third period in this history. People began to see the full range of plants which was available and all sorts of easy and inexpensive ways appeared for cultivating alpines without having to build a rockery. So interest switched to the plants and away from rock structures, and this is the key feature of this third period in the history of rock gardening. The term **Rock Garden Plants** is used in this book to describe the species and varieties involved.

CHAPTER 2
USING ROCK GARDEN PLANTS

Rock garden plants are a motley collection of species and varieties which includes alpines — see page 10 for details. Their traditional home is the rock garden or rockery — these terms are interchangeable. Here the plants look at home and the planting sites can be adapted to suit the needs of individual specimens. But the rock garden is not for everyone — it takes time, trouble and money to build and needs to be at least 8 ft x 4 ft to be really worthwhile.

Where space and resources are limited you can still enjoy rock garden plants by growing some of the carpeting varieties in cracks between paving stones or at the front of a mixed border. A flat bed with a gentle slope can be turned into a scree garden, and a patio can be graced with an alpine-filled trough.

A popular alternative to the rock garden these days is the raised bed. Easy to build and maintain, it is suitable for a wide range of rock garden plants. Its walls can be planted, or a special dry-stone wall may be constructed.

Some of the plants in this book require the humus-rich conditions of their woodland home, and here a peat bed is the ideal environment. Others need winter protection and an alpine house is the answer for the enthusiast.

Rockery Stones

Westmorland Stone

Mendip

Purbeck

Gloucester Red

BASIC RULES
- Don't steal stones from the countryside.
- Don't use broken concrete or pieces of reconstituted stone as a substitute.
- Use the same sort of stone for the whole of the rock garden.
- Buy stones from a local quarry if you can. Otherwise look up 'Stone Merchants' in Yellow Pages and ask for samples and quotes. Visit and select your own stones if possible.
- Choose a range of sizes in the ¼–2 cwt range — pick weathered pieces.
- Be on site when the stone is delivered.
- A 10 ft x 5 ft rock garden will require 1–2 tons of stone.

LIMESTONE
The great advantage of this type of stone is that it readily weathers, so the surface loses its sharp edges and both lichens and mosses soon appear. The drawback is that lime-hating plants may suffer. The colour is often (but not always) grey. The most popular type is weathered **Westmorland Stone** — white or grey and seen in rockeries everywhere. Not a good choice these days as its extraction damages environmentally-important sites — buy second-hand stones. Other grey Limestones include **Derby** and **Forest of Dean** — **Mendip** is bluish or golden. The cream-coloured ones (**Cotswold** and **Purbeck**) tend to split into plates.

SANDSTONE
The advantages here are that a number of attractive colours are available and there is generally a mellow appearance with a bold grain. Weathering usually takes a long time — the exception here is **Sussex Limestone** which loses its angular bits quite quickly and is popular in the South of England. Creamy-grey **Kentish Ragstone** is another type which is often found in southern rockeries. **Millstone Grit** is a good choice if you want a sand-coloured rockery — it is very coarse without obvious strata. For a brick-coloured rock garden choose **Gloucester Red** or **Monmouth Red**. **York Stone** is a poor choice — it is very hard and often splits into plates.

GRANITE
A very hard and fine-grained stone. It is not porous and weathers very slowly. Not a good choice.

SLATE
An attractive stone in shades of grey, green or purple. It is sharply cornered at first but weathers in time.

TUFA
A form of limestone which is porous and contains plant remains. The outstanding advantages are its lightness (half the weight of ordinary limestone) and its ability to support plant growth. See page 8.

York Stone

Granite

Slate

Tufa

The 11 Homes for Rock Garden Plants

ROCK GARDEN

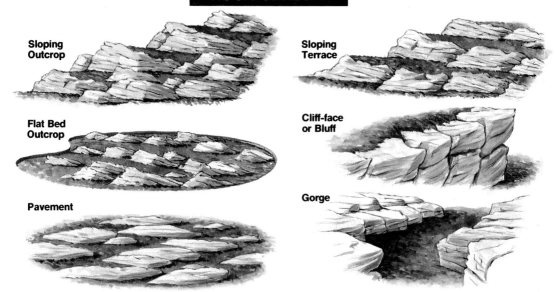

Sloping Outcrop

Sloping Terrace

Flat Bed Outcrop

Cliff-face or Bluff

Pavement

Gorge

Building a Rock Garden

1 **PLAN CAREFULLY** Careful planning is essential before you begin. Remember that the aim is to produce a rock garden which looks as natural as possible — avoid at all costs scattering stones at random over a flat bed. Choose one of the basic designs shown above — as a general rule a sloping rock garden is more attractive than a level one. The chosen site should be free from shade for most of the day — a background of trees and shrubs will improve the 'natural' feel, but trees must be far enough away to have no harmful effect on the plants. Visit a good rock garden or two to see how an outcrop or terraced rockery should look. Draw a rough sketch, but a detailed plan is impossible. Mark out an area with string which is slightly larger than the planned rock garden.

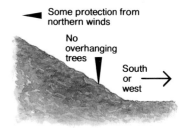

Some protection from northern winds

No overhanging trees

South or west

2 **PREPARE THE SITE** Choose a day when the soil is reasonably dry. Strip off turf if present and remove perennial weeds. This weed removal is absolutely vital as couch, bindweed etc can ruin a rock garden. Dig out the roots — if the site is badly infested you will have to use an appropriate weedkiller such as glyphosate and leave the site unplanted for the period recommended on the label. Good drainage is another vital need. With a sloping site in a non-clayey area no extra preparation will be required, but if the subsoil is heavy then a drainage layer will be necessary as shown on the right.

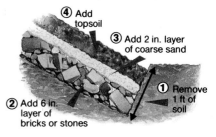

④ Add topsoil

③ Add 2 in. layer of coarse sand

① Remove 1 ft of soil

② Add 6 in. layer of bricks or stones

3 **MOVE THE STONES** You will be able to move small stones by simply carrying them, either alone or with assistance from a helper. Wear leather gloves and stout boots. Remember the golden rules — knees bent, back straight, hold the load evenly and then straighten knees with elbows close to your thighs. Never stoop over to grasp the rock and never jerk suddenly to raise it above ground. You will be able to tackle rocks weighing ½–1 cwt in this way, but in a large rockery you will need some stones which weigh appreciably more. One of the best aids for medium-sized rocks is a sack trolley — you will have to lay down a trackway of boards on soft ground. Do not use a single-wheeled garden wheelbarrow as the load can easily tip over. Some stones are too large for a sack trolley and these pose a problem. You can make a track of wooden planks and roll the rock along by turning it over with a crowbar, but it is often easier to use the method shown on the right.

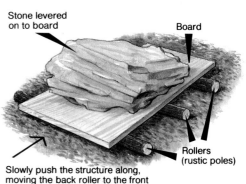

Stone levered on to board

Board

Rollers (rustic poles)

Slowly push the structure along, moving the back roller to the front

4 **SET THE STONES IN POSITION** You will need a crowbar, spade, some wooden planks and a stout stick for ramming soil between the stones. Unless the proposed rockery is tiny, you will also need one or more capable helpers. Ideally you will have chosen a bank with a gentle slope of about 10° — if the site is flat and you plan to build a sloping rock garden then you will require about 1 ton of topsoil for every 20 sq.ft. Buy good quality topsoil if the earth in your garden is clayey. Look at the stones and choose one which is large and has an attractive face — this will be the keystone and serve as the centre point for the first tier of stones. Dig out a hollow which is larger than the base of the keystone and roll this rock into place. Use the crowbar to lever it into its final position as shown on the right. Push rubble under this keystone and add soil both under and behind it. Ram this down firmly with a stick to ensure that there are no air pockets — stand on it to make sure it is firm. Follow the same procedure with stones of various sizes on either side of the keystone — this will complete the first tier. Some stones should be pushed tightly together using the crowbar but you should avoid a continuous line one stone high. It is much better to arrange the stones in groups, declining in height as the edges of the rock garden are reached. You must make sure that all the strata lines on the stones run in the same horizontal direction and soil should be pushed into the cracks. Alpines can be planted into these joints as you proceed — now move on to the second tier of stones. It may be necessary to put down wooden plank ramps to enable the stones to be rolled up to the upper tiers. Continue until all the stones have been set in position — stand back now and then to make sure that you are achieving the desired effect. The last step at this stage is to add some more soil between the stones, but do not fill the planting pockets to their final level — leave a space for the planting mixture.

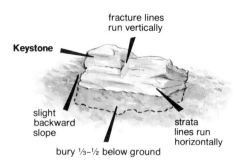

fracture lines run vertically

Keystone

slight backward slope

strata lines run horizontally

bury ⅓–½ below ground

Keystone

Small stones
Wedge together into a group — plant alpines in the crevices

Joints
These should run vertically — do not stagger the joints as if you were building a wall

5 **MAKE UP AND USE THE PLANTING MIXTURE** Nearly all rock garden plants need a soil which is both free draining and water retentive. Ordinary garden soil rarely matches these two requirements and so a planting mixture should be prepared. A standard mixture which is suitable for nearly all plants is shown on the right, but it can be adapted to meet special needs. For lime-hating plants (see the A–Z chapter) a better mixture is 1 part topsoil, 2 parts moist sphagnum peat and 1 part lime-free gravel or pea shingle. Note that fertilizer is not added, although you can add a sprinkling of Bone Meal. Many text-books recommend the use of planting mixture instead of topsoil for the whole of the rock garden making process. This may be ideal, but the cost and labour involved in mixing make it prohibitive unless the rockery is very small. It is more practical to use topsoil for stage 4 and then fill the planting areas with a layer of planting mixture. Let this settle for a few weeks and then add some more mixture which should be firmed so that it slopes gently backwards to the stone behind.

Standard Planting Mixture

1 part **Topsoil**

1 part **Grit** or **Stone Chippings**

1 part **Peat** or **Well-rotted Leaf-mould**

6 **PLANT AND MULCH** Some garden designers insist that the front of the rock garden should be planted with large specimens and the lowlier ones should be set at the back in order to give an impression of maximum depth. It is better to go for maximum interest — use some bold plants such as dwarf conifers and shrubs as single specimen plants here and there and grow smaller plants in groups in the spaces between. Aim to cover some but not all the rock faces with carpeting plants and also aim for year-round-colour. Never plant without checking the A–Z guide first — look at the plant's spread and its light/soil type needs. Do not plant rampant growers next to choice and delicate varieties. Plant lime-hating types at the top of the rockery if limestone rocks or chippings have been used in its construction. With pot-grown specimens you can plant at any time of the year if the ground is reasonably moist and not frozen. The experts prefer spring in cold areas and mid-autumn elsewhere. Water the pot and let it drain before removing the plant — loosen the roots. Planting in crevices should take place during construction — rooted cuttings are best but you can use pot-grown specimens if the root ball is trimmed to fit. Terraces and pockets between the stones should not be planted for a few weeks after the rock garden has been built. Dig a hole which is larger than the root ball and fill the hole with water. When this has drained away put in the root ball and fill the space around it with planting mixture. Firm the mixture with your fingers and water in. The final step is to cover the surface with a 1 in. layer of grit — ½ in. pea gravel can be used but the best choice is small chippings of the stone used in the construction of the rock garden.

SCREE

A scree in nature is an area of loose rock at the bottom of a gully or cliff. Small stones predominate, but there may be some sizeable boulders. In this competition-free environment a number of splendid alpines flourish, and there are several ways in which a scree can be created in a home garden.

The most satisfactory method is to dig out a strip of soil from a well-drained, shade-free part of a rock garden — ideally this should be between large stones and widen out as it descends. Inside this dug-out area place an 8 in. layer of scree compost — 1 part topsoil, 1 part peat or leaf-mould and 3 parts grit or gravel. Another place for a scree is the boundary between lawn and rock garden — provide an edging to keep the small stones off the grass. Where a rockery is absent you can create a scree bed in a sunny spot in the garden. Remove soil from the area and fill with an 8 in. layer of broken bricks or stones topped with a 2 in. layer of coarse sand or gravel. Add an 8 in. layer of scree compost to bring the level to the surface. When planting shake off as much compost as you can from the roots — when planting is finished place a 1 in. layer of chippings over the surface and under the leaves. A number of small stones bedded into the surface around the plants will improve the appearance of the scree. Recommended plants include Aethionema, Erodium, Penstemon, Phlox douglasii and Silene.

RAISED BED

An increasingly popular way of growing rock garden plants — easier, cheaper and less space-demanding than a rockery. A height of 1½–3 ft is recommended and the retaining walls can be made with bricks, stone, reconstituted stone blocks or railway sleepers. Where space permits an upper terrace or a series of terraces can be built on the bed to create extra interest and a place for trailing plants. Clear away perennial weeds before you begin and lay a concrete foundation if the walls are to be more than 1 ft high. Provide weep-holes at the base if mortar-bonded bricks, blocks or stones are the building material.

When the walls are finished, add a layer of bricks, rubble or stones if the soil below is not free draining. Cover with grit and fill with standard planting mixture — see page 6. Leave a 2 in. space between the surface and the top of the retaining wall and wait a few weeks before introducing the plants. Top up if necessary. Choice and planting technique are the same as for the rock garden — the use of trailing types to partially cover the top of the retaining walls is especially important. Cover the soil with a 1 in. layer of stone chippings — the use of larger stones is a matter of personal taste but is an aid to plant growth.

SINK or TROUGH

The idea of growing alpines in troughs and glazed sinks caught on in the 1930s. There are the obvious virtues. Using a container means rock garden plants can be grown anywhere, including on a patio or balcony. The plants are also raised from the ground, bringing them in easy reach. There is a less obvious virtue — some difficult alpines which often rot outdoors can survive the winter in the excellent drainage provided by a deep trough.

Many attractive reconstituted stone troughs are available these days — the key feature to look for is an adequate drain at the bottom. Old glazed sinks can be covered with hypertufa — 1 part cement, 1 part sand and 1 part fine peat blended to a moist mix with water. Place the sink or trough on firm supports in a sunny spot and cover the drainage hole or holes with crocks or rubble and fill to within 2 in. of the top with standard planting mixture — see page 6. Allow it to settle for a couple of weeks and then plant up, aiming for a mixture of shapes, sizes and colours. Here you can use choice and delicate types to maximum advantage — avoid rampant carpeters. Place some rocks between the plants and cover the surface with a 1 in. layer of stone chippings. Water regularly during the growing season — continue until water comes out of the drainage holes.

DRY-STONE WALL

A dry-stone wall is made without mortar. In northern rural areas you will see mile after mile of dry-stone walling built by bonding flat stones together — in the home garden soil or planting mixture is used to fill the spaces between the stones. In these cracks a wide range of rock garden plants can be grown.

There are two types of dry-stone wall — the free-standing double-faced one with a central core of soil and the retaining type used to support a raised bed or to face a bank. Building a free-standing wall should be left to the professional, but a retaining one is well within the scope of the home gardener. Use limestone or sandstone — an easier-to-handle alternative is the dry-walling variety of reconstituted stone blocks. A wall above 1 ft high will need a 6 in. foundation of rubble or concrete. Lay large and flat stones for the lower layers, pushing them together tightly with a fill of planting mixture (see page 6) between the sides and layers of stones. Each stone should slope downwards and backwards — a 10° slope is satisfactory. Plant as you go, placing the specimens sideways. Rooted cuttings are generally easier to use than plants which are pot-grown. Pack the mixture around the roots. When constructing a wall against an earth face, planting mixture should be packed firmly to fill the space between the back of the stones and the front of the bank. Spray the wall with water when planting is finished — water in dry weather until the plants are established. Recommended plants include Alyssum, Aubrietia, Dianthus, Helianthemum, Phlox and Thyme for a sunny face and Arabis, Campanula and Saxifraga for a shady one.

PEAT BED

It is distinctly odd that the peat bed and its associated plants should be traditionally included in books and catalogues dealing with rock gardens and their flora. Rock is not used in its construction and most of the plants come from woodland areas. The three features they share are a need for good drainage, a dislike of exposed windy sites and a preponderance of low-growing types.

The walls of the bed can be made of stone, brick etc but wood is better, especially logs or railway sleepers. Best of all are peat blocks, which must be soaked thoroughly and then laid in brick-like fashion. The base of the bed must be weed-free with unimpeded drainage. It must also be lime-free — there is no point in trying to create a peat bed if you live in a chalky area. Fill the bed with a suitable planting mixture — a popular one is 1 part topsoil, 1 part sphagnum peat and some grit as an optional extra. Let the soil mix settle for a couple of weeks before planting — top dress with peat or pulverised bark after planting and renew each year. Weed with care — remove by hand rather than hoeing. Avoid walking over the peaty soil — lay down stepping stones if the bed is large. Recommended plants include Astilbe, Cassiope, Dodecatheon, Gaultheria, Autumn-flowering Gentian, Hepatica and Primula.

TUFA

Truly a remarkable stone which can be used to make a spectacular rock feature. Tufa is a form of magnesium limestone which is suitable for lime-hating plants — the first surprising feature. Next, it is porous and can hold more than its own weight of water, and roots of plants will grow into it.

Pieces of tufa can be used in a scree, raised bed, rock garden, trough etc, but the most eye-catching use is as a piece of planted-up rock standing on a patio or balcony. The rock is quite soft and can easily be drilled or worked with a hammer or chisel. Make a series of downward-sloping holes 1½ in. wide and 3–5 in. deep. Use small plants — free the roots from compost and wrap in moist toilet paper and insert in the hole. Carefully fill the space around it with the paving-type planting mixture — see page 9. Water after planting up and keep moist in dry weather. To cut down the need for watering you can insert the bottom 1–2 in. of the rock into a bed or rock garden — tufa soaks up water like a sponge. The biggest surprise of all is that some difficult alpines will grow in tufa but may fail under all other conditions in the garden.

PAVING

Many rock garden plants can be grown in the cracks between the paving stones of paths and patios. They relieve the monotony of plain slabs, but only a few such as Thymus and Acaena can withstand regular brushing and foot traffic. Excavate soil between the slabs using an old kitchen knife and gently insert and shake down the roots of the small plant or rooted cutting. Fill the hole with a planting mixture of 1 part topsoil, 1 part fine peat and 1 part coarse sand. Do this in autumn — alternatively you can add planting mixture to the dug-out hole and sow seeds in spring. If the base is free-draining you can make a more spectacular display by removing one of the slabs and digging out enough foundation material for an 8 in. layer of planting mixture — see page 6. Plant up and treat like a raised bed (page 7). Recommended plants include Acaena, Antennaria, Arenaria, Armeria, Dianthus, Erica, Iberis, Lychnis, Saxifraga, Sedum and Thymus.

ROCKWORK

In rockwork it is the stones and not the plants which are the key feature. Grand rockwork is now a thing of the past, but you can still see examples at places like Chatsworth (illustrated), Sezincote, Biddulph Grange etc. In recent years there has been a revival on a modest scale as interest in Japanese gardening has increased. The most popular arrangement is the *sanzon* or Three Buddha Stones which can be seen in Buddhist temple gardens throughout Japan. It is a triangle of rocks, an upright pillar-like one at the centre and two recumbent rounded ones at the base. These stones must be weathered and naturally sculpted — hopefully they will be covered with moss and lichens. Use this *sanzon* as a lawn or patio feature — at the base you can plant low-growing carpeting plants such as Thymus or Acaena. Avoid any type which grows upright or has large flowers. You can extend this three-stone arrangement, but keep to odd numbers — five, seven etc.

ALPINE LAWN

It's a nice idea — a lawn composed of a low-growing, rock garden plant rather than grass. Unfortunately it is very difficult to create and even more difficult to maintain. Thymus serpyllum is the usual planting material, but you can try Antennaria. Obviously all traces of weed and grass must be removed and the alpine lawn material is planted in close groups. When established, hand weeding is necessary and even successful alpine lawns have to be renewed every few years. An easier alternative is the alpine wild flower garden — sow a mixture of low-growing grasses and alpines which bloom before midsummer. Mow the grass in July and again in September. Sounds easy, but even here the native grasses and weeds generally take over quite quickly.

ALPINE HOUSE

For nearly all gardeners who are keen on rock garden plants growing them outdoors is sufficient, but for the serious enthusiast an alpine house is essential. A custom-made alpine house is very expensive — the usual action is to buy a standard small green-house and have extra windows and louvres fitted to provide the additional ventilation required by alpines. In this unheated house the grower can enjoy his plants all year round, give the potted specimens individual attention and grow varieties which would die in the frost and rain outdoors in winter. Fill pots with J.I. No.1 compost or a Multipurpose peat compost with added grit — water quite sparingly in winter but more frequently and thoroughly during the active growth period. Pots can be plunged in a bed of moist sharp sand to cut down the need for frequent watering. Ventilate the house from spring to autumn and shade when the temperature nears 90°F.

CHAPTER 3
ROCK GARDEN PLANTS A~Z

The dividing line between rock garden plants and the other sorts grown in the garden is extremely blurred. The reason is simple — nobody has been able to produce a satisfactory definition of a rock garden plant, which means that nobody can be sure just where the rockery list begins and ends.

There is no problem with the alpines — an enormous group which is at the core of any rock garden plant list. Unfortunately 'alpine' is often used to cover *all* plants recommended for the rockery, and that is incorrect. This term has a specific meaning — **Alpines** are herbaceous or sub-shrubby plants which were originally collected from mountainous regions such as the Alps, Andes, Himalayas, Rocky Mountains etc. The natural home of the **True** or **High-mountain Alpines** is above the tree line. The Edelweiss of the Swiss Alps has become the classic representative of this alpine group — low-growing and extremely hardy with a passion for sun and gritty, free-draining soil. Many alpines appear in the following pages — Saxifraga, Alpine Poppy, Lewisia, Erinus, Androsace etc. It may seem surprising that some plants from the high mountains may require the shelter of an alpine house to protect them from the rain and frost of the British winter. The reason is that at home these plants spend the cold months tucked up under a thick blanket of unmelted snow.

Alpines make up a vital part but not all of the rock garden plant list. Rockery plants include species from the sea-shore, such as Frankenia, and others from woodland regions — Gaultheria and Vaccinium are examples. Many of the specimens you will find on the 'alpine' bench at your garden centre have no natural home — they are man-bred hybrids or varieties.

We must go beyond the alpines if we are to cover the full span of rock garden plants. Alpine and many lowland herbaceous and sub-shrubby perennials are grouped together as the **Rockery Perennials**, and nearly all the plants you will buy and grow belong here. The ones chosen for inclusion in this section are not necessarily the best or the easiest to grow — they are the plants you are most likely to find in the catalogues, garden centres and text-books. Be careful if you plant Cerastium, Aubrietia, Alyssum saxatile, Arabis and Saponaria. They are easy to cultivate but their invasive habit means that delicate types can be quickly overrun if these rampant species are not kept in check. The height and spread information given in this A–Z is what you can expect after 3 years' growth under average conditions.

Dwarf Conifers are an excellent way of providing an evergreen skeleton to the rock garden. Species of Chamaecyparis and Juniperus are included here, but there are others — look for Pinus mugo 'Gnom', Picea mariana 'Nana', Taxus baccata 'Standishii' and Thuja occidentalis 'Hetz Midget'. Make sure that the conifer you buy is labelled as a 'dwarf' variety. **Dwarf Shrubs** are another useful group for providing a woody backbone to the rockery. A number of the popular ones are included in this section, but you can also grow dwarf species and varieties of Azalea, Berberis, Betula, Pernettya, Prunus, Rhododendron, Rubus and Salix.

Dwarf Bulbs are an essential part of rockery planting and many varieties of the basic spring-blooming trio (Crocus, Narcissus and Tulip) can be found in any rock garden catalogue. Iris, Cyclamen and Oxalis are also included here, but there are many others to choose from — Allium, Chionodoxa, Eranthis, Galanthus, Leucojeum, Muscari, Scilla etc. **Ferns** were all the rage in Victorian times and still make a useful addition for the rock garden of today — look for Adiantum and Asplenium species.

So what *is* a rock garden plant? The definition — *A plant which looks at home and is at home in a rock garden* is too restrictive. Some need the protection of an alpine house and there are others which require the humus and shade of a peat bed to be successful. Another definition — *A low-growing perennial grown by alpine gardeners* — seems to beg the question. The definition adopted here is — *A plant you can expect to find listed in some of the alpine nursery catalogues and some of the text-books on rock gardening.* Not really satisfactory, of course, as it leaves out the annuals and biennials which are so useful to provide a splash of temporary colour — Antirrhinum, Bellis, Cheiranthus, Helichrysum, Limnanthes, Nemophila etc. Perhaps the absence of a clear-cut definition is a good thing. A rockery is an art form and should not be shackled by tedious scientific restrictions.

ACAENA New Zealand Burr

An easy-to-grow carpeting perennial with a number of uses — covering cracks between paving slabs, providing ground cover between plants and forming leafy blankets around dwarf bulbs. This hardy plant is low-growing (1–4 in.) and tolerant of poor and dry soil, but soon dies out in waterlogged ground. The dense mat of evergreen foliage spreads rapidly, so take care that choice plants are not swamped. The flowers are tiny and insignificant, but they are followed in late summer by burr-like seed heads which are often showy and colourful.

VARIETIES: For red burrs grow the popular **A. microphylla** — height 2 in., spread 2 ft. The foliage is silvery when young, becoming bronze. Another red-burred variety is **A. 'Blue Haze'** (blue-grey leaves). The most vigorous species is **A. novae-zealandiae** — the mat of silky green foliage is very invasive. For colourful foliage choose **A. buchananii** (silvery-green) or **A. 'Copper Carpet'** (coppery-purple).

SITE & SOIL: Any well-drained garden soil — thrives in sun or light shade.

PROPAGATION: Divide clumps in autumn or spring.

Acaena 'Blue Haze'

A. microphylla

ACER Japanese Maple

Most Acers are trees — these include the stately Maples and Sycamores. The Japanese Maples, however, are compact and slow-growing, and if you choose carefully they make splendid specimen shrubs for the larger rock garden. They are planted for their attractive growth habit and their divided leaves in green, red or purple — the colour of the non-green varieties may be year-round or appear only in autumn. This foliage needs some protection from morning sun and cold winds.

VARIETIES: It is surprising that Japanese Maples appear in so few catalogues offering rock garden plants, but you should have no difficulty in finding them at your garden centre. Pick a variety of **A. palmatum 'Dissectum'** — the shrub is very slow-growing, reaching 3–4 ft, and the branches spread horizontally. The leaves are deeply cut and divided. The year-round purple-leaved form is **A. palmatum 'Dissectum Atropurpureum'** — the variety **A. palmatum 'Osakazuki'** turns red in autumn.

SITE & SOIL: Requires a neutral or acid soil. Grows best in partial shade.

PROPAGATION: Buy from a garden centre or nursery.

Acer palmatum
'Dissectum Atropurpureum'

*A. palmatum
'Dissectum'*

ACHILLEA Alpine Yarrow

Most Achilleas grow several feet high and are found in the herbaceous border, but there are several dwarf species which are suitable for the rockery. They form a mat of silvery or green finely-divided foliage and during the summer flat heads of tiny white or yellow flowers appear. These Alpine Yarrows are useful for covering areas of dry sandy soil or crevices between rocks and the plants are easily propagated in the spring. Sprinkle Slug Pellets around the plants if leaf damage is seen.

VARIETIES: The most popular species is **A. tomentosa** — basic details are height 6 in., spread 1 ft, flowering period July-September. The downy greyish leaves form a dense carpet and the yellow flower-heads are 3 in. across. Remove dead flowers to preserve evergreen habit. Other yellow-flowering types include **A. chrysocoma** (**A. aurea**) (foliage highly aromatic when crushed) and **A. 'King Edward'** (long flowering season). For white flowers and silvery foliage pick **A. argentea** (**A. clavennae**) or **A. kellereri**.

SITE & SOIL: Requires well-drained infertile soil in full sun.

PROPAGATION: Divide clumps or take cuttings in spring.

Achillea kellereri

A. tomentosa

AETHIONEMA Aethionema

A low-growing shrubby evergreen which will flower for many weeks from early to late summer if the site is unshaded and the soil is free draining. All species thrive best in alkaline soil, but the popular types do well in neutral or even slightly acid soil. The grey, fleshy leaves form a dense carpet and the flower-heads cover the surface. Each head is a rounded cluster of tiny flowers, varying in colour from palest pink to deepest rose depending on the variety chosen.

VARIETIES: The popular one is **A. 'Warley Rose'** — an excellent choice for the rock garden or for growing on an old wall. The basic details are height 6 in., spread 1 ft, flowering period May–August — the flower colour is rosy red. **A. 'Warley Ruber'** is a similar plant with even more striking flowers, but is harder to find. **A. grandiflorum** (1 ft) is the tallest Aethionema, bearing pale pink blooms from May to August. **A. pulchellum** (9 in.) is a rather similar plant but is more compact.

SITE & SOIL: Any well-drained soil — full sun is required.

PROPAGATION: Easily raised from seed. With named varieties plant cuttings in a cold frame in early or late summer.

Aethionema pulchellum

A. 'Warley Rose'

AJUGA Bugle

Bugle will thrive almost anywhere — in dry or moist soil and in sun as well as shade. Plant it as ground cover or in the crevices between rocks well away from choicer and more delicate plants — Bugle spreads rapidly and can be invasive. The flowers which appear from April to August are usually blue and appear on 6 in. tall spikes. The decorative effect, however, is often derived from the foliage which forms dense mats — multicoloured and variegated forms are available.

VARIETIES: Most of the cultivated forms have been bred from the wild flower **A. reptans**. It grows about 4–6 in. high and leaf colour separates the different varieties — **'Burgundy Glow'** (leaves green, pink and red), **'Atropurpurea'** (leaves reddish-purple) and **'Multicolor'** (leaves green, mottled bronze and red). **'Alba'** is a white-flowered variety. **A. pyramidalis** is quite similar to A. reptans but usually taller — look for the variety **'Metallica Crispa'**.

SITE & SOIL: Any reasonable garden soil will do — thrives in sun or partial shade.

PROPAGATION: Divide clumps in autumn or spring.

Ajuga reptans 'Burgundy Glow'

A. reptans 'Multicolor'

ALCHEMILLA Alpine Lady's Mantle

Alchemilla mollis is the popular herbaceous border species, but it is too large for the rockery. The Alpine Lady's Mantles are much more compact, forming hummocks of lobed leaves. During the summer fluffy branching sprays of tiny yellow flowers appear, but Alchemilla is grown for its foliage rather than its blooms. Its advantage is that it is very easy to grow in either rock or peat gardens — its drawback is that self-seeding can mean unwanted plants appearing anywhere.

VARIETIES: **A. alpina** is a common wild flower in the Alps — height 6 in., spread 1 ft, flowering period June–August. The leaves are dark green above with silvery edges and silver below. Some of the foliage dies down in winter. Other miniature Alchemillas include **A. erythropoda** (similar to but less invasive than A. alpina), **A. conjuncta** and **A. ellenbeckii** (long trailing stems).

SITE & SOIL: Any well-drained garden soil will do — thrives in sun or light shade.

PROPAGATION: Easily raised from seed sown in spring. Divide clumps in spring.

Alchemilla alpina

A. conjuncta

ALLIUM Flowering Garlic

Many species of Allium are available — tall ones for the border and dwarfs for the rock garden. Leaves and petals may be wide or narrow, and flower-heads may be loose or tightly packed. Some are sold as bulbs for planting in the autumn but many of the choice types have rhizomatous roots and are bought as growing plants. Choose with care as a few popular Alliums such as A. moly (1 ft, loosely-packed heads of yellow stars) and A. pulchellum self-seed very freely and are invasive.

VARIETIES: A. beesianum is a tall rockery Allium with 1 ft stalks bearing clusters of pendant blue flowers in midsummer. Another species which bears hanging bell-like flowers in June is the pink or purple **A. narcissiflorum** (8 in.). **A. ostrowskianum** (6 in.) carries its wide-petalled carmine flowers in flat clusters — for late summer blooms choose the small **A. amabile** (5 in., grassy foliage, red-purple blooms). **A. cyaneum** (6 in.) has small heads of upright blue flowers.

SITE & SOIL: Any well-drained soil will do — thrives best in full sun.

PROPAGATION: Divide clumps every few years in autumn.

Allium narcissiflorum

A. ostrowskianum

ALYSSUM Alyssum

Don't reject this plant because you see it in rockeries everywhere — in spring it provides a bright yellow splash which blends well with the blues and pinks of Aubrieta. But don't let it run riot — it can soon spread and choice alpines may be swamped. When not in flower it is a greyish shrubby perennial which flourishes in poor soil. Trim back once the flowers have faded — this will keep it in check and also prolong the life of the plant.

VARIETIES: A. saxatile (Gold Dust) is the basic species — height 6 in.-1 ft, spread 1½ ft, flowering period April–June. The tiny bright yellow flowers form large heads which often completely cover the foliage. There are a number of named varieties — look for **'Citrinum'** (pale yellow), **'Dudley Neville'** (buff), **'Plenum'** (double yellow), **'Compactum'** (neat growth habit) and the dwarf **'Tom Thumb'**. Another miniature is **A. montanum** — height 4 in., spread 1 ft. **A. spinosum (Ptilotrichum spinosum)** is a spiny white- or pink-flowering dwarf shrub.

SITE & SOIL: Any well-drained soil — thrives best in full sun.

PROPAGATION: Sow seeds under glass in spring. With named varieties plant cuttings in a cold frame in early summer.

Alyssum saxatile 'Citrinum'

A. saxatile

ANACYCLUS Mt. Atlas Daisy

A beauty for the sink garden, scree or rockery. The Carrot-like root produces a rosette of prostrate stems, each stem bearing grey-green ferny foliage and a Daisy-like flower at the tip. In bud only the red undersides of the petals can be seen, but when open the flower is a pure white Daisy. This plant from the Atlas Mountains of N. Africa is hardy and not difficult to grow if you meet its two basic needs — free-draining, gritty soil with a covering of gravel and a sheltered site which is unshaded.

VARIETY: Unless you are willing to search through the specialist catalogues you will find just one species — **A. depressus**, sometimes listed as **A. pyrethrum depressus**. The basic details are height 2 in., spread 1 ft, flowering period May–August, flowers 1–2 in. across. Avoid overwatering at all times and dead-head after flowering. Other species are rare, and are no better than A. depressus.

SITE & SOIL: Requires well-drained open soil — full sun is essential.

PROPAGATION: Sow fresh seeds under glass in autumn or plant cuttings in a cold frame in spring.

Anacyclus depressus

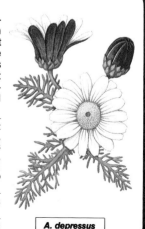
A. depressus

Androsace sarmentosa

ANDROSACE Rock Jasmine

There are 150 species of this splendid alpine and you can find a score or more in the specialist catalogues. You must choose with care — most of them are too delicate and susceptible to rain to grow outdoors, but the four species described below will succeed in the open garden. Some produce neat rosettes of foliage, others are tightly-packed mounds of narrow leaves and the remainder have a trailing growth habit. All bear tiny, Primrose-like flowers.

VARIETIES: A. sarmentosa is a popular species — it grows only 4 in. high but the spread of the neat foliage rosettes is up to 2 ft. Pink flowers appear from April to June. **A. carnea** is a cushion-forming type — 4 in. high with pink flowers in spring. The easiest one is **A. carnea rosea** (other name **halleri**). **A. lanuginosa** is a trailer for growing over rocks — pink flowers are produced in July and August. **A. sempervivoides** bears yellow-eyed flowers of delicate pink in spring.

SITE & SOIL: A well-drained gritty soil is essential. Thrives in sun or light shade.

PROPAGATION: Use rosettes or basal shoots as cuttings — plant in a cold frame in early summer.

A. sarmentosa

Anemone blanda

ANEMONE Windflower

A popular group of garden flowers — the smaller ones make good rock garden plants with showy blooms (usually blue) in early spring. The three you are most likely to find are A. blanda, apennina and nemorosa — all produce rhizomes underground and the 'bulbs' of A. blanda can be bought for planting out in September. The leaves of these small Anemones are deeply cut and the flowers are either starry or Daisy-like.

VARIETIES: A. blanda is the one you are most likely to find. Basic details are height 4 in., flowering period February–April, Daisy flowers 1½ in. across. Named varieties include **'Atrocaerulea'** (deep blue), **'Blue Star'** (mid blue), **'Charmer'** (rosy red) and **'White Splendour'** (white). **A. apennina** is very similar, but the flowers are rather smaller and appear later (March–April). **A. nemorosa** (Wood Anemone) is taller (6–8 in.) and bears glossy starry flowers in spring. The wild species is white, but blue, pink and red named varieties are available.

SITE & SOIL: Well-drained, humus-rich soil is required — thrives in sun or light shade.

PROPAGATION: Divide mature clumps in late summer.

A. nemorosa

Antennaria dioica 'Rosea'

ANTENNARIA Cat's Ear

There is nothing showy about this lowly plant, but it does have one useful property — it can be walked on without harm. This means that it can be used as a crack filler between paving stones and as the basic material for an alpine lawn. Its mat of creeping stems can also be used as ground cover around bulbs. It is tough, hardy and flourishes in poor soil. In May and June the small flower-heads open with blooms in white, pink or red.

VARIETIES: The only species you are likely to find in the catalogues — **A. dioica**, sometimes offered as **A. tomentosa**. It spreads to form a mat of silvery leaves, reaching about 1½ ft across. The tiny flowers are of the 'everlasting' type — they appear in clusters on top of erect flower-stalks. The height of these stalks and the colour of the blooms depend on the variety chosen. Look for **'Aprica'** (4 in., cream), **'Nyewoods Variety'** (4 in., deep pink), **'Rosea'** (4 in., pink), **'Rubra'** (6 in., crimson) and **'Minima'** (2 in., pink).

SITE & SOIL: Any well-drained garden soil will do — thrives best in full sun.

PROPAGATION: Divide clumps in early autumn or spring.

A. dioica

AQUILEGIA   Alpine Columbine

The Aquilegia of the herbaceous border is A. vulgaris and its hybrids — 1½–3 ft plants which are too tall for the average rock garden. Choose instead one of the attractive Alpine Columbines with flowering stems between a few inches and 1 ft high. Each pendant flower bears 5 spurs and the foliage is finely divided. One or two problems — Aquilegias are not long-lived, they require copious watering in dry weather and cross-fertilization means that seeds may produce plants you don't expect. Flowers appear in June and July — dead-head when they fade.

VARIETIES: Some experts consider **A. flabellata (A. akitensis) pumila** to be the queen of the crop. The white and violet flowers are borne on 6 in. stalks above bluish-green leaves. Another 6 in. dwarf is the blue-flowered **A. bertolonii**. For red and gold flowers choose **A. canadensis**, a variable species producing stems between 6 in. and 1½ ft high. A choice but difficult species is **A. jonesii** with 3 in. stems and blue flowers.

SITE & SOIL: Thrives in well-drained moist soil and light shade.

PROPAGATION: Sow seeds outdoors in April. Mature Aquilegias dislike transplanting.

Aquilegia flabellata pumila

A. flabellata pumila

ARABIS   Rock Cress

A very easy plant to grow with leaves which are usually jagged and hairy. Masses of small, four-petalled flowers appear in loose clusters in the spring. Common Rock Cress is useful for covering a large area of bare rock or for clothing a bank, but all too often it is allowed to run wild in a small rock garden. The foliage is generally evergreen, but stems can die back in wet and cold winters. To keep the plant in check, cut back after flowering. The fruit pods are long and narrow — an easy way to distinguish Arabis from the rather similar but even more popular Aubrieta.

VARIETIES: The Common Rock Cress is **A. albida (A. caucasica)** — height 9 in., spread 2 ft, leaves downy and grey-green, flowering period March-April with sporadic blooms until June, flower colour white. The more compact double form (**'Flore Pleno'**) is popular — the blooms are larger but the plant is less free-flowering. White is not the only colour — there are pink varieties such as **'Pink Pearl'** and **'Rose Frost'**. There is also a slow-growing variety with cream-splashed leaves — **A. albida 'Variegata'**. Avoid A. albida if you want a low-growing compact plant — choose instead a prettier and less rambling species. Examples include **A. blepharophylla** (height 3 in., spread 9 in., leaves grey-green, flower colour deep rose), **A. Ferdinandi-coburgii 'Variegata'** (height 4 in., spread 1 ft, fleshy leaves brightly variegated all year round, flower colour white) and **A. alpina** (height 6 in., spread 1 ft, flower colour white or pink).

SITE & SOIL: Any well-drained garden soil will do — thrives in sun or light shade.

PROPAGATION: Divide clumps in autumn or plant cuttings in a cold frame in summer. Species (not named varieties) can be raised from seed sown under glass in spring or summer.

Arabis albida 'Flore Pleno'

Arabis blepharophylla

A. albida

Arabis Ferdinandi-coburgii 'Variegata'

Arenaria balearica

ARENARIA   Sandwort

There is nothing eye-catching about the lowly Sandworts. The prostrate stems form a mat of foliage and the small white flowers borne on upright stalks are nothing special. Not for a prominent planting pocket, but a good choice for covering rocks or filling cracks between paving slabs. The leaves are evergreen and although the plant can be left to spread over a wide area it can easily be kept in check.

VARIETIES: For covering damp or dry rocks which receive little or no sun choose **A. balearica** (height 1 in., spread 1½ ft, flowering period March–July). The tiny green leaves give the plant a mossy appearance. For rocks which face the sun choose instead **A. montana** (height 4 in., spread 1½ ft, flowering period May–June). **A. caespitosa 'Aurea' (Sagina glabra 'Aurea')** bears golden grassy leaves. **A. purpurascens** is the odd man out — pale purple instead of white flowers above green leafy cushions.

SITE & SOIL: Requires well-drained moist soil. Sun or shade requirement depends on the species.

PROPAGATION: Divide clumps in autumn or spring.

A. montana

Armeria caespitosa

ARMERIA   Thrift, Sea Pink

You will find Armeria growing wild around the sea-shore and in countless rock gardens. The evergreen grassy leaves form dense mounds and tiny flowers in ball-like papery heads appear on top of thin stalks — a good plant for a sunny spot. It will naturalise on stone walls and in rocky crevices. The only problem is a tendency for the middle of the clumps to die out.

VARIETIES: Our native Thrift is **A. maritima** (height 8 in., spread 1 ft, flowering period May–July). The flower-heads are about 1 in. in diameter — the colour of the species is pink and so are some of the named varieties such as **'Merlin', 'Laucheana'** and **'Perfection'**. Other colours are available — look for **'Dusseldorf Pride'** (crimson), **'Vindictive'** (bright red), **'Bloodstone'** (deep red) and **'Alba'** (white). For a more compact Thrift choose **A. caespitosa (A. juniperifolia)** — height 3 in., spread 9 in., flowering period April–May. The pink or white flower-heads are almost stemless.

SITE & SOIL: Any well-drained soil will do — thrives in sun.

PROPAGATION: Divide clumps or plant basal cuttings in a cold frame in summer.

A maritima

Artemisia pedemontana

ARTEMISIA   Artemisia

This extensive group of herbaceous perennials and shrubs are grown for their silver feathery foliage rather than their small, button-like yellow flowers which appear between July and September. Most are large and belong in the herbaceous border, although A. stellariana (Dusty Miller) is sometimes grown in large rockeries. There are a few dwarf and compact species for the average rock garden. Like the other species they may lose their leaves in winter, but are quite hardy if the roots are not waterlogged.

VARIETIES: A. schmidtiana 'Nana' is a good choice for a sunny scree or a gritty pocket between the rocks. It forms a mound of silvery-grey ferny leaves about 6 in. high and 1 ft across. The young growth is particularly attractive. **A. pedemontana** (also sold as **A. lanata, A. assoana** and **A. caucasica**) is a tiny shrub which grows only 2 in.-high and bears finely divided leaves clothed with white hairs. Other alpine Artemisias such as **A. glacialis** and **A. mutellina** are harder to grow.

SITE & SOIL: Requires well-drained soil — thrives in full sun.

PROPAGATION: Plant stem cuttings in a cold frame in spring.

A. schmidtiana 'Nana'

ASPERULA   Alpine Woodruff

The weak stems of the Alpine Woodruffs form clumps or loose mats and bear the tiny leaves in whorls. These leaves are of two types — there are smooth-surfaced species which can be grown fairly easily outdoors and the woolly ones which hate winter rain and need either protection or the comfort of an alpine house. The flowers are borne in clusters and are distinctly tubular. Pink is the usual colour, but white and yellow Woodruffs are available. The flowering season is early summer.

VARIETIES: A. lilaciflora caespitosa is a prostrate plant, forming cushions of glossy green leaves and an abundance of 1 in. long lilac-pink flowers. Grow it in an open spot in the rock garden — an even easier plant to grow outdoors is **A. gussonii** which produces 4 in. high woody-based tufts. The flowers are flesh-pink. The most popular woolly-leaved species is **A. suberosa** which produces 3 in. high cushions in the alpine house. The flowers are short (⅓ in.) and pale pink.

SITE & SOIL: Requires well-drained gritty soil in full sun.

PROPAGATION: Divide clumps or take cuttings in spring.

A. lilaciflora caespitosa

Asperula suberosa

ASTER   Mountain Aster

The Asters are well represented in the garden by the Michaelmas Daisies in the herbaceous border, but there are some dwarf species which belong in the rock garden. They are spreading plants with greyish leaves, and in summer the flowers are large and colourful. By far the most popular is A. alpinus which is an easy plant to grow. If you don't mind having a mixture of colours you can raise this plant from seed, but it is better to buy a named variety from your garden centre or catalogue.

VARIETIES: A. alpinus has a basal rosette of hairy leaves above which are the solitary Daisy-like flowers — 1½ in. across with pale purple ray petals surrounding the golden eye. Basic details are height 6 in., spread 1½ ft, flowering period May–July. Choose a good named variety — **albus** (white), **'Beechwood'** (blue) or **'Happy End'** (pink). **A. natalensis** is a sky-blue species which blooms rather later — **A. tibeticus** (blue flowers) is noted for its free-flowering habit.

SITE & SOIL: Any well-drained garden soil — thrives in full sun.

PROPAGATION: Divide clumps every 3 years in spring.

A. alpinus

Aster alpinus albus

ASTILBE   Rockery Astilbe

The popular Astilbes are stately plants with 3 ft high feathery plumes in summer, but there are several rockery varieties which grow less than 1 ft tall. They differ in a number of interesting ways from the run-of-the-mill alpines. Astilbes thrive best in cool, damp and slightly shady places, they have a flower structure which makes a pleasant change from the standard rockery plant form and these flowers appear in midsummer when so many alpines have passed their flowering season.

VARIETIES: One of the most popular Rockery Astilbes is **A. chinensis pumila** — height 9 in., spread 1 ft, flowering period July–October. Its miniature ostrich plumes are mauve. The baby of the family is **A. glaberrima 'Saxatilis'** (height 5 in., spread 6 in., leaves bronzy, flowers pink in June and July). A number of colourful and highly recommended hybrids of **A. simplicifolia** are available — **'Aphrodite'** (deep rose), **'Willy Buchanan'** (creamy-white), **'Sprite'** (pale pink) etc. A word of warning — Astilbes fail miserably in dry soil.

SITE & SOIL: Requires moist soil — thrives in light shade.

PROPAGATION: Divide clumps every 3 years in spring.

A. chinensis pumila

Astilbe simplicifolia 'Aphrodite'

AUBRIETA Rock Cress, Aubrietia

It is perhaps not surprising that Aubrieta is the most widely grown of all rock garden plants. It is vigorous, tolerant of a wide range of conditions and extremely colourful when covering a sloping bank in spring. In the average-sized rockery it certainly has a place, but it should not be allowed to take over. Cut back hard after flowering to keep it in check and to induce a second flush of flowers in autumn.

VARIETIES: The basic species is **A. deltoidea** (height 3–5 in., spread 2 ft, flowering period April–June). The grey-green leaves are downy and the blooms about ¾ in. across. The species is not grown — the garden varieties are hybrids and there are many from which to choose. A few popular ones are **'Aureovariegata'** (lavender flowers, gold variegated leaves), **'Bressingham Pink'** (double pink), **'Doctor Mules'** (purple), **'Red Carpet'** (red), **'Carnival'** (deep violet), **'Gloriosa'** (rose-pink), **'Wanda'** (double pale red) and **'Dream'** (pale blue).

SITE & SOIL: Any well-drained, non-acid soil in full sun.

PROPAGATION: Divide clumps in autumn or plant cuttings in a cold frame in summer. Sow seeds in spring for a mixture of colours.

Aubrieta deltoidea 'Aureovariegata'

A. deltoidea

CALCEOLARIA Slipperwort

The large pouched flowers of the half hardy Calceolaria made this plant a favourite in Victorian times, but it is the few hardy species which are grown in the rock garden and peat bed. Yellow is the usual flower colour and the flowering period is June to August. They are short-lived perennials — a few will grow quite happily outdoors if the soil has ample humus and is kept moist, but others need an alpine house.

VARIETIES: The largest Calceolaria for growing outdoors is **C. biflora**. The 1 in. bright yellow flowers are carried on 1 ft stalks above the hairy toothed leaves. **C. tenella** is much more compact — the tiny leaves form a dense carpet and the yellow flowers are borne on 2 in. stalks. For something really different grow **C. darwinii** (height 4 in., spread 6 in.). Each yellow flower is speckled with brown and the lower lip has a broad white band. Unfortunately it is difficult to grow outdoors.

SITE & SOIL: Requires moist soil — thrives in light shade.

PROPAGATION: Divide clumps or sow seeds under glass in spring or summer.

Calceolaria biflora

C. darwinii

CALLUNA Heather, Ling

There are scores of named varieties of the Common Heather which grows on our northern and western moors. These miniature shrubs grow 4 in.–2½ ft high and bloom in late summer — choose one or more of the dwarf types if you have a spot to fill where the soil is infertile and acid. Rather like Erica, but the flower parts are separate and not fused into a bell. Trim the plants after flowering to keep them compact.

VARIETIES: There is only one species (**C. vulgaris**) but there is a wide assortment of varieties. Many have coloured foliage — golden, silvery, bronze or red. There is also a range of flower colours from pure white to deep red. Varieties which grow less than 1 ft high include **'Foxii Nana'** (4 in., purple), **'J. H. Hamilton'** (8 in., double pink) and **'Joan Sparkes'** (9 in., double purple). For coloured foliage choose **'Gold Haze'** (bright yellow) or **'Blazeaway'** (red in winter).

SITE & SOIL: Well-drained acid soil is essential — thrives best in full sun.

PROPAGATION: Layer shoots in spring or plant stem cuttings in a cold frame in summer.

Calluna vulgaris 'Gold Haze'

C. vulgaris

CAMPANULA Bellflower

Campanula is an important genus of alpines and offers something for everyone. Amongst the many dwarf types there are difficult tender species which are a challenge even for the experts and there are popular ones which are both easy and reliable in the open garden. All need well-drained soil and the addition of lime if the ground is acid. June and July are the peak flowering months, and Campanulas have a well-earned reputation for bearing masses of blooms. Praised in all of the books, there are still a number of limitations. Colours are almost entirely restricted to white and blue, and the young foliage is especially susceptible to slug damage in spring. In addition, a few species can be invasive and a threat to surrounding plants.

VARIETIES: There are two distinct flower types, depending on the species. The usual form is a bell, sometimes held erect but more commonly pendant. The other form is a star-like bloom. **C. carpatica** is the most popular Campanula — height 9 in., spread 1 ft, flowering period June–September. It bears cup-shaped bells, 1½–2 in. across, in shades ranging from pure white to deep blue. **C. cochlearifolia** (Fairy Thimbles) is a much daintier plant — it spreads as wide as C. carpatica and flowers during the same period, but it forms a ground-covering mat and the 3 in. high flower-stalks bear small pendant bells in blue or white. If the site is shady you can grow **C. muralis (C. portenschlagiana)** — height 4 in., spread 1 ft. But do remember that it is a rampant grower producing purple bells on trailing stems. Another vigorous species is the starry **C. poscharskyana** — if you want a starry-flowered Campanula which will not spread everywhere then choose **C. garganica** which produces compact tufts with blue or white flowers. **C. zoysii** with its urn-shaped flowers is an example of a hard-to-grow Campanula.

SITE & SOIL: Any well-drained, non-acid soil — thrives in sun or light shade.

PROPAGATION: Sow seeds under glass or divide clumps in spring. Alternatively plant stem cuttings in a cold frame in late spring.

Campanula carpatica

Campanula cochlearifolia

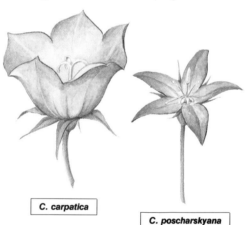

C. carpatica

C. poscharskyana

Campanula garganica

CASSIOPE Cassiope

Wiry stems with small bell-like flowers and a need for moist, cool and lime-free conditions. It is easy to see that Cassiope belongs to the Heather family, and it is easy to spot the difference. With these plants the leaves are scale-like and clasp the stem, giving a whipcord appearance. The white or pink blooms appear in late spring or early summer — the buds are damaged by frost so choose a sheltered spot.

VARIETIES: The easiest one to grow is **C. lycopodioides**, a prostrate mat-forming species which grows only 2-3 in. high but spreads 1½ ft or more. The cord-like stems are clothed with tiny ¼ in. flowers, each one white with a red calyx. Another easy one is the erect hybrid **C. 'Edinburgh'**, a free-flowering plant with white-edged leaves and white flowers. One of the parents of this hybrid is **C. tetragona** — the tallest of the rockery Cassiopes with clusters of ¼ in. pink-tinged white bells on the 1 ft high stems in April and May.

SITE & SOIL: Humus-rich acid soil is required — thrives in light shade.

PROPAGATION: Plant stem cuttings in a cold frame in summer.

Cassiope lycopodioides

C. 'Edinburgh'

CERASTIUM Snow-in-summer

This popular rock garden plant has few friends amongst the experts. Only a small minority of alpine nursery catalogues list it and the books which mention it issue a stern warning. The silvery-leaved sheets which bear white flowers in early summer will soon spread like a weed and choke out other plants. This is true and Cerastium has no place in an average-sized rockery, but there is little to beat it for quickly covering a large dry bank.

VARIETIES: The ordinary Cerastium is **C. tomentosum** — height 4 in., spread 2 ft or more, flowering period May–July. The white flowers (½–1 in. across) have notched petals and are borne in loose clusters above the woolly oblong leaves. The dwarf variety **C. tomentosum columnae** is equally rampant. The only restrained variety is **C. alpinum lanatum**, a compact grey-leaved Cerastium which forms neat mats, but it needs protection against winter rain and is not really worth the trouble.

SITE & SOIL: Any well-drained soil — thrives best in full sun.

PROPAGATION: Sow seeds or divide clumps in spring.

Cerastium tomentosum

C. tomentosum

CHAMAECYPARIS False Cypress

Chamaecyparis is one of the most popular conifers in Britain. Several types are just too quick-growing for the rock garden — don't be tempted to plant C. lawsoniana 'Allumii', 'Columnaris' or 'Fletcherii' because it looks small and attractive in the garden centre. There are, however, a number of dwarfs which are highly recommended for the rock garden. Leaves are scale-like and the branchlets form flattened sprays. The cones are small (½ in. or less) and round.

VARIETIES: C. obtusa has several good rockery varieties — **'Nana'** (round, dark green), **'Nana Gracilis'** (round, shell-shaped sprays of branchlets, dark green) and **'Nana Lutea'** (round, yellow). C. lawsoniana also has a number of slow-growing varieties — **'Ellwood's Gold'** (columnar, yellow-tipped green), **'Minima Aurea'** (conical, yellow) and **'Minima Glauca'** (round, green). Finally there are several varieties of C. pisifera — the popular and feathery **'Boulevard'** (conical, silvery-blue) and **'Plumosa Compacta'** (round, blue-green).

SITE & SOIL: Well-drained acid soil — thrives best in full sun.

PROPAGATION: Plant stem cuttings in a cold frame in autumn.

Chamaecyparis lawsoniana 'Minima Aurea'

C. lawsoniana 'Minima Glauca'

CORYDALIS Corydalis

The foliage of Corydalis is ferny and delicate and each tubular bloom is spurred at the rear and lipped at the front. Some are fibrous-rooted — the rest arise from tubers. There is no basic colour — one species is bright blue, some are yellow and others are white or pink. One species will spread and flower everywhere but another one may fail to flower even in expert hands.

VARIETIES: Pride of place must go to the much-praised **C. cashmeriana** with clusters of pure blue flowers — height 6 in., spread 6 in., flowering period April–June. There is a problem — it is difficult and needs peaty, well-drained and cool soil. **C. lutea** is much easier to grow — the flowers are just ordinary yellow but they appear from March to October. Others include **C. wilsonii** (blue foliage, yellow flowers, needs winter rain protection) and **C. solida** (rose, purple or white flowers).

SITE & SOIL: Requires well-drained open soil — thrives in sun or partial shade.

PROPAGATION: Sow seeds under glass or divide clumps in spring.

Corydalis cashmeriana

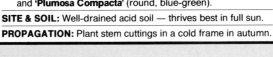

C. lutea

COTONEASTER   Cotoneaster

Cotoneaster microphyllus

The favourite garden Cotoneaster is C. horizontalis — a spreading 3 ft high bush grown against house walls or between taller shrubs. This one has no place in the average rock garden, but there are several dwarf Cotoneasters which are useful for clothing rocks or bare patches of soil. These ground-hugging types have small white flowers in summer followed by an abundance of showy berries and rich foliage colours in autumn. All are hardy and are tough enough to grow anywhere.

C. dammeri

VARIETIES: C. congestus nanus is a fine evergreen — less than 1 ft high with blue-green foliage and red berries. **C. adpressus** is even more prostrate — a deciduous species with Holly-like berries amongst the bronzy-red leaves in autumn. **C. dammeri** is perhaps the best of the lot — it grows only a few inches high but spreads up to 7 ft. The oval leaves are glossy and the bright red berries are borne singly or in pairs. The variety of **C. microphyllus** to choose is **thymifolius**.

SITE & SOIL: Any garden soil — thrives in sun or light shade.

PROPAGATION: Plant cuttings in a cold frame in late summer.

CROCUS   Crocus

Crocus chrysanthus 'Cream Beauty'

All the Crocus species and hybrids can be grown in the rock garden. Goblet-shaped flowers appear in many colours — bronze, white and blue as well as the too-familiar purple or yellow. Several types are described below, and the ones recommended for the rockery are not the large-flowered Crocuses seen everywhere in spring.

C. speciosus

VARIETIES: There are three basic groups. The favourite ones for the rock garden are the *Winter Flowering* species, planted in September and blooming in February. All are small, 3–4 in. high, and include **C. imperati** (striped white and purple), **C. susianus** (the Cloth of Gold Crocus with bronze and golden petals) and **C. chrysanthus** with its host of hybrids. The *Spring Flowering* Dutch hybrids grow about 5 in. high and bloom in March and April. Scores of varieties are available in a wide range of colours. The *Autumn Flowering* species, blooming between August and October, offer a much more restricted choice. **C. speciosus** varieties are the most popular, producing attractive flowers in white, lilac or purple.

SITE & SOIL: Any well-drained soil in sun or light shade.

PROPAGATION: Divide overcrowded clumps in autumn.

CYANANTHUS   Trailing Bellflower

Cyananthus microphyllus

This low-growing alpine appears in most text-books but it is hard to find in the catalogues and garden centres. It should be better known, as it is an excellent choice if there is a damp but well-drained spot to fill and if you live in a cool district. The prostrate matted stems bear solitary flowers at their tips. Cyananthus is closely related to Campanula, but it usually bears funnel-shaped blooms with wide-open lobes rather than bells or stars. Slugs can be a problem.

C. lobatus

VARIETIES: C. microphyllus is the one most likely to survive the British climate in winter. Basic details are height 3 in., spread 1 ft, flowering period August–September. The clear blue flowers are tubular with five narrow petal lobes spreading about 1 in. across. White and dark blue varieties are available. **C. lobatus** is also quite reliable — It is taller than the previous species and the flowers bear wide petal lobes. The usual colour is bright blue. **C. sherriffii** needs to be kept indoors.

SITE & SOIL: Requires well-drained, humus-rich soil — thrives in light shade.

PROPAGATION: Sow seeds under glass in spring or plant stem cuttings in a cold frame in late spring.

Cyclamen coum

CYCLAMEN Cyclamen

Cyclamen is generally thought of as a pot plant — large, long-stemmed flowers with swept-back petals. If this flower form appeals to you there are hardy dwarfs with 1 in. flowers to grow outdoors. The foliage is often marbled with silver and the blooms are sometimes fragrant. Buy growing plants rather than dried corms.

VARIETIES: There are winter-, spring-, summer- and autumn-flowering Cyclamens — the four varieties described below will provide blooms almost all year round. **C. hederifolium** (**C. neapolitanum**) is the easiest and most popular — the Ivy-shaped marbled leaves appear after the first flowers have opened. The flowering time is September to November — for flowers to follow in January to March grow **C. coum** (round leaves, flowers white, pink or red). Plant **C. repandum** (purple twisted petals) for blooms in April and May. **C. purpurascens** provides the July to September blooms.

SITE & SOIL: Well-drained, humus-rich soil in partial shade is required.

PROPAGATION: Sow seeds under glass in summer — plants cannot be divided.

C. hederifolium

CYTISUS Broom

The Brooms bear whippy stems with tiny leaves which are almost completely clothed with Pea-like flowers in either spring or summer, depending on the variety. They are easy plants to grow, thriving in dry and starved soils, but Cytisus cannot tolerate root disturbance, so buy pot-grown plants and do not try to transplant established specimens. Yellow is the usual flower colour but there are one or two whites, pinks and reds.

VARIETIES: Choose a dwarf species. Even here you must be careful — some of the so-called dwarfs such as **C. kewensis** (spreading, April flowering) and **C. beanii** (upright, May flowering) can reach 2 ft. For the average-sized rock garden there are **C. decumbens** (6 in. high, prostrate, bright yellow flowers in May and June), **C. ardoinii** (8 in. high, arching, golden yellow flowers in April and May) or the larger **C. purpureus** (1½ ft high, semi-prostrate, lilac flowers in May). The baby Broom is **C. demissus** (3 in.).

SITE & SOIL: Thrives best in poor, sandy soil in full sun.

PROPAGATION: Sow seeds under glass or plant cuttings in a cold frame in summer.

Cytisus demissus

C. purpureus

DAPHNE Daphne

It is not difficult to understand why the experts heap so much praise on the dwarf Daphnes when you see and smell the fragrance of a well-grown specimen in full flower. But it is not trouble free — some species are hard to grow and all are difficult to propagate. They can be short-lived and all parts are poisonous. Still, the starry flowers borne in profusion in spring easily outweigh the drawbacks.

VARIETIES: There is a small group of easy dwarf Daphnes and beginners should pick one of them. The most popular and perhaps the best is **D. cneorum** — height 6 in., spread 6 ft, flowering period April–May. The sweet-smelling pink flowers may cover the whole shrub — recommended varieties include **'Eximia', 'Variegata'** and **pygmaea**. Another excellent 6 in. high species is the pink-flowered **D. arbuscula** (April–June). **D. retusa** is rather different — it grows about 1½ ft high and the flowers which appear in April and May are white or purple. **D. neapolitana** can reach 2 ft or more.

SITE & SOIL: Well-drained, humus-rich soil is required — thrives best in full sun.

PROPAGATION: Plant stem cuttings in a cold frame in summer.

Daphne cneorum

D. arbuscula

Dianthus deltoides 'Flashing Light'

Dianthus caesius

DIANTHUS   Rockery Pink

Flower beds and borders are the place for the larger members of this genus — the Carnations, Sweet Williams and the Old-fashioned Pinks. This leaves scores of dwarfs, and there are species suited to screes, troughs, paving and walls as well as the planting pockets between the stones in the rock garden. The Rockery Pinks form either neat cushions or spreading carpets of grey or green grassy foliage. These leaves are covered by the sweet-smelling and generally fringed flowers in May or June, just as the display of the popular spring-flowering alpines comes to an end. Pink is the usual colour, but whites, reds, purples and even one yellow (D. knappii) are available. As a general rule the Rockery Pinks like but do not insist on chalky soils but they all hate clayey ones.

VARIETIES: Choose **D. alpinus** (Alpine Pink) if you want large 1 in. flowers on neat cushions of green foliage — height 4 in., spread 6 in., flowering period May–August. The dark-eyed blooms are available in pink, white or purple. **D. deltoides** (Maiden Pink) is an old favourite — height 8 in., spread 10 in., flowering period June–September. Pink is the usual colour, but there is also white (**'Albus'**) and bright red (**'Flashing Light'**). For covering large areas pick the carpeter **D. caesius** (**D. gratianopolitanus**) — height 8 in., spread 2 ft, flowering period May–July. Miniatures for the trough or sink garden include **D. erinaceus** and **D. freynii** (height 2 in., flowers small and pink). **D. neglectus** (**D. pavonius**) is unusual — the flowers do not appear until July and August and the pink petals have a biscuit-coloured reverse. In addition to the species there are many miniature hybrids, such as **'Little Jock'** (pink), **'La Bourbrille'** (pink) and **'Nellie Clark'** (red).

SITE & SOIL: Requires well-drained open soil — thrives in full sun.

PROPAGATION: Sow seeds under glass in spring or plant cuttings in a cold frame in summer.

D. alpinus

Dianthus 'Little Jock'

DIASCIA   Twinspur

Some plants decline in popularity as the years go by, but others such as this S. African sprawling rockery plant quite quickly move from being a rarity to appearing in most of the catalogues. Just two are offered for planting in the rock garden — both are dwarf and quite hardy but may die out if the winter is exceptionally cold. The flowering period is long and the flat-faced pink blooms are borne in great profusion. Look for the two spurs at the back of the flower which give this plant its common name.

VARIETIES: D. cordata forms a mat of wiry stems which reach about 8 in. high. Loose heads of Nemesia-like flowers appear in June and continue to appear until September. Throughout this long flowering period the plant is covered with these rosy-pink flowers. The hybrid of D. cordata and D. barbarae was launched as **D. 'Ruby Field'** in the 1970s and has become popular. It is taller than D. cordata (9–10 in.) and the flowers are larger.

SITE & SOIL: Requires well-drained soil and a sunny site.

PROPAGATION: Plant stem cuttings in a cold frame in spring.

D. cordata

Diascia 'Ruby Field'

DICENTRA Bleeding Heart

The Common Bleeding Heart (D. spectabilis) belongs in the bed or border — there are smaller, feathery-leaved species for the rock garden. The popular dwarfs are easy to grow provided the soil is reasonably fertile and is kept moist in dry weather. In early summer the flowering sprays appear — arching stems bearing pendant locket-like flowers in white, pink or red.

VARIETIES: D. cucullaria (Dutchman's Breeches) is a popular 6 in. high rockery type — the flowers are white with yellow tips and appear in April and May above mounds of ferny foliage. As with all of the Dicentras, the leaves die down shortly after flowering. **D. canadensis** is quite similar, but the flowers are all-white with just a touch of green. **D. eximia** (1 ft) is a taller plant with pink-purple flowers from May to midsummer. **D. formosa** (1½ ft) produces pink blooms in early summer. **D. peregrina** is a difficult beauty — popular in the text-books but rare in the catalogues.

SITE & SOIL: Any well-drained garden soil will do — thrives best in light shade.

PROPAGATION: Divide clumps after flowering.

Dicentra eximia

D. cucullaria

DODECATHEON Shooting Star

A plant for a moist and shady spot — often grown with Primulas as they both thrive under the same conditions. The common name comes from the shape of the flowers — the petals are swept backwards, revealing the anthers. These Cyclamen-like blooms are borne in clusters on top of an upright stalk. Eye-catching in summer when the flowers are present, but in winter the leaves die down.

VARIETIES: The most popular species is **D. meadia** (American Cowslip), but it is not the best one for the rock garden. Basic details are height 1½ ft, spread 1½ ft, flowering period June–July. The usual colour is rose-purple, but a white variety (**album**) is available. A better choice is **D. pulchellum**, also sold as **D. pauciflorum** and **D. radicatum**. The foliage is neater, the flower-stalks shorter and the fine crimson variety (**'Red Wings'**) grows only 8 in. high. At the mouth of the flower there is a group of purple stamens.

SITE & SOIL: Requires a moist but well-drained spot — thrives best in light shade.

PROPAGATION: Sow seeds under glass or divide clumps in spring.

Dodecatheon meadia

D. pulchellum 'Red Wings'

DRABA Whitlow Grass

Some of the plants in the A–Z guide are too large or too invasive to be grown in a trough or small rock garden. Draba has the opposite problem — it is so small and delicate that it would be lost in an extensive open space. It belongs in a trough, scree, a small crevice between rocks or in a pot in the alpine house. No more than a couple of inches high, the mounds of tiny leaves bear clusters of white or yellow flowers in spring.

VARIETIES: The easiest one to grow is also the largest — **D. aizoides.** The basic details are height 3–4 in., spread 6 in., flowering period April. The greyish leaves are borne in rosettes which are clustered together to form a bristly cushion. The yellow flowers are borne on wiry stems. **D. bryoides imbricata** is a choicer variety, with a height and spread of only 2 in. Bright yellow flowers appear in April. Don't be tempted to buy the lovely cushioned and wide-spreading **D. mollissima** — it's one for the specialist and the alpine house.

SITE & SOIL: Any well-drained soil — thrives best in full sun.

PROPAGATION: Sow seeds under glass in spring or plant rosettes in a cold frame in summer.

Draba bryoides imbricata

D. aizoides

DRYAS Mountain Avens

An excellent prostrate plant for ground cover or clothing bare rocks. The creeping woody stems bear leathery evergreen leaves which are shiny green above and silvery below. Above this Oak-like foliage the large flowers appear on short stalks in late spring or early summer, and these blooms are followed by attractive silky seed heads in summer. Do not feed — flowering is disappointing in rich soil.

VARIETIES: The popular species is **D. octopetala**, which grows wild in the mountainous regions of Britain and other European countries. The basic details are height 4 in., spread 2 ft, flowering period May-June. The blooms are about 1½ in. in diameter and look like small Shrub Roses. There are eight white petals and a golden centre. Where space is limited grow the miniature variety **'Minor'**. The American species **D. drummondii** bears yellow flowers. The hybrid of these two species is **D. suendermannii** with cream-coloured blooms.

SITE & SOIL: Thrives in well-drained soil and full sun.

PROPAGATION: Plant stem cuttings in a cold frame in summer.

Dryas octopetala

D. octopetala

EDRAIANTHUS Edraianthus

It is easy to see the family resemblance to the Campanulas. This low-growing plant produces tight clumps of tufted foliage from which trailing stems arise. The flowers are open bells of blue, white or occasionally purple — they appear on short stalks in June and July. Not a difficult plant, but it is occasionally short-lived. Its deep-rooting habit makes it a good choice for dry situations.

VARIETIES: E. pumilio is the pick of the bunch. It is compact — 3 in. high with a 6 in. spread, and a mass of violet-blue flowers. These almost stemless blooms cover much of the silvery-grey foliage. The bells are 1 in. across. For flowers which are 2 in. wide choose **E. serpyllifolius** (**Wahlenbergia serpyllifolia**) — height 6 in., spread 1 ft. The large violet blooms form a ring around the edge of the tufted clumps. The variety **'Major'** has the largest blooms. **E. graminifolius** has grassy leaves and almost stemless blue-purple flowers.

SITE & SOIL: Requires well-drained gritty soil — thrives in full sun.

PROPAGATION: Sow seeds or plant stem cuttings in a cold frame in summer.

Edraianthus serpyllifolius

E. pumilio

ERICA Heather

For some reason Ericas are rejected by some of the experts as suitable plants for the rock garden. Yet these woody evergreens with their needle-like leaves and bell-like flowers have a number of distinct advantages. They are easy to obtain and grow, are not rampant spreaders and are available in a wide range of flower and foliage colours. By choosing varieties with care, you can have Ericas in flower nearly all year round.

VARIETIES: Pick **E. carnea** (**E. herbacea**) for blooms between January and April — height 9 in., spread 2 ft. The blooms are borne on one side of the stem and there are many varieties ranging from pure white to deep red. A few well-known ones are **'Vivellii'** (red foliage and flowers), **'Springwood White'** and **'Springwood Pink'**. This species does not demand acid soil — the others do. The Bell Heather **E. cinerea** (in bloom June-September) has many varieties, ranging from white to near-black. **E. tetralix** (in bloom June-October) has grey foliage.

SITE & SOIL: Requires well-drained soil and a sunny site.

PROPAGATION: Layer shoots in spring or plant stem cuttings in a cold frame in summer.

Erica carnea

E. cinerea

ERIGERON Fleabane

There are several dwarf Fleabanes for the rock garden, all with golden-centred flowers with several whorls of ray florets in white, blue, pink, purple or yellow. They are easy to grow if the site is sunny and there is a long flowering season, but the smaller species tend to be short-lived. Choose with care — some species form neat clumps but one or two can be very invasive.

VARIETIES: E. mucronatus (**E. karvinskianus**) is the most popular species but it is also the most invasive, spreading by runners and self-seeding. Keep it out of the rockery — use it instead in paving cracks and crevices between walling stones. Basic details are height 6 in., spread 2 ft, flowering period June–October. Flowers darken from white to deep pink with age. Other species include **E. aureus** (height 4 in., spread 9 in., golden flowers in June and July), the tiny **E. compositus** (height 3 in., spread 5 in., pale blue flowers in June–October) and the much larger **E. aurantiacus** (height 1 ft, spread 1½ ft, orange flowers in June–August).

SITE & SOIL: Thrives best in well-drained gritty soil in full sun.

PROPAGATION: Sow seeds or divide clumps in spring.

Erigeron aureus

E. mucronatus

ERINUS Summer Starwort

The species grown in rock gardens is a true alpine, growing wild in the mountains of Europe and sometimes seen as a naturalised plant in cracks and crannies in old buildings and walls. It is small and short-lived, but this is not a problem as self-sown seedlings take over, providing small mounds of tiny green leaves. Clusters of small starry flowers appear on short wiry stalks — a splash of pink, white or red which lasts until midsummer or even longer.

VARIETIES: There is just one species — **E. alpinus**. The basic details are height 3 in., spread 4 in., flowering period April–August. The toothed leaves are dark green and the flower colour is pink. At first glance the flowers look like five-petalled stars, but on closer examination they are seen to be two-lipped, with two lobes above and three lobes below. You can buy named varieties in different colours, such as **'Albus'** (white), **'Dr Hanele'** (crimson) and **'Mrs Charles Boyle'** (pink).

SITE & SOIL: Requires well-drained infertile soil — thrives in sun or light shade.

PROPAGATION: Sow seeds in spring where the plants are to flower.

Erinus alpinus 'Albus'

E. alpinus

ERODIUM Storksbill, Heron's Bill

A number of species are available for growing in a sunny rock garden or trough. They are long-lived and not fussy about soil type, and the foliage as well as the blooms is generally attractive. The usual flower colour is white or pink with a network of red veins, but there are exceptions. The common name relates to the long and beaked fruits.

VARIETIES: The plants are nice but the names in the catalogues are often muddled. The most important species is listed as **E. reichardii** (**E. chamaedrioides**). It is a ground-hugging plant which produces almost stemless flowers in June and July. Choose one of the varieties — **'Album'** (white), **'Roseum'** (pale pink) or **'Bishop's Form'** (deep pink). All have reddish-purple veins on the petals. **E. chrysanthemum** (6 in. high clumps) has yellow flowers in May and June. An odd point — male and female flowers occur on separate plants. **E. corsicum** is a silvery-leaved pink-flowered species which forms a mat rather than a clump. Others to look for are **E. guttatum** and **E. petraeum**.

SITE & SOIL: Any well-drained garden soil — thrives in full sun.

PROPAGATION: Sow seeds or divide clumps in spring.

Erodium reichardii 'Roseum'

E. corsicum

EURYOPS Euryops

This member of the Daisy family from S. Africa has become increasingly popular in recent years, but it is still missing from many catalogues and garden centres. It forms a rounded bush with attractive foliage and in late spring bright yellow flowers appear. When conditions are right the whole bush may be covered by the blooms, but in some seasons the number of flowers may be disappointing. Dead-head when flowers fade and cut the plant back hard every few years to maintain the compact growth habit.

VARIETY: There is just one species for the outdoor garden — **E. acraeus**, sometimes sold as **E. evansii**. Basic details are height 1 ft, spread 1½ ft, flowering period May–June. The ends of the branched stems are crowded with silvery-grey narrow leaves. This foliage is evergreen and the bush is hardy, making Euryops a useful addition to any rock garden in winter. The flowers are about 1 in. across and are borne on 1½ in. stalks. Other Euryops species need an alpine house.

SITE & SOIL: Requires well-drained gritty soil in full sun.

PROPAGATION: Easy. Plant cuttings in a cold frame in summer.

E. acraeus

Euryops acraeus

FRANKENIA Sea Heath

Sea Heath is an appropriate name for this carpeting plant — it looks like Heather when not in bloom and its natural home is the seaside. One of the species grown (F. laevis) is found growing wild in coastal areas. Frankenia is a prostrate shrubby plant with wiry stems and tiny leaves. In summer small pink flowers appear above the foliage, each one bearing five petals around a yellow centre. In autumn the foliage is often tinged with reddish tones.

VARIETIES: F. laevis is the smaller of the two species offered for sale. The prostrate reddish stems bear small narrow leaves with inrolled edges — this foliage is green and slightly downy. Solitary pink flowers, about ¼ in. across, appear in July and August. **F. thymaefolia** is easier to obtain and to grow. This native of Spain and Morocco differs in a number of ways. The flowers are larger, more numerous and are borne in clusters. The plant grows about 3 in. high.

SITE & SOIL: Requires well-drained open soil — thrives in full sun.

PROPAGATION: Divide clumps or plant cuttings in a cold frame in summer.

F. laevis

Frankenia thymaefolia

GAULTHERIA Wintergreen

Many species of this dwarf shrub are listed in the specialist catalogues. One of the smaller species is an excellent choice if you want an evergreen carpeter which bears bell-like flowers in summer and showy berries in autumn. Don't bother with Gaultheria, however, unless you can provide it with acid, humus-rich soil in a partly shaded position. It is one for the peat bed rather than the rock garden.

VARIETIES: The best-known Gaultheria is the Partridge Berry (**G. procumbens**). The spreading branches bear shiny, dark green leaves and this neat mat grows about 6 in. high. In July the pink-flushed white blooms appear and these are followed by bright red berries and reddish foliage in autumn. **G. cuneata** and **G. miqueliana** grow 1 ft high and bear white flowers which turn into white berries. **G. nummularoides** is quite different — the leaves are downy rather than leathery and it rarely grows over 3 in. high. The white or pink flowers are succeeded by blue-black berries.

SITE & SOIL: Requires well-drained acid soil in partial shade.

PROPAGATION: Layer shoots in spring or plant stem cuttings in a cold frame in summer.

G. procumbens

Gaultheria cuneata

GENISTA Broom

This group of Brooms generally have wiry stems, tiny leaves and a mass of yellow flowers in June. There the generalisations end — Genista species may be evergreen or deciduous, spiny or thornless and heights range from 2 in. to 12 ft. All bloom freely if given plenty of sun and no food — fertile soil reduces flowering. After flowering, spreading plants can be kept in check by cutting back stems which have borne blooms, but do not prune into old wood.

VARIETIES: The most popular one for the rock garden is **G. lydia**, a spreading shrub growing about 2 ft high. Its arching stems are covered with golden yellow flowers in May and June. **G. hispanica** (Spanish Broom) is a 1 ft high, densely branched and spiny species which is excellent for ground cover. **G. pilosa** is a prostrate thornless species — **G. pulchella** (2 in.) is even shorter. **G. sagittalis** is unusual — the young stems are flattened and winged, and the bright yellow flowers are borne in terminal spikes.

SITE & SOIL: Requires well-drained open soil in full sun.

PROPAGATION: Sow seeds or plant stem cuttings in a propagator in summer.

G. lydia

Genista hispanica

GENTIANA Gentian

For most people this is the queen of the alpines — to attempt to create a truly impressive rock garden without at least one Gentian would be unthinkable. The blue trumpets can provide colour from May to October if you choose a selection of spring-, summer- and autumn-flowering types. Unfortunately most Gentians are rather temperamental and cannot be regarded as 'grow anywhere' plants. You should always check the likes and dislikes of a particular species before you buy it, and even then it can be flower-shy for no particular reason. Lime is a problem — spring-flowering types may either tolerate or require it, but the autumn-flowering Gentians cannot stand it. All demand free-draining but not impoverished soil. Add peat and some grit before planting firmly in spring.

VARIETIES: The easiest one to grow is the summer-flowering **G. septemfida** which gives a good display of 1–2 in. long purple-blue trumpets in any sunny well-drained spot. The basic details are height 9 in., spread 1 ft, flowering period July–August. The popular **G. acaulis** (Trumpet Gentian) is a smaller plant (3 in. high) and blooms earlier (May–June), but its flowers are much more eye-catching — 3 in. long almost stemless trumpets standing upright above the glossy oval leaves. Unfortunately it is unpredictable — in some situations it will not bloom and nobody knows why. If your plant is flower-shy, simply move it to another spot in autumn. **G. verna** is another spring-flowering Gentian — height 3 in., spread 6 in., flowering period May–June. Its starry flowers are bright blue — an attractive evergreen which is unfortunately short-lived. The most popular autumn-flowering Gentian is **G. sino-ornata** — height 6 in., spread 1 ft, flowering period September–October. The 2 in. long trumpets are bright blue with pale green stripes. For many experts the white-throated **G. farreri** is the best of all.

SITE & SOIL: Well-drained soil is essential — thrives in sun or light shade.

PROPAGATION: Divide clumps in spring (autumn-flowering Gentians) or midsummer (spring-flowering Gentians). Sow seeds for G. verna.

Gentiana septemfida

Gentiana acaulis

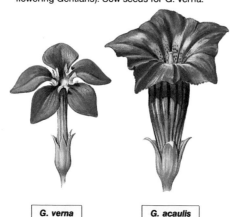
G. verna   G. acaulis

Gentiana farreri

GERANIUM Rockery Cranesbill

The Garden Geraniums should not be confused with the bedding and house plant 'Geraniums' with their large heads of showy flowers. The plants described here are low-growing perennials which die down in winter and then produce divided or lobed leaves in spring and bowl-shaped flowers in summer. The foliage may be green or grey and the white, pink or red flowers are usually prominently veined. All are easy to grow as long as the site is free draining and not too shady. Watch out for slugs.

VARIETIES: **G. cinereum** is an attractive species — height 6 in., spread 1 ft, flowering period May–August. It is best known through its variety or hybrid **G. 'Ballerina'** — this plant has ashen grey foliage and large pink flowers. There is a white type (**'Album'**) and a crimson one (**G. subcaulescens**). **G. dalmaticum** reaches the same height and spread as G. cinereum and its varieties, but the flowering period is shorter (June–August) and the pale pink flowers are not veined.

SITE & SOIL: Any well-drained soil — thrives best in full sun.

PROPAGATION: Sow seeds or divide clumps in spring.

Geranium subcaulescens

G. 'Ballerina'

GEUM Alpine Avens

Most of the ordinary Geums, such as Mrs Bradshaw, are too tall for the rockery, but there are a few dwarfs which are excellent for filling planting pockets and should be more widely grown. They are true alpines, growing wild in the Swiss Alps. The flowers are large, usually yellow, and bear a prominent mass of stamens at the centre. These Rose-like blooms are followed by fluffy seed heads.

VARIETIES: **G. montanum** produces clumps of rough and wrinkled leaves, and in summer a mass of golden yellow flowers on short stalks. The basic details are height 9 in., spread 1 ft, flowering period May-July. It is an easy and reliable plant to grow, but **G. reptans** is not. This temperamental Geum produces long Strawberry-like runners which spread out, producing rosettes of leaves where rooting takes place. Bright yellow flowers, 1½ in. across, appear on 6 in. stems. A much better choice is its hybrid **G. 'Borisii'** — clump-forming, easy to grow, and with masses of orange flowers all summer long.

SITE & SOIL: Any well-drained soil — thrives best in full sun.

PROPAGATION: Sow seeds or divide clumps in spring.

Geum 'Borisii'

G. montanum

GYPSOPHILA Baby's Breath

All the dwarf Gypsophilas have narrow greyish leaves and form clouds of tiny white or pink flowers in summer. The most popular one is G. repens, which looks like a scaled-down version of the herbaceous border Gypsophila. It is ideal for trailing over rocks, and like the other dwarf species it is both hardy and easy to grow. Gypsophilas are lime lovers but an alkaline soil is not essential.

VARIETIES: The basic details of **G. repens** are height 6 in., spread 2 ft, flowering period June–August. It is quick-growing, the carpet of stems of grey-tinged foliage soon spreading over quite a large area. It is usual to grow a named variety. **'Dorothy Teacher'** is a good compact form with bluish-grey leaves and pink flowers, **fratensis** and **'Letchworth Rose'** are other single pinks and **'Rosea'** is a double pink. For white flowers grow **alba** or **'Monstrosa'**. Other species include the loosely cushioned **G. cerastioides** with its red-veined white flowers or the tightly cushioned **G. arietioides**.

SITE & SOIL: Any well-drained soil — full sun is required.

PROPAGATION: Plant stem cuttings in a cold frame in early summer.

Gypsophila 'Dorothy Teacher'

G. repens
fratensis

HABERLEA Haberlea

Many of the rock garden plants listed in this section are easy to grow and not at all fussy about location. This attractive alpine, like its close relative Ramonda, is quite different — it will not grow unless the conditions are just right. This calls for acid soil in a shady spot and water must not be allowed to stand in the heart of the rosette of leaves in winter. The usual advice is to plant it sideways in a crack between the stones on the north-facing side of the rockery, but the best place of all is between peat blocks.

H. rhodopensis

VARIETIES: The one you are most likely to find in the garden centre or catalogue is **H. rhodopensis**. Basic details are height 4 in., spread 8 in., flowering period May–June. There is a rosette of leathery toothed leaves and the stalks bear clusters of lilac flowers which are tubular and about 1 in. across. A white variety (**'Virginalis'**) is available. **H. ferdinandi-coburgii** is larger and the lilac flowers are flecked with gold.

SITE & SOIL: Requires well-drained but damp soil with little or no direct sun.

PROPAGATION: Divide clumps in autumn or plant leaf cuttings in a cold frame in summer.

Haberlea rhodopensis

HEBE Veronica

A large genus of evergreen shrubs from New Zealand, once grouped with Veronica and this still remains the common name. The usual pattern is a neat bush with either scale-like or oval leaves and spikes of tiny white or blue flowers. They come in all sizes, but only the popular dwarfs are described here.

H. pinguifolia 'Pagei'

VARIETIES: One of the best for the rock garden is **H. pinguifolia 'Pagei'**. The bush is about 9 in. high and the branches are clothed with greyish-green leaves. Between May and August floral spikes densely crowded with white flowers appear. **H. 'Carl Teschner'** is another popular Hebe — a prostrate plant with dark green leaves on near-black stems and white-throated mauve flowers in June and July. **H. 'Green Globe'** is an 8 in. ball of tiny Box-like foliage. **H. epacridea** is different — the stems are clothed with scale-like leaves and these 'whip-cord' branches bear white fragrant flowers in July. **H. 'Boughton Dome'** is another Whipcord Hebe, grown solely for its conifer-like appearance.

SITE & SOIL: Any well-drained soil in sun or light shade.

PROPAGATION: Plant stem cuttings in a cold frame in summer.

Hebe 'Carl Teschner'

HELIANTHEMUM Rock Rose

Few plants can match the ability of the lowly Rock Rose to provide such a long-lasting sheet of orange or yellow flowers during the summer months. Each flower lives for only a day or two, but new ones are borne in profusion between May and July. The spreading wiry stems become straggly and invasive if wrongly treated — once the first flush of flowers has faded you must cut them back hard to prolong the life of the plant and to induce another flush.

H. nummularium 'Ben Hope'

VARIETIES: Nearly all the Helianthemums grown in the rock garden are named varieties of **H. nummularium**. The basic details are height 6–9 in., spread 2 ft, papery flowers 1 in. across. The varieties may be single or double, and the colours range from white to deep red. Well-known ones include **'The Bride'** (white), **'Fire Dragon'** (orange) and **'Wisley Primrose'** (yellow). The 'Ben' series (**'Ben Hope'**, **'Ben Ledi'** etc) are reputed to be the hardiest. **H. alpestre** (height 4 in., spread 1 ft, yellow flowers) is an uncommon alpine relative.

SITE & SOIL: Requires free-draining gritty soil in full sun.

PROPAGATION: Plant stem cuttings in a cold frame in late summer.

Helianthemum 'Wisley Primrose'

HELICHRYSUM Rockery Helichrysum

The well-known annual Helichrysum grown for its 'ever-lasting' flowers is H. bracteatum — the blooms are cut and dried for floral decoration. This plant has a number of dwarf perennial relatives and a few of them can be used for ground cover in the rock garden. The ones described below are suitable for growing outdoors — there are others which need the protection of an alpine house. The Rockery Helichrysums are usually grown for their silvery foliage rather than their drab flowers.

VARIETIES: The species you are most likely to find is **H. bellidioides** — height 3 in., spread 1½ ft, flowering period June–August. It forms a mat of small woolly grey leaves which can be invasive if not kept in check. The white strawy-petalled flowers appear on short stalks. **H. coralloides** is grown for its curious coral-like appearance — branched and gnarled stems covered with scale-like leaves. **H. milfordiae** has the most colourful blooms — red buds and large silvery-white flowers.

SITE & SOIL: Any well-drained soil — full sun is essential.

PROPAGATION: Plant cuttings in a cold frame or divide clumps in summer.

Helichrysum bellidioides

H. milfordiae

HEPATICA Hepatica

A good choice for the rockery or peat bed as it begins to flower in late winter before the usual spring flowers (Aubrietia, Arabis etc) appear. But Hepatica has a special need — the soil must be kept moist at all times. It thrives best in partial shade — add peat or leaf-mould at planting time. The Anemone-like flowers are followed by stalked lobed leaves and in time the plants form large and dense clumps.

VARIETIES: The most popular species is **H. nobilis** (**H. triloba**). The basic details are height 3 in., spread 1 ft, flowering period February–April. The mauve starry flowers, measuring 1 in. across, are on short stalks above the tri-lobed leaves. Single and double varieties are available in white (**alba**), blue, pink or purple. **H. transsylvanica** (**H. angulosa**) is similar in appearance but is larger and the leaves are more rounded with scalloped edges. Best of all is the hybrid of these two species (**H. media 'Ballardii'**) with large, pure blue flowers.

SITE & SOIL: Well-drained but damp soil is required — thrives in light shade.

PROPAGATION: Divide large clumps in autumn.

Hepatica transsylvanica

H. nobilis

HUTCHINSIA Chamois Cress

Hutchinsia is a European alpine, growing wild high up in the Alps and Pyrenees. In early summer the leaves are covered by clusters of white flowers, but these blooms are much smaller than those borne by its more popular relatives Arabis and Iberis. This easy-to-grow and hardy alpine can be lost if planted between large rocks — the best place for it is in a trough, raised bed or crevice in a dry wall. Hutchinsia is short-lived but it readily self-seeds.

VARIETY: There is a single species — **H. alpina**. The basic details are height 2 in., spread 9 in., flowering period May–July. The rosette of evergreen leaves gives the plant a tufted appearance — this foliage is dark green, shiny and divided into small leaflets. The short flower-stalks appear in profusion and at the top of each one is a crowded 1 in. cluster of small, pure white flowers. Each bloom has the usual Crucifer pattern of four petals. The variety **brevicaulis** (1 in. high) is even smaller than the species.

SITE & SOIL: Requires well-drained gritty soil — thrives in sun or light shade.

PROPAGATION: Sow seeds as soon as they are ripe.

Hutchinsia alpina

H. alpina

Hypericum coris

HYPERICUM   St. John's Wort

The Hypericum you see everywhere is the bushy H. calycinum (Rose of Sharon). Growing about 1½ ft high, it can be used to clothe a large bare bank, but avoid it like the plague in an average-sized rockery — its highly invasive nature will soon swamp choicer plants. There are a number of dwarf Hypericums — all have large five-petalled flowers with a prominent central boss of stamens. Yellow is the standard colour and the ones listed below make excellent rockery plants.

VARIETIES: The most popular one is **H. olympicum**, which is almost identical to and frequently sold as **H. polyphyllum**. The basic details are height 6 in., spread 1 ft, flowering period July–August. The variety **'Citrinum'** is rather smaller and bears lemon-yellow flowers. **H. coris** is an evergreen Heather-like plant (6 in. high) which bears yellow star-shaped flowers in midsummer. **H. reptans** and **H. trichocaulon** bear yellow flowers preceded by red buds.

SITE & SOIL: Any well-drained soil — thrives best in full sun.

PROPAGATION: Plant stem cuttings in a cold frame in early summer.

H. olympicum

Iberis sempervirens 'Snowflake'

IBERIS   Perennial Candytuft

Iberis is one of the basic ingredients of the non-specialist rock garden. The popular forms are evergreen, hardy and easy to grow. In late spring the plant is covered with flat clusters of white flowers. Each has the four-petalled arrangement of the Cabbage family, but there are two long petals and two short ones. Iberis does need room to spread — it is best grown where it can tumble over rocks, spread over paving or grow down a wall. Dead-head regularly in order to extend the flowering period.

VARIETIES: **I. sempervirens** (**I. semperflorens**) is the popular one — height 9 in., spread 2 ft, flowering period May–June with a second flush in autumn if the summer has been warm. The flat clusters of flowers are about 2 in. across. It is better to grow a named variety rather than the species. **'Snowflake'** (10 in.) is considered the best — where space is a problem choose the more compact **'Little Gem'** (4 in.) or **pygmaea** (3 in.). If you want an unusual Iberis, there are **I. saxatile** (4 in., tiny leaves, white flowers) and **I. gibraltarica** (9 in., white or lilac flowers).

SITE & SOIL: Any well-drained soil — thrives best in full sun.

PROPAGATION: Plant stem cuttings in a cold frame in summer.

I. sempervirens

Iris reticulata

IRIS   Rockery Iris

The general flower form of the Iris is three erect inner petals ('standards') and three pendant outer petals ('falls'). There may be fleshy hairs on the falls ('beards'). The best-known Irises are the large ones which grow in the herbaceous border or at the edge of the pond, but there are also some splendid dwarf ones which belong in every rock garden.

VARIETIES: The *Bulb* group contains such rockery favourites as **I. danfordiae** (5 in., yellow flowers in February–March) and **I. reticulata** (5 in., yellow-marked purple flowers in February–March). Best, perhaps, is the beautiful blue and gold **I. histrioides 'Major'**. The *Rhizomatous/Fibrous-rooted* group has a wide variety of heights and colours. Included here are the hybrids of the bearded **I. pumila** (4–6 in.), **I. cristata** (6 in., purple and gold flowers), **I. lacustris** (3 in., lilac, yellow and white flowers) and **I. innominata** (6 in., gold and brown flowers).

SITE & SOIL: Well-drained soil is required — it can be alkaline for the Bulb group but not for the others. Sun requirement depends on the species.

PROPAGATION: Depends on the species. Divide bulbs when foliage has died down — divide rhizomes after flowering.

I. danfordiae

JUNIPERUS Juniper

Juniper is the star of the rockery conifers — the low-growing types with their tiered branches provide excellent ground cover. Juvenile leaves are Heather-like but adult ones are tiny green scales. The cones are green and berry-like, made up of fleshy fused scales. One of the most popular garden Junipers is the Pfitzer (J. media 'Pfitzeriana'), but it is too vigorous for most situations.

VARIETIES: The Spanish Juniper (**J. sabina 'Tamariscifolia'**) is an old favourite — horizontal branches of feathery foliage with an 8–10 ft spread if left unpruned, but only 1 ft high. **J. horizontalis** is even smaller (height 6 in., spread 5 ft) and the leaves have a distinct bluish tinge. **J. communis 'Depressa Aurea'** is a 1–2 ft high spreading bush — golden in summer and bronze in winter. There are a number of others which will not exceed 3 ft when mature — choose from **J. media 'Old Gold'** (golden, spreading), **J. squamata 'Meyeri'** (blue-green, upright with drooping branches) and **J. communis 'Compressa'** (greyish-green, column-like).

SITE & SOIL: Well-drained acid soil — thrives best in full sun.

PROPAGATION: Plant stem cuttings in a cold frame in autumn.

J. communis 'Compressa'

Juniperus communis 'Depressa Aurea'

LEONTOPODIUM Edelweiss

You will find Edelweiss described in every book on rock garden plants, and it is listed in most alpine catalogues. This is not due to its beauty — many more attractive plants hardly get a mention. The simple reason is that Edelweiss is the symbol of the Alps and their flowers. It is an interesting rather than an attractive plant — greyish-white, flat flower-heads are borne on short stalks above the greyish-green leaves. It flourishes quite happily if the site is sunny and well-drained.

VARIETIES: You are likely to be offered only a single species — **L. alpinum**. The basic details are height 6 in., spread 9 in., flowering period June–July. The narrow leaves are hoary on top and densely woolly below. They form a rosette from which the flower stems arise. The curious flower-heads are about 2 in. across — a central group of small, rayless Daisy-like flowers surrounded by a number of long, flannel-like bracts. The variety **'Mignon'** is recommended — more compact and longer-living than the species.

SITE & SOIL: Requires well-drained gritty soil in full sun.

PROPAGATION: Sow seeds under glass in early spring.

L. alpinum

Leontopodium alpinum

LEWISIA Lewisia

Lewis and Clark were the first explorers to cross and map America from the Mississippi to the Pacific — this alpine of the Rockies honours Lewis and the annual Clarkia honours his partner. Lewisia is one of the most colourful of rockery plants — flowers in pink, peach, orange or white with petals which are often striped. Unfortunately, it is not easy to keep alive in the rockery as water in the heart of the plant causes it to rot in winter. The answer is to plant Lewisia sideways in a crack or crevice, to cover the plant with glass during the winter months or to grow it in an alpine house.

VARIETIES: **L. cotyledon** is the most popular species. The basic details are height 1 ft, spread 9 in., flowering period May–June. Choose one of the showy hybrids, such as the **'Sunset'** strain. The other species are more difficult to grow and are not really reliable outdoors. **L. brachycalyx** blooms in May and **L. rediviva** bears 2 in. wide flowers in June. The aristocrat is **L. tweedyi** with 2½ in. wide apricot blooms in April and May.

SITE & SOIL: Requires well-drained gritty soil in full sun.

PROPAGATION: Sow seeds under glass in early spring.

L. cotyledon

Lewisia cotyledon

Linaria alpina

LINARIA   Alpine Toadflax

The small Toadflaxes are eye-catching perennials with Snapdragon-like flowers. These blooms are generally bicoloured or multicoloured and are borne in clusters along the trailing stems. The leaves, which are borne in whorls, die down in winter. The popular species has two key features. The flowering span is long, extending from late spring to early autumn, but the life span of the plant is short, often no more than a couple of years.

VARIETIES: The usual one is **L. alpina**, which grows wild in the European Alps. It is an attractive creeper growing about 5–6 in. high, the trailing stems bearing bluish-grey fleshy leaves and forming a neat mat. The flowering season is May–September, each bloom gaily painted in violet and orange. There is a pink (**rosea**) variety. L. alpina self-seeds readily so there is usually a supply of new plants — another species which produces new plants from self-sown seeds is the yellow-flowered **L. supina**. The brightest Linaria is **L. tristis 'Toubkal'** with blooms in yellow, red and purple.

SITE & SOIL: Any well-drained garden soil — thrives in full sun.

PROPAGATION: Sow seeds or divide clumps in spring.

L. alpina

Linnaea borealis

LINNAEA   Twin Flower

This native of the colder areas of Northern Europe was named in honour of Linnaeus, one of Europe's most renowned naturalists. It is an old favourite which produces a tangled mat of slender stems and rounded evergreen leaves. It spreads quickly and can become invasive, but it is easily kept in check. During the summer months the dainty, bell-like flowers appear above the foliage. A good choice if you have a large damp and shady area to cover.

VARIETIES: There is just one species — **L. borealis**. The basic details are height 2 in., spread 2 ft, flowering period May–July. From the prostrate carpet of stems and leaves the flower-stalks appear, each one topped by a pair of pale pink flowers — hence the common name. An easy plant if the conditions are right — but a disappointment on a sandy, sunny or chalky site. If you can find it, choose the variety **americana** — the plant is bigger and less temperamental and the flowers are deeper pink.

SITE & SOIL: Requires moist, humus-rich soil in partial shade.

PROPAGATION: Sow seeds or plant stem cuttings in a cold frame in spring.

L. borealis

Linum arboreum

LINUM   Perennial Flax

The dwarf varieties of Flax are tufted plants with wiry stems which are easy to grow but are usually short-lived. They produce their flowers in summer — five-petalled and nearly always blue or yellow. The blooms fade quickly, but there are always more buds to open — the best displays occur in sandy soil and hot weather. The two enemies of Linum are waterlogged soil in winter and slugs in spring.

VARIETIES: L. perenne alpinum is one of the sky-blue varieties — height 6 in., flowering period June–August. Another blue variety for the rock garden, this time with white-centred blooms, is **L. narbonense 'Heavenly Blue'** (1 ft). **L. arboreum** is quite different — it is a woody species with grey-green leaves and terminal clusters of large, golden yellow flowers. Like another yellow Flax (**L. flavum**) it is only moderately hardy and is sometimes listed as a plant for the alpine house. The best of the yellow Flaxes is **L. 'Gemmell's Hybrid'** — a 6 in. grey-green mound bearing large flowers.

SITE & SOIL: Well-drained garden soil in full sun.

PROPAGATION: Sow seeds under glass or plant stem cuttings in a cold frame in early summer.

L. perenne
alpinum

LITHOSPERMUM Gromwell

Lithospermum (or Lithodora) is a ground cover plant with creeping stems and clothed with slender leaves. A mass of open-faced funnel-shaped flowers appear in summer. The colour of the popular species and its varieties is Gentian blue — as bright as anything you will find in the summer rock garden. Lithospermum requires a sunny spot and humus-rich soil. Do not grow L. diffusum if your soil is chalky — choose instead the lime-tolerant L. oleifolium.

VARIETIES: The favourite Gromwell for the rock garden is **Lithospermum diffusum (Lithodora diffusa)** — height 6 in., spread 2 ft, flowering period June-September. Its outstanding feature is the pure blue of its flowers. Two named varieties rather than the species are grown — **'Heavenly Blue'** and **'Grace Ward'**. Both are very similar despite the claim of obvious differences in some catalogues. **L. oleifolium** is quite different — the leaves are silvery-grey and the pink buds open into pale blue flowers.

SITE & SOIL: Well-drained moist soil in full sun is essential.

PROPAGATION: Plant stem cuttings in a cold frame in midsummer.

Lithospermum diffusum 'Heavenly Blue'

L. oleifolium

LYCHNIS Dwarf Campion

The Campions are generally too tall for the rock garden and most of them belong in the herbaceous border, but there are a few dwarfs. The most popular one (L. alpina) is a tiny plant which is easy to grow in the cracks between paving stones or in a sink garden. It is not difficult as long as the land is reasonably fertile. Unfortunately it is not long-lived, but the plants are easily raised from seed.

VARIETIES: The usual Lychnis in the rockery is **L. alpina**, the Alpine Campion, which is sometimes listed as **Viscaria alpina**. The basic details are height 4 in., spread 4 in., flowering period May–July. The flower-stalks are just a couple of inches high and each one is crowned with a group of pink flowers. For other colours choose the variety **'Alba'** (white) or **rosea** (deep pink). The other Dwarf Campions are taller. **L. viscaria 'Splendens Plena'** is a showy plant for the larger rock garden — heads of crimson double flowers on 1 ft stalks. **L. Flos-jovis** bears its carmine flowers on 8 in.–1 ft stalks above grey-felted foliage.

SITE & SOIL: Requires well-drained soil — thrives best in full sun.

PROPAGATION: Sow seeds under glass in early spring.

Lychnis alpina rosea

L. alpina

LYSIMACHIA Creeping Jenny

There is nothing choice about Creeping Jenny — it grows wild in damp woodland and its vigorous trailing stems will soon spread everywhere if not cut back after flowering. However, it is a good choice if you want to cover an area of bare soil, especially at the edge of a pond. Lysimachia flowers are bowl-shaped and usually yellow, although both white and red forms are available.

VARIETIES: The common-or-garden Creeping Jenny (Moneywort) is **L. nummularia** — height 2 in., spread 2 ft, flowering period May–August. The ½ in. flowers are yellow and the round leaves are bright green. It is a dense carpeter which stifles weeds, but is far too invasive for a small rockery. Choose instead the yellow-leaved variety **'Aurea'** — it is much less vigorous than the species and the foliage is attractive all year round. For a ground-hugging miniature grow the shade-loving **L. japonica 'Minutissima'**.

SITE & SOIL: Requires well-drained, humus-rich soil in sun or partial shade.

PROPAGATION: Plant cuttings in a cold frame in spring or divide clumps in autumn.

Lysimachia nummularia

L. nummularia

MAZUS Mazus

Mazus reptans

A low creeper which is closely related to Mimulus, but it is a sun-lover and the flowers are in white or purple rather than red or gold. It is an easy plant to grow in a fertile spot and will tolerate light shade, but it has never become popular as a rock garden plant. The flowers which appear in summer are unusual — they are two-lipped (a short one above and an extended and lobed lip below) and are attractively spotted.

M. reptans

VARIETIES: The only one you are likely to find is **M. reptans** — height 2 in., spread 1½ ft, flowering period June-August. The slender stems hug the ground and the large purple flowers are spotted and marked with white and yellow. There is a white-flowered variety (**'Albus'**) — like the species this plant is a lime-hater. **M. radicans** is different — the foliage is bronzy-green and the flowers white with a purple centre. It blooms in June and July — flowering rather later is the dark green **M. pumilio** which bears yellow-centred white flowers on short stalks.

SITE & SOIL: Requires well-drained soil — thrives in sun or light shade.

PROPAGATION: Sow seeds or divide clumps in spring.

MECONOPSIS Meconopsis

Meconopsis cambrica

There are numerous species but not many are suitable for the rock garden. As a general rule the flowers are blue and the plants require acid soil. Both blooms and plants are short-lived, and so the stock has to be regularly replenished from seed. Best-known is the Himalayan Blue Poppy — a beautiful plant but too tall for the modest rockery. The odd one out is the Welsh Poppy — the flowers are yellow and it is easy to grow.

M. quintuplinervia

VARIETIES: The Welsh Poppy (**M. cambrica**) is an undemanding plant which is not fussy about soil type and produces a succession of 2 in. wide clear yellow Poppies all summer long. The variety **aurantiaca** is orange and **'flore pleno'** is semi-double. The basic details are height 1 ft, spread 9 in., flowering period June–September. A word of warning — the Welsh Poppy seeds very freely and is therefore invasive. **M. quintuplinervia** (Harebell Poppy) is the one to choose — lavender-blue 1 in. wide Poppies which droop gracefully.

SITE & SOIL: Requires well-drained, lime-free soil in light shade.

PROPAGATION: Sow seeds under glass in spring.

MIMULUS Monkey Flower

Mimulus 'Andean Nymph'

A showy plant which needs moisture-retentive soil and regular watering in dry weather — grow it in a peat bed or at the side of a pond. The trumpet-shaped flowers have an open-faced Snapdragon appearance — the basic colour scheme is either red blotched with yellow or a shade of yellow blotched with red, purple or brown. You can grow a variety of the popular bedding plant M. cupreus as a short-lived perennial or you can plant a rock garden species.

M. burnettii

VARIETIES: There are many varieties of **M. cupreus** from which to make your choice — **'Red Emperor'**, **'Whitecroft Scarlet'**, etc. Basic details are height 9 in., spread 9 in., flowering period June-September. **M. primuloides** is a smaller plant with bright yellow flowers on short stalks. Grow **M. 'Highland Red'** for hardiness, and for novelty choose **M. 'Andean Nymph'** which bears pale cream blooms which are marked with pink (May-July). **M. burnettii** is copper, spotted with yellow.

SITE & SOIL: Requires moisture-retentive soil — some shade is desirable.

PROPAGATION: Sow seeds under glass or divide clumps in spring.

MORISIA Morisia

This low-growing plant is not a true alpine — it grows wild along the coast of Sardinia and Corsica. As you would expect from its natural habitat, it requires sandy soil and full sun — planting Morisia in heavy soil is a waste of time. When conditions are right it forms a neat and compact cushion with numerous yellow flowers arising from amongst the tiny leaves. Do not feed Morisia — it does best in poor soil.

VARIETY: There is a single species — **M. monanthos** which is sometimes listed as **M. hypogaea**. The basic details are height 1 in., spread 6 in., flowering period March-May. The dark and shiny leaves form a rosette and the flowers are stalkless. The early flowering habit is a welcome feature and the four-petalled cross-shaped nature of the blooms shows that it is a member of the Cabbage family. Morisia is quite a small subject and looks best when grown in a trough, sink, scree or pot.

SITE & SOIL: Requires well-drained light soil in full sun.

PROPAGATION: Plant root cuttings in a cold frame in late winter.

Morisia monanthos

M. monanthos

NARCISSUS Dwarf Narcissus

In a large rockery it is perfectly practical to grow any Narcissus including the large-cupped ones which reach 1½ ft or more. In an average-sized rock garden you should restrict yourself to the dwarfs which grow to 9 in. or less. Plant bulbs as soon as you can in autumn and then leave them undisturbed for years. Do not remove the foliage after flowering until it is completely brown.

VARIETIES: Some of the dwarf ones are Narcissus species rather than named varieties, flowering between March and April. Examples include **N. bulbocodium** (Hoop Petticoat) — 3–6 in., all-yellow, narrow petals, **N. cyclamineus** — 6–8 in., drooping flowers with swept-back petals and **N. triandrus albus** (Angel's Tears) — 4 in., drooping creamy flowers. Named dwarf varieties include **N. 'Beryl'** (8 in., creamy petals, orange cup), **N. 'Jack Snipe'** (8 in., creamy petals, yellow cup), **N. 'February Gold'** (8 in., yellow petals and cup) and **N. Tête-a-Tête** (8 in., yellow petals and cup).

SITE & SOIL: Requires well-drained soil in sun or light shade.

PROPAGATION: Lift overcrowded or 'blind' clumps in late summer. Divide and plant individual bulbs.

Narcissus cyclamineus

N. 'Jack Snipe'

OENOTHERA Evening Primrose

A large American genus with a few species which are short enough to grow in the rock garden. The silky cupped blooms are remarkably large for such low-growing plants, but these yellow or white flowers generally open in the evening and close at dawn. Oenothera is not a long-lived plant, but it does produce a fine display if plentifully supplied with sun, sand and an adequate amount of water in dry weather. Cut back stems in late autumn.

VARIETIES: The largest blooms, 4 in. or more across, are borne by the trailing **O. missouriensis** (Ozark Sundrops). The basic details are height 6 in., spread 1½ ft, flowering period July–September. The yellow flowers are borne above the sprawling stems. **O. acaulis** is more temperamental but is considered by many experts to be a better plant. White flowers (2–3 in. across) which turn pink with age appear above the Dandelion-like leaves. **O. caespitosa** (4 in. high) has similarly coloured flowers, but the petals are notched.

SITE & SOIL: Requires well-drained open soil — thrives in full sun.

PROPAGATION: Sow seeds under glass in spring.

Oenothera acaulis

O. missouriensis

OMPHALODES Omphalodes

The flowers of Omphalodes are borne in loose clusters above the foliage, each one looking like a large blue or white Forget-me-not. No more generalisations can be made as the time of flowering, ease of cultivation and conditions required for success differ widely from one species to another. O. verna in woodland conditions can be vigorous enough to be invasive, but O. luciliae is so fussy that it needs to be grown in a pan in the alpine house if you want to be sure to enjoy this beauty.

VARIETIES: O. verna (Blue-eyed Mary) is the one you are most likely to find. The flowers are blue with a white throat — an all-white variety (**'Alba'**) is available. The basic details are height 6 in., spread 1½ ft, flowering period February–May. This plant needs humus-rich soil and partly shady conditions, as does the more compact **O. cappadocica**. **O. luciliae** is quite different — it needs a gritty, well-drained soil and plenty of sunshine. The sky-blue flowers are borne above the blue-grey foliage from May to July.

SITE & SOIL: Depends on the species — see above.

PROPAGATION: Sow seeds or divide clumps in spring.

Omphalodes verna

O. luciliae

ORIGANUM Marjoram

Apart from one colourful variety the ordinary Marjoram (O. vulgare) is too coarse for the rock garden, but there are several rockery varieties. The growth habit is shrubby and in summer pink or purple flowers appear. These small and rather insignificant flowers are partly covered by bracts. These dwarf Origanums are sun-lovers and are only moderately hardy — either cover with a cloche during frosty weather or grow in an alpine house.

VARIETIES: The best rockery species for growing outdoors is **O. amanum** — height 3 in., spread 6 in., flowering period July–September. During this period the ground-hugging mat of leafy stems is covered by elongated pink flowers. **O. dictamnus** (**Amaracus dictamnus**) is different — the plant is larger and forms a woolly-leaved clump. The pink flowers are borne in Hop-like heads of large purplish bracts. **O. vulgare 'Aureum'** is grown for its yellow foliage which is especially bright in spring.

SITE & SOIL: Requires well-drained soil in full sun.

PROPAGATION: Plant stem cuttings in a cold frame in late summer.

Origanum amanum

O. vulgare 'Aureum'

OXALIS Oxalis

Oxalis is well-known to nearly every gardener, unfortunately as a weed more often than as an attractive rock garden plant. This does not mean that you should avoid Oxalis — the species listed below will provide attractive foliage and in summer colourful funnel-shaped flowers in white, pink, yellow or lilac. These plants will not become aggressively invasive, but unfortunately there are many species which will become rampant, so never introduce an Oxalis unless you know its growth habit.

VARIETIES: The most popular rockery species is **O. adenophylla** — the basic details are height 3 in., spread 6 in., flowering period June–July. The grey-green pleated leaves form a neat clump — the flowers are white with pink edging and veining. **O. enneaphylla** is even more restrained and even more attractive — white, pink and red varieties are available. **O. laciniata** is another choice species — the flowers are rich purple. The white-flowered **O. magellanica** is a prostrate creeper but is not invasive.

SITE & SOIL: Requires well-drained soil in full sun.

PROPAGATION: Divide clumps in autumn.

Oxalis laciniata

O. adenophylla

PAPAVER   Dwarf Poppy

The showy Poppies of the annual bed and the herbaceous border do not belong in the rock garden, but there are a few dwarfs which are right for this situation. They are short-lived, but the ones below do produce self-sown seedlings without becoming invasive. These dwarf types look like miniature Iceland Poppies with petals in a wide range of colours and with the appearance of crinkled tissue-paper.

VARIETIES: A number of species which are native to the European Alps are grouped together and listed as **P. alpinum** (Alpine Poppy). The basic details are height 6 in., spread 4 in., flowering period May–August. White, pink, yellow or orange flowers are borne on short stalks above ferny grey leaves. An easy-to-grow plant unless the soil is heavy, but it blooms itself to death in two or three years. An alternative dwarf for the rock garden is **P. miyabeanum** (Japanese Alpine Poppy). Large, nodding yellow flowers are borne on 6 in. stems.

SITE & SOIL: Requires well-drained soil — thrives best in full sun.

PROPAGATION: Dislikes root disturbance — sow seeds in late summer where the plants are to grow.

Papaver alpinum

P. alpinum

PARAHEBE   Parahebe

Some time ago the genus Veronica was split into the Hebes (woody plants) and the Veronicas (herbaceous plants). A few, the Parahebes, didn't fit neatly into either group, but do fit into the rock garden. They are semi-woody plants which grow less than 1 ft high and produce small white, blue or pink Speedwell-like flowers. These blooms are borne in loose clusters and appear in late summer and early autumn.

VARIETIES: P. catarractae is an upright bush — basic details are height 10 in., spread 1 ft, flowering period August–October. The blooms are white with a crimson eye. **P. lyallii** is another species which is available from large garden centres and is an easier plant to grow. It is a spreading bush 8 in. high, with leathery leaves and pink-veined white flowers in July and August. Another easy one, **P. bidwillii**, is rather more difficult to find in the catalogues. Pink-veined white flowers appear above a 6 in. high rounded bush.

SITE & SOIL: Requires well-drained soil and a sunny site.

PROPAGATION: Plant stem cuttings in a cold frame in early summer.

Parahebe lyallii

P. catarractae

PENSTEMON   Rockery Penstemon

You will find a number of rockery species and varieties listed in the alpine catalogues and on the benches of larger garden centres. They may be herbaceous or shrubby, and all bear tubular, two-lipped flowers in large clusters in summer. The usual colours are pink or purple, but blue and white ones are available. The Penstemons are showy plants, but they do tend to be delicate.

VARIETIES: The hardiest species is **P. pinifolius** — height 6 in., spread 1 ft, flowering period June–September. Dark orange blooms are borne above the needle-like foliage. There is much confusion over the naming of Penstemons, and even the experts are confused. There is a group which grows about 9 in. high with a spread of about 1 ft and produces lots of flowers in midsummer. Included here are **P. roezlii** (red), **P. newberryi** (pink or red) and **P. menziesii** (violet). A distinct species is the prostrate **P. rupicola** (3 in. high) with crimson flowers.

SITE & SOIL: Requires light, well-drained soil — thrives best in a sheltered site in full sun.

PROPAGATION: Plant stem cuttings in a cold frame in early summer.

Penstemon roezlii

P. newberryi

Phlox douglasii 'Crackerjack'

PHLOX   Dwarf Phlox

You will find numerous Dwarf Phlox varieties in catalogues and garden centres, and any one of these plants will provide you with a flat sheet of white, pink, blue, lavender or red flowers. Phlox will grace any rock garden — it is easy to grow and will cover rocks or tumble over walls, bearing masses of ½ in. blooms in late spring or early summer.

VARIETIES: P. subulata is one of the two basic species — height 4–6 in., spread 1½ ft, flowering period May–June. There are many named varieties, such as **'Scarlet Flame'** (red), **'Vivid'** (pink, compact), **'Temiscaming'** (pale red, vigorous) and **'G. F. Wilson'** (blue). The other basic species **P. douglasii** (Alpine Phlox) also has many varieties, such as **'Apollo'** (violet, compact), **'Crackerjack'** (red) and **'Iceberg'** (white). The height and spread of this species are similar to P. subulata, but the clumps are tidier and the flowers appear later. Other types include **P. kelsyi 'Rosette'** (violet-pink, miniature) and **P. amoena variegata** (bright pink, leaves in green and cream).

SITE & SOIL: Requires well-drained, moisture-retentive soil — thrives best in full sun.

PROPAGATION: Plant stem cuttings in a cold frame in summer.

P. subulata
'Vivid'

Pleione bulbocodioides

PLEIONE   Rockery Orchid

There is something especially satisfying about growing an Orchid in the rockery. Cost is not a problem — you will have to pay no more for a suitable Pleione than you would for some Primulas. The problems are that you will have to search through a number of catalogues to find a supplier, and you will need a sheltered site in a mild locality in partial shade. No specialist compost is needed — just enrich the soil with peat and leaf-mould plus some sharp sand. Cover with a pane of glass in winter. There is a risk, but you may well be rewarded with true Orchid flowers. Grow in an alpine house if the site is unsuitable.

VARIETIES: P. bulbocodioides (P. formosana) and its varieties are the Pleiones which are usually chosen for growing outdoors — height 3 in., spread 6 in., flowering period April–May. The showy 3 in. blooms bear narrow white, pink or purple petals and a large yellow or white central tube.

SITE & SOIL: See above for details.

PROPAGATION: Plant detached pseudobulbs in a cold frame in spring.

P. bulbocodioides

Polygonum vaccinifolium

POLYGONUM   Rockery Knotweed

Polygonums bear tiny flowers in white, pink or red in clusters above the foliage. The growth habit is wide-spreading, and the flowers appear in spring or autumn, depending on the species. Numerous species are sold for garden use and you must choose with care — most of them are far too invasive for growing in a rock garden.

VARIETIES: Polygonum is sometimes listed as Persicaria. The pink-flowered **P. affine 'Donald Lowndes'** (height 1 ft, spread 2 ft or more, flowering period June–October) is frequently recommended for rockery use, but you will have to keep it in check. **P. vaccinifolium** is the common rock garden type — height 4 in., spread 2 ft, flowering period September–December. The pale pink flowers are borne on upright spikes and the leaves are tinged red in autumn. For something smaller choose **P. tenuicaule** — height 4 in., spread 1 ft, flowering period March–April. The white flowers are borne on small upright spikes.

SITE & SOIL: Requires well-drained soil in full sun.

PROPAGATION: Divide clumps in autumn or spring. Alternatively plant stem cuttings in a cold frame in autumn.

P. affine
'Donald Lowndes'

POTENTILLA   Rock Cinquefoil

The Shrubby Potentillas which are so popular in beds and borders are generally too large for the rock garden. Still, there are numerous species which are suitable and some are described below. These Rock Cinquefoils are generally mat-forming plants with the long period of flowering associated with their shrubby cousins, but sometimes without their free-flowering habit.

VARIETIES: **P. 'Sunset'** (1½ ft) is a compact variety of the Shrubby Potentilla **P. fruticosa** — useful for the larger rock garden. A typical rockery one is **P. aurea** (Golden Cinquefoil) — height 4 in., spread 1 ft, flowering period June–September. The flowers are yellow and appear above creeping stems — for yellow flowers on a small upright bush grow **P. crantzii** (6 in.). **P. eriocarpa** is becoming popular — lots of pale yellow flowers throughout the summer. **P. nitida** has silvery leaves, pink flowers and low-growing stems, but it does not flower freely. **P. tonguei** bears orange blooms with a red centre.

SITE & SOIL: Requires well-drained soil in full sun.

PROPAGATION: Sow seeds under glass in spring or divide clumps in autumn.

Potentilla aurea

P. tonguei

PRIMULA   Rockery Primrose

Hundreds of species and varieties are dwarf enough to be grown in the rock garden or alpine house. There is a basal rosette of leaves and from this the flower-stalks arise, bearing Primrose-shaped blooms which may be pendant or upright. There are few general rules about cultivation. Most types require humus-rich soil, plenty of moisture during the growing season and a little shade during the day. But there are Primulas which thrive only when exposed to full sun and others which require shady and swampy conditions. Some will grow almost anywhere but a number need to be pampered in an alpine house. The Primulas chosen here are all relatively easy to grow and are suitable for outdoors.

VARIETIES: Border types, such as the Common Primrose (**P. vulgaris**), Polyanthus (**P. variabilis**), Cowslip (**P. veris**) and the Drumstick Primrose (**P. denticulata**), are often planted in rock gardens — see The Flower Expert for details. The fleshy-leaved Auricula (**P. auricula**) is an old favourite — height 6 in., spread 6 in., flowering period March–April. Large flowers are borne in clusters on top of the flower-stalks. **P. juliae** has a different growth habit — it is a low carpeter flowering in March–May. Short-stemmed flowers nestle in the leaves — well-known hybrids include **P. 'Wanda'** (purple-red) and **P. 'Lady Greer'** (yellow). **P. pubescens** is the group name for many 4–6 in. high hybrids blooming in April–May. Several favourites belong here — **P. 'Harlow Carr'** (cream), **P. 'Faldonside'** (white-eyed pink), **P. 'Mrs Wilson'** (white-eyed purple) etc. **P. marginata** is a small plant flowering in April — the best-known variety is **'Linda Pope'** (mauve-blue). **P. vialii** is the odd one out — 1 ft tall and flowering in June–July. **P. rosea** (6 in.) needs very moist soil, **P. sieboldii** needs a peat bed and **P. edgeworthii** is very early but needs winter protection from rain. The baby is **P. minima** — height 2 in., spread 5 in.

SITE & SOIL: Well-drained, moisture-retentive soil in light shade is the usual requirement.

PROPAGATION: Plant stem cuttings under glass in summer or divide clumps after flowering.

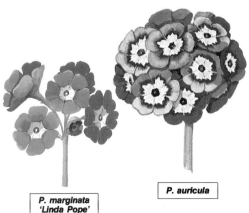
P. marginata 'Linda Pope'

P. auricula

Primula 'Wanda'

Primula vialii

Primula marginata

PULSATILLA   Pasque Flower

The Common Pulsatilla or Pasque Flower grows wild on the meadows and downs over limestone — in the garden it is easily raised from seed and is a welcome sight on any rockery at Easter. In spring the flower-stalks push up through the earth, each one crowned by a silky bud. The buds open into 3 in. wide cup-like flowers and later into flat stars. The flowers are followed by ferny foliage and then by attractive silky seed heads.

VARIETIES: The Pasque Flower is **P. vulgaris (Anemone pulsatilla)** — height 9 in., spread 1 ft, flowering period April–May. The flower colour is pale purple but you can buy varieties in white (**alba**) or red (**rubra**). **P. vernalis** is even more attractive — the flowers are pearly white inside, flushed purple on the outside and with a prominent boss of golden stamens. It grows about 6 in. high. **P. alpina** is a taller white-flowering Pulsatilla — **sulphurea** is a yellow-flowering variety.

SITE & SOIL: Requires well-drained soil and a sunny site. P. vulgaris and P. vernalis need alkaline soil.

PROPAGATION: Sow seeds under glass in summer.

Pulsatilla vulgaris

P. vernalis

RAMONDA   Ramonda

Most alpines need sunny conditions in order to flourish, but Ramonda hates prolonged direct sunlight. The place for it is on the north side of a rock garden, and as with the closely-related Haberlea (page 30) it should be planted sideways in a crack or crevice. The reason for this sideways planting is that it cannot tolerate water standing in the crown in winter.

VARIETIES: The easiest species to grow and to find is **R. myconi** which grows wild in the Pyrenees. The basic details are height 5 in., spread 9 in., flowering period April–May. The evergreen leaves are rough and crinkled and the large flat-faced flowers are lavender with a boss of golden stamens. The varieties **'Alba'** (white), **'Rosea'** (pink) and **'Coerulea'** (blue) are available. **R. nathaliae** is smaller but similar to R. myconi — **R. serbica** differs by having purple stamens.

SITE & SOIL: Requires well-drained but damp soil with little or no direct sun.

PROPAGATION: Divide clumps in autumn or plant leaf cuttings in a cold frame in summer.

Ramonda myconi

R. myconi

RANUNCULUS   Dwarf Buttercup

There are a number of Dwarf Buttercups which can be grown in the rock garden, but you should make your choice with care. Despite being closely related to some rampant weeds, a few are hard to grow outdoors and need alpine house conditions. At the other end of the scale are the invasive varieties of R. ficaria which can overrun nearby choice specimens.

VARIETIES: R. montanus 'Molten Gold' (Mountain Buttercup) is a showy miniature — height 4 in., spread 4 in. and shiny yellow flowers, 1 in. wide, in spring. **R. crenatus** is another tiny one — 3 in. high with pure white flowers in May. **R. calandrinioides** (height 6 in., spread 6 in.) bears its white flowers as early as January which makes it a useful out-of-season plant. For 1 ft tall Buttercups there are **R. gramineus** (yellow blooms in May–July) and some **R. ficaria** varieties — **aurantiacus** (orange), **cupreus** (copper), **albus** (white) and **'flore pleno'** (double, yellow).

SITE & SOIL: Requires well-drained gritty soil in full sun.

PROPAGATION: Sow seeds under glass in spring or divide clumps in autumn.

Ranunculus calandrinioides

R. montanus

RAOULIA Scabweed

Raoulia australis

Some of the Raoulias grow into 3 ft high mounds in their native home in New Zealand, but the ones grown in British rock gardens are carpets with a pile which is no higher than ½ in. when in full flower. The tiny leaves and tiny blooms form a useful ground-hugging cover for areas in which dwarf bulbs have been planted. Unfortunately Raoulia is never fully at home in our climate. A very hard winter can be fatal, and a pane of glass should be placed over the plant from late autumn to spring to keep off winter rain.

VARIETIES: The best-known variety is **R. australis** — basic details are height ½ in., spread 1 ft, flowering period May. It is grown mainly for its silvery foliage rather than its minute pale yellow flowers. **R. tenuicaulis** is easier to grow — the green mossy mat is covered with fine wool. The best floral show comes from **R. lutescens** — height ½ in., spread 1 ft. From April to June the flower-heads turn the surface into a bright yellow carpet.

SITE & SOIL: Requires well-drained gritty soil in full sun.

PROPAGATION: Divide the mats in autumn.

R. australis

RHODOHYPOXIS Rhodohypoxis

Rhodohypoxis baurii

This South African alpine has none of the robust hardiness found in some of the popular plants which have come to us from the European Alps. It is not, however, quite as delicate as some text-books claim, and there is no reason why you should not try this small beauty in a sheltered site in Central and Southern England. Add peat at planting time, top dress around the crown with grit, and water in the growing season during periods of dry weather.

VARIETIES: Choose a variety of **R. baurii** — height 2 in., spread 3 in., flowering period April–September. White, pink, rose and purple are the colours available. Tufts of narrow leaves are produced by the corm-like roots and the flowers are unusual — there is an outer ring of three petals and an inner ring of three petals. The attractive flower form and the exceptional length of the flowering season make Rhodohypoxis an excellent subject for a pot, sink garden or a tiny pocket in the rock garden.

SITE & SOIL: Requires well-drained gritty soil which is lime-free. Full sun is essential.

PROPAGATION: Divide clumps in autumn.

R. baurii

SANGUINARIA Bloodroot

Sanguinaria canadensis 'Flore Pleno'

This woodland plant from N. America is easy to grow in the rock garden if you can supply its basic needs — peaty, acid soil and some shade. As you would expect from its common name, red sap oozes from the root if it is severed. Sanguinaria is a wide-spreading perennial which belongs to the Poppy family, and unfortunately inherits the drawback of having flowers with a very brief life span. The flowers may be fleeting but the large blooms nestling amongst the greyish lobed leaves are extremely attractive.

VARIETIES: There is a single species — **S. canadensis**. The basic details are height 6 in., spread 1½ ft, flowering period April–May. The single white flowers with a central boss of golden stamens look like Anemones, but they last for less than a day. Choose instead the double form **'Flore Pleno'** — the plants are easier to grow and the flowers are larger, showier and longer-lasting. The leaves start to die down once flowering has finished.

SITE & SOIL: Requires humus-rich soil which is lime-free. Thrives best in light shade.

PROPAGATION: Not easy — divide clumps carefully in spring.

S. canadensis

SAPONARIA Soapwort

Every rock garden needs reliable plants which are low-growing but can spread widely enough to fill bare patches of earth or to clothe rock faces. They must also be free-flowering enough to form a sheet of colour during the flowering season. For spring we rely on Aubrietia, Arabis and Phlox — for summer Saponaria is a good and popular choice. For maximum display avoid over-rich soil and shade, and cut back the stems after flowering.

VARIETIES: S. ocymoides is the favourite species — height 4 in., spread 2 ft, flowering period May–August. The flat-faced tubular flowers are about ½ in. across and are borne in loose clusters — the usual colour is pale pink. Not all Saponarias are vigorous trailers. **S. ocymoides 'Rubra Compacta'** is a non-invasive plant with reddish-pink flowers — **S. 'Bressingham'** is another slow-spreading type which bears white-eyed bright pink blooms. **S. olivana** is worth looking for — 6 in. wide cushions with 1 in. wide pink flowers.

SITE & SOIL: Requires well-drained soil in full sun.

PROPAGATION: Plant stem cuttings in a cold frame in summer or divide clumps in spring.

Saponaria ocymoides

S. 'Bressingham'

SAXIFRAGA Saxifrage

The large area devoted to Saxifrages in the rockery plant section of your garden centre clearly indicates the variety and importance of this genus. Most of the Saxifrages come from mountainous regions (the word Saxifraga means 'stone breaker') and the usual growth pattern of these perennials is small and spreading. A group of leafy rosettes or a mossy mat is formed and from this arise upright flower-stalks bearing loose clusters of starry flowers. Spring or early summer is the usual flowering season and the blooms may be white, pink, red, yellow or purple. But these are generalisations and all sorts of variations occur. Botanists divide the Saxifragas into 16 groups, but for ordinary garden purposes only four need to be considered.

VARIETIES: The *Border* group consists of large and invasive types which are more suited to the flower border than a modest rockery. **S. urbium** (London Pride) is the best-known example — height 1 ft, spread 1½ ft, flowering period May–July. The *Encrusted* or *Silver* group contains plants which have rosettes of lime-encrusted leaves and star-shaped flowers in May–July. Examples are **S. aizoon** (**S. paniculata**) with its sprays of white flowers and **S. cochlearis** (height 8 in., spread 9 in.) with clusters of white flowers on red stalks. **S. cotyledon** is very tall — choose instead one of the compact Encrusted hybrids such as **S. 'Whitehill'** (white) or **S. 'Esther'** (cream). The *Mossy* group contains plants which form moss-like hummocks and flower in April–May. Popular ones include **S. 'Hi-Ace'** (pink), **S. 'Pixie'** (rose red), **S. 'Cloth of Gold'** (white, leaves golden) and **S. 'Peter Pan'** (pink). Finally, there is the *Cushion* group with a low mound of lime-encrusted leaves and early flowers in February–April. **S. burseriana** (2 in., white) is a popular beauty which blooms in late winter — **S. apiculata** (4 in., yellow) blooms a little later. Other popular Cushion Saxifrages include **S. 'Jenkinsae'** (pale pink) and **S. 'Cranbourne'** (pink).

SITE & SOIL: All require well-drained soil. Provide a moist spot with some shade from the midday sun — only the Encrusted group will thrive in full sun.

PROPAGATION: Separate rosettes or detach part of a clump and plant in a cold frame in early summer.

Saxifraga cochlearis

Saxifraga 'Peter Pan'

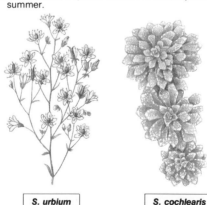
S. urbium

S. cochlearis

Saxifraga 'Jenkinsae'

Sedum acre aureum

SEDUM Stonecrop

The low-growing succulent leaves of Sedum can be seen in rockeries everywhere, but far too often it is one of the weedy varieties such as S. acre and S. album. There are many well-controlled and much more attractive types — so choose with care. The general features are a prostrate mat of fleshy leaves from which arise five-petalled starry flowers, borne either singly or in flat heads. Most of them are evergreen and they are amongst the easiest of rock garden plants, flourishing in dry and poor soils where little else will grow. They are also very easy to propagate and so deserve their popularity as carpeters for cracks and crevices.

VARIETIES: Only grow the Common Stonecrop **S. acre** if you have a large area to clothe — height 2 in., spread over 2 ft, flowering period June–July. The variety **aureum** has yellowish leaves. **S. album** is another invasive species, but it does have several well-behaved varieties such as **'Coral Carpet'** and **murale** which have colourful leaves. **S. spathulifolium** is an old favourite — height 3 in., spread 1 ft, flowering period June–July. The leafy mound is made up of silvery rosettes and the yellow flowers are borne in flat heads. The variety **'Purpureum'** has large purple leaves and **'Cappa Blanca'** has foliage which is almost white. The flowers of **S. spurium** (height 3 in., spread 1 ft) are white, pink or red — a change from the usual yellow. There are other unusual ones. **S. cauticolum** is deciduous, with grey leaves in summer and red flowers in autumn. **S. humifusum** bears solitary yellow flowers in late spring above reddish leaves, and **S. kamtschaticum 'Variegatum'** is an eye-catcher — yellow and golden flowers above cream and red-edged leaves. **S. ewersii** is a trailer with paired leaves and pink or red flowers.

SITE & SOIL: Requires well-drained soil — thrives best in full sun.

PROPAGATION: Very easy — divide clumps in autumn or spring.

Sedum spathulifolium 'Cappa Blanca'

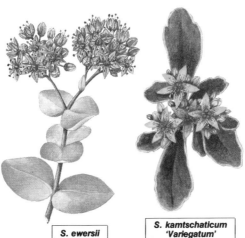
S. ewersii

S. kamtschaticum 'Variegatum'

Sedum spurium

SEMPERVIVUM Houseleek

Houseleeks can grow in the tiny amount of earth in the cracks in old walls and the small crannies between close-fitting rocks. Thick flower-stalks bearing a number of multi-petalled flowers in yellow, red or purple appear in summer or autumn, but Sempervivum is usually grown for its foliage. The leaves are fleshy and grouped into a ball-like rosette — there is a wide variation in colour, texture, size, hairiness etc. This rosette quickly produces offsets at the end of short runners — the mother rosette dies when flowering comes to an end.

VARIETIES: The Common Houseleek **S. tectorum** is the best-known one — height 3 in., spread 1 ft or more, flowering period July. The flowers are deep pink or pale purple and are borne on 1 ft flower-stalks. Leaves are purple-tipped. For a smaller plant with hairy leaves but similar flowers choose **S. montanum**. The decorative foliage ones include **S. arachnoideum** (small rosettes covered with web-like hairs), **S. 'Jubilee'** (green/red rosettes) and **S. calcaratum** (purple-tipped rosettes).

SITE & SOIL: Requires well-drained soil — full sun is essential.

PROPAGATION: Plant offsets in autumn or spring.

S. tectorum

Sempervivum arachnoideum

Silene acaulis

SILENE Rockery Campion

The Campions are lovers of dry, sandy soils and will grow in the cracks and crevices of a stone wall. The stems and soft, hairy leaves spread slowly to form a low carpet. In summer or autumn the flat-faced tubular flowers appear — the petals are blunt-ended and often notched. Silene is a useful carpeter as it provides late summer colour when many of the more popular mat-forming plants have passed their flowering season. You will be disappointed if you grow it in a shady, poorly-drained spot.

VARIETIES: **S. acaulis** is the popular Moss Campion — height 2 in., spread 1 ft, flowering period May–June. The tiny green leaves form a cushion — the notched pink flowers are almost stemless. **S. alpestris** is a creeping plant with sticky, lance-shaped leaves and white flowers in loose clusters between June and August. **'Flore Pleno'** is a double-flowered variety. **S. maritima** is a prostrate grey-green spreading plant — grow the white double-flowered **'Flore Pleno'**. Best of all, choose the bright pink **S. schafta** for July–October display.

SITE & SOIL: Requires well-drained soil in full sun.

PROPAGATION: Plant stem cuttings in a cold frame in summer.

S. schafta

Sisyrinchium brachypus

SISYRINCHIUM Sisyrinchium

Clumps of Iris-like leaves and open star-shaped flowers make Sisyrinchium an easy plant to recognise, but it is not a common sight in the rock garden. The blooms are not long-lived but they appear in regular succession through-out the flowering season. It is not difficult to grow in a shade-free site but there is a problem. Some of the species produce self-sown seedlings very freely — the answer is to remove flowers when they fade.

VARIETIES: The smallest one is **S. brachypus** — height 4 in., spread 6 in., flowering period June–September. The blooms are yellow — for a similar but taller plant choose **S. californicum**. Two species have the common name Blue-eyed Grass. They are **S. angustifolium** and **S. bermudianum** — height 9 in., spread 1 ft, flowering period June–September. Both bear blue flowers and are not easy to tell apart — the key is to look for the yellow eye in the bloom of S. bermudianum. **S. 'Mrs Spivey'** has white flowers — **S. douglasii** has purple bell-shaped blooms.

SITE & SOIL: Requires well-drained, humus-rich soil in full sun.

PROPAGATION: Divide clumps in autumn or spring.

S. angustifolium

Soldanella montana

SOLDANELLA Snowbell

The catalogues are right when they describe the Snowbell as one of the prettiest of all early spring alpines. In its native mountain home it can be seen blooming at the edge of the snowfields — hence the common name. Dainty bell-like flowers with deeply fringed margins droop gracefully from the tops of the upright flower-stalks. Lavender-blue is the usual colour but varieties in other shades are available. Soldanella needs some care — protection against winter rains is advisable and you will need to keep slugs away as they devour the flower buds in late winter or spring.

VARIETIES: **S. alpina** (height 4 in., spread 9 in., flowering period March–April) has all the features of the genus — rounded leathery leaves and pale purple, fringed bells which appear in the spring. Unfortunately it is not free-flowering — you will have more success with **S. montana** — height 6 in., spread 1 ft. The most floriferous and the easiest to grow is **S. villosa** (height 6 in., spread 1 ft). It flowers later than the others (May–June) and is more robust.

SITE & SOIL: Requires well-drained moist soil in light shade.

PROPAGATION: Divide clumps in summer.

S. alpina

TANACETUM Tansy

A large genus of plants usually associated with the large-flowered representatives such as T. coccineum grown in the herbaceous border. Only two or three species have a place in the rock garden — these are generally grown for their silvery leaves rather than their white or yellow flowers. The blooms are button-like with only disc florets or distinctly Daisy-like with both disc and ray florets. Tanacetum must have good drainage — it does well in pots of compost outdoors or in the alpine house.

VARIETIES: T. densum amani is the one you are most likely to find in the catalogues — it may be listed as **Chrysanthemum haradjani**. Feathery silver-grey leaves which look like filigree form dense 6 in. high mounds. The summer flowers are small yellow buttons surrounded by grey woolly bracts. **T. herderi** is a 9 in. bush which bears silvery foliage and small heads of yellow flowers.

SITE & SOIL: Requires well-drained open soil — full sun is essential.

PROPAGATION: Plant stem cuttings in a cold frame in early summer.

Tanacetum densum amani

T. densum amani

THYMUS Thyme

Thyme can be as useful in the rock garden as in the herb garden. There are two basic groups — the small bushy ones for planting in pockets between the stones and the carpeters which produce large mats of aromatic leaves and a covering of tiny flowers. These prostrate ones can be used to fill gaps between paving stones or as leafy blankets to clothe rocks. Cut back the stems in spring.

VARIETIES: T. serpyllum is the basic carpeter — height 1–3 in., spread 2 ft, flowering period May–July. The small flowers are borne in round heads. Named varieties are grown — **albus** (white), **'Annie Hall'** (pale pink), **coccineus** (red), **'Goldstream'** (mauve) etc. The basic bushy Thyme is **T. citriodorus** — height 9 in., spread 1 ft, flowering period May–July, lemon-scented foliage, lavender flowers. There are excellent varieties and hybrids which are shorter and more compact — **'Aureus'** (yellow leaves), **'Silver Queen'** (silver/green leaves) and **'E B Anderson'** (golden leaves) are examples.

SITE & SOIL: Requires well-drained light soil in full sun.

PROPAGATION: Divide clumps in autumn or spring or plant stem cuttings in a cold frame in summer.

Thymus citriodorus 'Silver Queen'

T. serpyllum

TRILLIUM Wood Lily

A beautiful plant for humus-rich soil and partial shade — good in a large rockery and excellent in a peat bed. A thick underground rhizome produces several fleshy stems which bear the foliage and flower parts in threes — three leaves, three petals, three sepals and three cells in the berry. The flowers which appear in spring are white, red, purple or more rarely yellow. Worth looking for, as it is eye-catching and long-lived once established.

VARIETIES: T. grandiflorum is the one you are most likely to find. It is also perhaps the easiest and the most attractive. The basic details are height 1 ft, spread 1 ft, flowering period April–June. The 2–3 in. wide blooms are white, turning pink with age. A double-flowered variety (**flore pleno**) is available. **T. ovatum** is rather similar but the leaves and flowers are smaller. **T. erectum** is different — the leaves are dark green and mottled, and the flowers are reddish-purple. The yellow-flowered Trillium is **T. luteum** (height 8 in.).

SITE & SOIL: Requires well-drained moist soil — thrives in light shade.

PROPAGATION: Divide clumps in autumn.

Trillium grandiflorum

T. erectum

TULIPA Species Tulip

For the rock garden we turn to the dwarfs amongst the Species Tulips rather than to the popular Garden Hybrids. November to December is the usual time for planting. Bedding Tulips are lifted when flowering is over and the foliage has turned yellow, but some Species Tulips are left in the ground over winter.

VARIETIES: The list is enormous if you wish to be adventurous, but only tried and tested ones are included here. **T. pulchella** is a tiny 4 in. dwarf — white, pink and violet varieties are available. **T. tarda** is another miniature, with several star-shaped white and yellow flowers on each stem. It blooms in April to May like nearly all Tulips — for March flowers grow **T. kaufmanniana** (6–10 in.). This is the Water-lily Tulip which has many varieties. **T. praestans 'Fusilier'** (orange-red) has become popular — **T. greigii** (8 in.-1 ft) with brown-mottled foliage is an old favourite. Others to look for are **T. clusiana**, **T. vyedenski**, **T. batalini** and **T. aucheriana**.

SITE & SOIL: Requires well-drained soil in full sun.

PROPAGATION: Remove bulblets when lifting clumps. Dry, store and replant in late autumn.

Tulipa pulchella

T. tarda

VACCINIUM Vaccinium

Vaccinium is a large and commercially important genus, as it includes the Cranberry, Blueberry and Bilberry. They are all lime-hating shrubs — some are bushy and upright but many are low and spreading. There are a number of dwarfs, but you must choose with care. Vacciniums growing 3 ft or more are listed as rock garden plants in some of the text-books — the ones described below are ground-hugging prostrate plants or dwarf bushes.

VARIETIES: **V. vitis-idaea** is the Cowberry — height 6 in., spread 1½ ft, flowering period May–June. The creeping stems and glossy oval leaves provide good ground cover — the small white or pink flowers are urn-shaped and are followed by red berries. Several varieties such as **'Koralle'**, **minus** and **compactum** are available. **V. praestans** is another prostrate Vaccinium with white flowers and red edible berries, but it loses its leaves in winter. **V. nummalaria** is a 1 ft high evergreen bush with pink flowers and black berries.

SITE & SOIL: Requires well-drained acid soil in light shade.

PROPAGATION: Plant stem cuttings in a cold frame in late summer.

Vaccinium vitis-idaea

V. nummalaria

VERBASCUM Rockery Mullein

The Mulleins are generally associated with the herbaceous border — there you will find the 3-6 ft high varieties of V. hybridum. There are just three species which are small enough for the rock garden, and they are worth growing in a sunny spot. Most of the basic family traits are there — leaves which are hairy or spiky, a profusion of bowl-shaped yellow blooms and a dislike of shade and heavy soil, but only one has the characteristic poker-like flower-head.

VARIETIES: The rockery species which is closest in growth habit to the border Mulleins is **V. dumulosum** — height 9 in., spread 1 ft, flowering period July–August. The upright flowering spikes bear purple-eyed yellow flowers above the grey hairy leaves. **V. spinosum** is different — the leaves are tiny and spiny, and the flowers are borne in loose clusters. The most popular one is a hybrid of these two species — **V. 'Letitia'**. It is a shrubby perennial which is covered by ½ in. yellow flowers from June to August.

SITE & SOIL: Requires well-drained soil in full sun.

PROPAGATION: Plant root cuttings in a cold frame in late winter.

Verbascum 'Letitia'

V. dumulosum

Veronica pectinata

VERONICA Rockery Speedwell

Speedwells make a useful addition to the rock garden as they supply midsummer colour and are easy to grow in a well-drained site. Several species are available and the popular ones are spreading plants which form a leafy mat. A word of caution — some can become as invasive as Speedwells on the lawn, so pick a restrained one where choice plants are grown nearby. The rampant species include V. filiformis and V. prostrata.

VARIETIES: V. prostrata (**V. rupestris**) is the most popular Rockery Speedwell — height 4 in., spread 1½ ft or more, flowering period May–August. Blue is the species flower colour, but there is white (**'Alba'**), pink (**'Mrs Holt'**) and pale blue (**'Spode Blue'**). A good choice between paving stones but too invasive for a small rockery. **V. pectinata** provides non-aggressive ground cover — the pink variety **'Rosea'** is the usual selection. Other Speedwells include **V. fruticans** (red-eyed blue flowers) and **V. cinerea** (grey foliage).

SITE & SOIL: Requires well-drained soil — thrives best in full sun.

PROPAGATION: Divide clumps in spring.

V. prostrata

Viola lutea

VIOLA Rockery Violet

The Violas are an extensive genus and are instantly recognisable. For maximum display the familiar biennial Violas and Pansies are sometimes bedded out into planting pockets, but it is preferable to grow the perennial species. Two (V. odorata and V. cornuta) have long been associated with the herbaceous border, but the others described below are true Rockery Violets.

VARIETIES: V. cornuta (Horned Pansy) — height 6–9 in., flowering period May–August has many varieties, such as **'Alba'** and **'Minor'. V. odorata** (Sweet Violet) is earlier (March–May) and smaller (4–6 in. high). For yellow flowers throughout the summer grow **V. aetolica** or **V. biflora** — for purplish-blue flowers and foliage choose the late spring-flowering **V. labradorica 'Purpurea'**. Perhaps the easiest to grow is **V. lutea** and the smallest one you are likely to find is the mauve-coloured **V. jooi**. Varieties of **V. gracilis** are noted for their daintiness — look for **'Major'** (yellow-eyed purple) and **'Moonlight'** (yellow).

SITE & SOIL: Requires well-drained soil in sun or light shade.

PROPAGATION: Plant stem cuttings in a cold frame in summer.

V. cornuta

Zauschneria californica 'Solidarity Pink'

ZAUSCHNERIA Californian Fuchsia

An uncommon but valuable plant for the rock garden, as it produces bright flowers late in the year. Unfortunately this small shrub from N. America is not for everyone — it does need a warm and dry spot if it is to flourish. Abnormally cold winters are a killer, but it is well worth a trial if you have a sheltered spot. It is listed by some of the alpine nurseries and is offered by larger garden centres. The flowers are tubular and red is the usual colour.

VARIETIES: The only species you are likely to find is **Z. californica**, sometimes listed as **Epilobium canum**. The basic details are height 1 ft, spread 1½ ft, flowering period August–October. Along the branched stems are grey hairy leaves and at each tip a cluster of 1 in. long tubular flowers. It is deciduous. The species bears red blooms, but several varieties are available with slightly different colours. **'Glasnevin'** is orange-red, and so is the hardiest one under our conditions — **'Dublin'. 'Solidarity Pink'** is pink. **Z. cana** is a rare species with narrow leaves.

SITE & SOIL: Requires well-drained gritty soil in full sun.

PROPAGATION: Plant stem cuttings in a cold frame in summer.

Z. californica

CHAPTER 4
ROCK GARDEN MAINTENANCE

If you have made a rock garden or raised bed by following the basic rules set out in Chapter 2, then routine maintenance should be a straight-forward task. It will not call for skill as required in the pruning of fruit trees nor the heavy work demanded in the vegetable plot. You should not be troubled by weeds for some time and the plants will flourish in the well-drained, gritty conditions you have provided for them. But regular maintenance is not something you can ignore. Leave a shrub border untended for a season and no great harm may result, but leave a rock garden for a year and it may well be ruined.

Treat rock garden care as a routine once-a-week job during the growing season, in the same way as you may treat house plant and lawn maintenance. Weed control will be the major task — read the sections on Weeding and Mulching on page 51. Keep the area free from dead plants and debris, and water only when necessary. Dead-head spent flowers where practical, especially if the variety can become a nuisance by self-seeding. Label plants which die down for part of the year. Trim back unwanted growth.

Autumn is the major overhaul time of the year. All fallen leaves must be removed and the stems of rampant plants must be cut back — do not leave this job for the spring. Cover winter-sensitive plants. In spring renew the grit mulch, feed, remove winter protection, firm plants which have been lifted by frost and look for slug damage.

All this advice may have come too late — the rockery may be overrun by weeds and it is covered with straggly rampant alpines due to past neglect. There is no easy answer. You will have to start again. Remove the soil from the affected area, replace it with new planting mixture (see page 6) and then replant.

BUYING

Buying specimens in 3 in. pots is the most usual way of obtaining new plants — you can also propagate your own or receive them as gifts, but you should never dig them up from their natural habitat. Most garden centres offer the widest range in spring, but you should also call to see what is available and what is in bloom at different times of the year. Look for a good example of the variety you have chosen (see below) — it may well not be the largest on offer. Keep it in a shady spot if you cannot plant immediately and water daily if the weather is dry.

Good signs — Bad signs

Clear labelling

Firm top-growth

Absence of pests and diseases

Wilted leaves

Dry soil

Long roots growing through drainage holes

Specialist nurseries carry a much larger range of rock garden plants than general-purpose garden centres, and skilled advice is usually available. This is the place to go to if you are looking for rarities, but you cannot necessarily expect to find an alpine nursery within easy driving distance. Many offer catalogues and mail order service — deliveries are generally made in spring and autumn. This is not the cheapest method — you have to pay for postage and packing. Remember to unpack immediately and wait a few days before planting.

REPLANTING

No matter how perfect your rock garden may look today, you will be involved in some replanting in the future and the introduction of new plants will become a fairly regular routine. There are several reasons for this. An obvious one is that there may be an empty planting pocket or area — equally obvious is the failure of a plant which needs to be thrown away or be moved to a spot which may offer a better home. Less obvious is the limited decorative life span of many alpines — the average is about 5 years. After this time the plant will need to be either discarded and replaced or else lifted, divided and replanted. Finally, there will be times when you see a plant at the garden centre or nursery which you simply must have, even though it means removing an old friend from the rock garden.

Whatever the reason for replanting, do make a good job of it. It is vital that the environment should be right. Nearly all rockery perennials are sun-lovers, but a few require shade and these can be accommodated against a rock-face which receives little sun during the day. A few plants in this section cannot stand winter rain on their leaves and should be planted vertically in cracks between the rocks.

When planting a group it is wise to place the pots in position before you begin in order to make sure you are happy with the arrangement. It is customary to plant large plants before small ones and to place upright, conical conifers at a lower level than spreading ones. Follow the basic planting technique described on page 6. The trickiest job is to firm the planting compost around the root ball with sufficient but not too much pressure — use your fingers rather than the back of the trowel.

WEEDING

Weeding is the most tedious of all the maintenance jobs, and prevention is so much easier than cure. Begin at construction time — make sure that the planting site is free from all perennial weeds and that weed roots are absent from the topsoil used for making the planting mixture. As described below, a mulch of grit on rockery and raised bed gardens or bark on peat gardens will help to prevent annual weeds.

It is unfortunate that however careful you are at the construction stage, weeds will still appear and they must be tackled promptly as dwarf plants such as alpines can be easily swamped by them. There are a number of sources of these weeds, and you can cut down the work of weeding if you take preventive measures. Firstly, weeds are often brought in with the plants — always check carefully and pull out stems and roots of any weeds which are growing on the soil surface of the pot.

Next, perennials can creep in from surrounding land — create some form of weed-proof barrier if this is likely. Finally, weed seeds are blown on to the site — remember that this includes the seed from nearby rock garden plants which readily produce self-sown seedlings. Dead-heading and weed control in surrounding land will reduce this problem.

Hoeing is not practical where a grit mulch is used. Pulling out weeds by hand is the usual way to tackle the problem — you may need a narrow trowel if the roots are firmly anchored. Of course not all self-sown alpines are 'weeds' — you will only need to pull out seedlings which are growing where they are not wanted. Perennial weeds are a difficult problem when the roots are too deep and widespread to be removed. The answer here is to paint the leaves very carefully with glyphosate — never spray weedkillers and never use lawn-type ones.

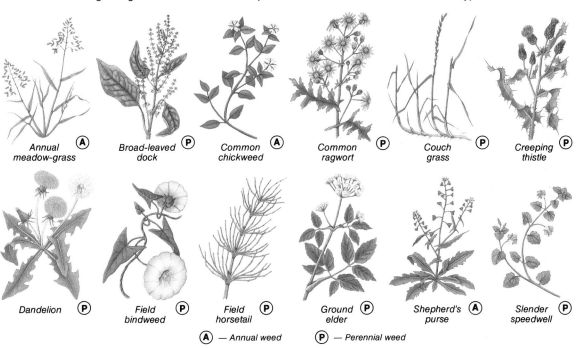

Annual meadow-grass (A)   Broad-leaved dock (P)   Common chickweed (A)   Common ragwort (P)   Couch grass (P)   Creeping thistle (P)

Dandelion (P)   Field bindweed (P)   Field horsetail (P)   Ground elder (P)   Shepherd's purse (A)   Slender speedwell (P)

(A) — Annual weed   (P) — Perennial weed

WATERING

During the first few weeks after planting you should water regularly even if the weather is not particularly dry — once a plant is established it will only need watering during prolonged dry weather. A plant should never be left to show visible signs of distress during a period of drought — the time to water is when the soil at a few inches depth is dry and the foliage looks unusually dull. Once you decide to water then do it thoroughly — a light sprinkling will do more harm than good. Apply 2–4 gallons per sq. yard — a hose pipe is much better than a watering can unless your rockery is a very small one. Do water carefully and slowly so that the plants are not dislodged and repeat the watering a week later if rain has not fallen. Of course this only applies to open ground — troughs, sinks and pots will need watering much more frequently than once a week in dry weather. For the enthusiast a sprinkler system is a boon.

MULCHING

A mulch is a layer of bulky material spread on the surface of the soil around the plants, and nowhere is it more beneficial than in the rock garden, raised bed, sink or trough. The list of advantages is a long one — slugs and weeds are deterred, moisture loss is reduced, surface panning by rain is eliminated, roots are kept cool in hot weather, water is kept away from the neck of the plants in winter and the scree-like effect gives a more natural look to the rock garden ... a long list indeed! This rockery mulch consists of a 1 in. layer of gravel, chippings or grit which is pushed under the leaves of the plant and over the soil surface — topping-up time is early spring. Just two rules. Use a mulch which is in keeping with the rock — grey grit amongst red sandstone would be distinctly out of place. Secondly, do not use limestone chippings around acid-loving plants. The type of mulch has to be changed for the peat bed — here the right material is a 2 in. layer of shredded bark — renew in spring. Ordinary peat is not a good choice.

PROPAGATION

Propagation is a highly desirable but not essential part of rock gardening. It is not just a matter of money — there is a great deal of satisfaction to be gained from raising your own plants and increasing your stock. **DIVISION** is the easiest method — clump-forming rockery perennials often deteriorate after a few years if not lifted and divided. In this way you can increase your stock and rejuvenate the plant at the same time.

SEED can be obtained from some garden centres and specialist nurseries. Follow the instructions on the packet — the seed of many 'true alpines' (see page 10) need a period of freezing before sowing. Other sources of seed include the exchange scheme run by the Alpine Garden Society and your own plants — remember that this seed may not breed true and it should generally be sown as soon as it is ripe.

Striking **CUTTINGS** is the most widely used method of propagation as it can be used for nearly all types and the resulting plant is identical to its parent. Stem-tip cuttings (short pieces of non-flowering shoot tips) are taken from herbaceous and some woody plants. Some plants such as Armeria produce young shoots around the base and these are cut off at ground level and used as basal cuttings. With woody plants a cutting is sometimes obtained by gently pulling off a non-flowering side-shoot from a main stem, making sure that some of the stem ('heel') remains.

Don't guess which method to use — look up the plant in the A–Z guide in Chapter 3 and see the recommended technique or techniques and their timing. Consult Chapter 4 in The Flower Expert for more details on the craft of propagation.

Stem Cuttings

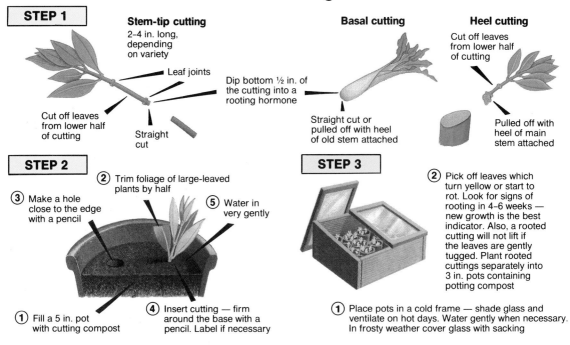

STEP 1

Stem-tip cutting
2–4 in. long, depending on variety

Leaf joints

Cut off leaves from lower half of cutting

Straight cut

Dip bottom ½ in. of the cutting into a rooting hormone

Basal cutting

Straight cut or pulled off with heel of old stem attached

Heel cutting
Cut off leaves from lower half of cutting

Pulled off with heel of main stem attached

STEP 2

② Trim foliage of large-leaved plants by half

③ Make a hole close to the edge with a pencil

⑤ Water in very gently

① Fill a 5 in. pot with cutting compost

④ Insert cutting — firm around the base with a pencil. Label if necessary

STEP 3

② Pick off leaves which turn yellow or start to rot. Look for signs of rooting in 4–6 weeks — new growth is the best indicator. Also, a rooted cutting will not lift if the leaves are gently tugged. Plant rooted cuttings separately into 3 in. pots containing potting compost

① Place pots in a cold frame — shade glass and ventilate on hot days. Water gently when necessary. In frosty weather cover glass with sacking

FEEDING

Plants growing in the rock garden do not need frequent feeding. Newly-planted specimens do not need fertilizing at all — established ones should be fed just once a year. The best time is in early spring just before the grit layer is topped up and before active growth starts. Leave it to the rain to wash the nutrients slowly down into the soil. Choose your fertilizer with care — never pick one where the nitrogen content is higher than the other elements — Bone Meal is a popular choice, but you can use Growmore or any other balanced NPK granular (not powder) fertilizer. Take care to keep the granules off the leaves.

The once-a-year programme outlined above does not apply where the amount of growing medium is restricted as in a raised bed, trough or pot. In these cases in-season balanced liquid feeds should be applied as well as the spring dressing.

WINTER PROTECTION

Nearly all rock garden plants listed in this book will quite happily survive the rigours of winter, but may suffer if not given some shelter from northerly icy winds. Some choice varieties in the catalogues, however, are only moderately hardy and need the protection of a cloche when frost is expected — remove the cloche when the danger of frost has passed. A number of other non-robust types are susceptible to winter rains rather than frost, and some form of more permanent winter protection is required, as shown below.

Do not place the glass over the plant until the cold weather arrives — remove as soon as the weather turns mild in spring

PESTS & DISEASES

One of the fortunate aspects of rock gardening is that you don't have to wage the constant battle against pests and diseases which bedevils the vegetable and fruit grower. The range of insects and fungi which can cause a serious problem is limited and the likelihood of an attack by more than one or two of them is not common. Even so, you should do all the cultural things which are necessary to prevent problems from arising.

The rules for pest and disease prevention are the same as for the rest of the garden. Prepare the ground as instructed in Chapter 2 — poor drainage is the main cause of root rots. Make sure the plants you buy are free of insects and leaf diseases, and follow the correct planting procedure. Be careful not to overfeed and always clear away rubbish and dead plants promptly — slugs are attracted by damaged rather than healthy leaves. Finally, keep watch for trouble and if pests appear, remove them or the badly affected leaves by hand picking if practical. If not it may be necessary to spray where there is a large infestation — always read the instructions and precautions on the pack before use.

The problems described below are the ones which are most likely to call for action. Other troubles occasionally occur — mice may dig up bulbs, and roots may be damaged or disturbed by ants, root aphids or cutworms. In the alpine house the plants may be afflicted by red spider mite, mildews and whitefly — the use of proper cultural techniques is the way to keep down pests and diseases under glass as it is outdoors. One final point — don't assume that all leaf discoloration is due to disease. Yellow leaves on lime-hating plants indicate iron or manganese deficiency — spray with sequestrene.

SLUGS & SNAILS

A serious pest of many rock garden plants in late winter or early spring — the result of an attack on young plants can be devastating. Irregular holes are formed and tell-tale slime trails can be seen. Damage is worst when the site is poorly drained and the weather is unsettled. Keep the area clear of rubbish — scatter Slug Pellets around plants. Follow the precautions.

APHIDS

Greenfly and blackfly may appear in large numbers when the weather is warm and settled. Young growth is distorted and weakened — leaves are covered with sticky honeydew which later becomes covered with sooty mould. They also transmit virus diseases. Keep plants watered in dry weather. Spray if necessary with a systemic insecticide or horticultural soap.

CATERPILLARS

Many different leaf-eating caterpillars may attack rockery perennials. Some are uncommon, but angle shades moth and cabbage white butterfly can be a nuisance. Pick off the caterpillars if this is practical — where damage is widespread it will be necessary to spray with an insecticide such as Long-last or Fenitrothion. Ready-to-use Pest Pistols are available.

BIRDS

Several birds such as sparrows, blackbirds and bullfinches can be troublesome every spring in your rockery and yet your neighbour's rock garden may be spared. Primulas and Crocuses are favourite targets but all types of cushion-forming plants may be disturbed in the hunt for grubs. Control is difficult — repellents are rarely effective and black cotton or netting is unsightly.

VINE WEEVILS

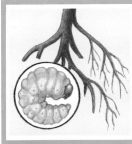

These wrinkled white grubs are the larvae of the adult dark brown vine weevil. They are extremely destructive underground both outdoors and under glass, eating the roots of many rockery perennials. If a plant suddenly dies, look in the compost for the rolled-up grub. Difficult to control — spray with HCH or add Nemesys to potting compost.

BOTRYTIS

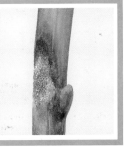

Botrytis or grey mould is a destructive disease in a wet season. The fluffy mould appears on the leaves and stems — flower petals become spotted and then rotten. Pick off and destroy mouldy leaves and flowers. Improve ventilation if it is an alpine house problem. Spray infected and surrounding plants with a systemic fungicide.

CATS

Cats are a pest of new rock gardens and newly-planted specimens. The new plants are disturbed by their scratching and the resulting root damage can lead to the death of the recently introduced plants. Pepper Dust applied liberally around the plants may help, but the real answer is to cover all bare soil with a 1 in. grit mulch.

MOLES

Perhaps the worst headache of all — an invasion by moles can cause havoc. The hills thrown up by their tunnelling are unsightly and cause severe root damage. Eradication is not easy — smokes and sonic deterrents should be tried first. It may be necessary to set traps or to gas them — this work is best carried out by a professional exterminator.

CHAPTER 5

LOOKING AT WATER GARDENS

Your fascination with water began a long time ago. As a toddler you stamped into every rain puddle you could find, and at the sea-shore you ran to the water's edge and played in the incoming waves. Now as an adult it is the pond, fountain or waterfall which acts like a magnet when you visit a garden for the first time, drawing you away from bed or border.

It is therefore not surprising that water has been a basic feature of Grand Gardens from the very beginning. Nobody knows when it all began — perhaps with the Incas or Chinese 4,500 years ago. What we do know for certain is that at the start of Western gardening, water was the *only* essential ingredient. The Ancient Persians had their tiled canals and tinkling fountains, Moorish Spain inherited the style and the mastery of water gardening passed to the Italians in the 16th century. Then along came Le Nôtre with his magnificent formal stretches of water at Versailles, and in Britain whole valleys were filled with water by Capability Brown to create his informal pools.

These superb waterworks were designed to show off water at its best — the widespread use of water as a home for decorative plants and fish came later. It was in the middle of the 18th century that books first began to describe the growing of aquatic plants, and it was not until the latter part of the 19th century that the great craze for water gardening began. A number of things stimulated this upsurge in interest. Joseph Paxton induced the Giant Water Lily (Victoria amazonica) to flower in the pool within the vast conservatory at Chatsworth. The Frenchman Joseph Bory Latour-Marliac produced the first coloured hybrid Water Lily before 1880 and scores more followed during the next 30 years. New aquatic plants arrived from all over the world and new ideas about water gardening came in from the Orient.

So people with money and space were able to build ponds of concrete or puddled clay and add extra interest with fountains and cascades. A wide variety of aquatic plants and fancy fish was available, but from the start of the craze in Victorian times until the 1960s all of this was generally outside the scope and pocket of the average ordinary gardener.

It was the introduction of flexible liners which brought pond-making within the do-it-yourself gardener's scope. No longer was it necessary to use concrete to make a pond which was large enough to house fish and a wide range of plants. In addition ready-made pools in a range of sizes and shapes became increasingly available, and so did an array of water features. Inexpensive submersible pumps, floating lights, pre-formed cascades and self-contained fountains are now in every garden centre, and so it is not surprising that the number of ponds and associated items has increased in recent years.

'Pond' or 'pool'? Dictionary definitions don't help very much as they are not clear-cut — in this book a simple distinction has been adopted. Where water is the only feature or is by far the most important one we generally talk about a 'pool' — for instance, a swimming pool. On the other hand we refer to a pond where there is an appreciable living element — a fish pond, lily pond, wildlife pond etc.

So here we are mainly dealing with ponds — fish and aquatic plants and water. Wildlife comes as a bonus, and even a small pond will attract dragonflies and frogs and perhaps newts and toads. A thing of beauty, then, to provide so much interest during the summer months — but *only* if it is the type of water garden you wanted to create and then only if it was constructed, stocked and cared for in the right way. All too often we see murky green water, overrun with weeds and infested with midges and mosquitoes. The cause is generally a combination of doing the wrong things at the start and later failing to do a few essential tasks.

Put away your cheque book or credit card if you have thoughts about a new pond or a new water feature — rushing out and buying things just because you can afford them and because they 'look good' is a recipe for failure. Careful planning is absolutely vital, and the rules are set out on pages 56-57. There are four basic questions to answer. Just what sort of water garden do I want, what space have I got available, and what are the conditions like in that space? Finally, can I afford it?

So what sort of water garden do you want? Probably a pond, with a variety of fish, a number of aquatic plants and clear water. For this you will need a pond which is large enough for the plants and deep enough for the fish. You will also need to grow a number of underwater plants which are of no decorative value at all. It's not just a matter of size — the pond must be in the right location. Maybe a beautiful display of Water Lilies is a prime objective — then you will have to keep rapid water currents and fountain droplets well away from the leaves. You have a different problem if Koi Carp rather than Water Lilies are to be the main purpose of the pond. Koi need a special home. You will then need a depth of about 4 ft and a large surface area plus a good filtration system. It may be that you have no particular fancy, but would like a natural-looking water area. Fine, but you will need a lot of space for a large, informal pond made with a flexible liner. A rockery, waterfall and bog garden would all be attractive extensions, and should wherever possible be created at the same time as the pond.

At the other end of the scale it may be shortage of space rather than shortage of ideas or money which is the problem. A minipond is the answer, housing a Water Lily or two with perhaps a few other aquatic plants and Goldfish. Unfortunately chemicals and careful management cannot be relied upon to keep the water clear if the pond is too small, but you can still have the charm of moving water even if your plot is tiny. These days there are all sorts of self-contained fountains and other features available in kit form for the patio or small garden.

If you are new to ponds and aquatic life, welcome to the world of water gardening. If you already have a pond but need fresh ideas or answers to your problems, you should find most of the information in the following pages. But you will never learn *everything* — according to an old Japanese saying "Water has secrets it will tell to no man".

Water in the Grand garden
The Sea-horse Fountain Canal Pond and the 300 ft high Emperor Fountain at Chatsworth, Derbyshire.
Vast and impressive

Water in the Home garden
A Formal raised pond with Water Lilies, Iris, Petunias and Marigolds in a suburban garden.
Compact and colourful

CHAPTER 6
MAKING A WATER GARDEN

Before you write a cheque or dig the first spadeful of soil you must plan carefully. It is essential to make sure that you have chosen the most satisfactory type of pond for your needs and situation. This, of course, should be obvious — a lot of money, time and effort are involved and you can't simply alter things if you've made a mistake.

The problem is that there is no such thing as the 'right' type of pond for everyone — the perfect choice in one situation would be a disaster elsewhere. An added complication these days is that there are all sorts of shapes, styles and materials from which to make a choice — so where do you begin?

The first step is to study each of the guide paragraphs on these two pages. Then go back to the Size and Style sections to make your first basic decision. Do you have the space for a pond which is at least 40 sq.ft? If not, your choice of style is quite limited. A small formal pond or minipond is the usual answer, or perhaps an informal wildlife pond. For a patio think about a raised pond, and with all small ponds you must keep your stocking plans simple.

The choice is much larger if you can devote more than 40 sq.ft to the pond. With care you can have a balanced arrangement of clear water, aquatic plants and fish. There are still basic rules — the pond size and style must be in keeping with the size and style of the garden, and the site must be suitable.

You should now have a fairly clear idea of size, construction material and where the pond will go. The next thing is to mark out the outline with either rope or a hose pipe, and look at it from the house and other parts of the garden. Changes can be made at this stage, but not afterwards. The final planning stage has now been reached — it is time to think about features. These additional features will probably call for electricity, and that means an electric cable will have to be laid. The most important additions (fountains and waterfalls) involve ways of making the water move. Finally there is lighting — even a few simple lights can bring a pond to life at night.

SIZE

Miniponds such as half-barrels, deep sinks and small rigid liners can be used to house aquatic plants and a few Goldfish, but for a proper pond which can be expected to stay clear you should aim for a water surface of at least 40 sq.ft. The minimum depth of water should be 1½ ft at some point. If the surface area is 50 sq.ft or more and if you plan to have various types of fish, then a depth of 2 ft is better. For large ponds of several hundred sq.ft a depth of 2½ ft is desirable.

A shelf is necessary for housing Marginal plants which need their crowns to be covered with water — this shelf may run around a part or the whole of the pond. It should be at least 10 in.–1 ft wide and will need to be 9 in.–1 ft below the water surface.

STYLE

Few of us are fortunate enough to have a **Natural pond** fed from a stream or underground spring. Do not interfere with its shape or depth — just carry out a programme of careful planting and judicious stocking with fish.

There are two basic styles of man-(or woman-) made pond. One is no better than the other — the correct choice depends on the situation. With the **Formal pond** the outline is clearly defined and the shape is either geometrical (square, oblong etc) or gently curved. It is generally separated from other garden features and is often used as a centrepiece. Three types of plants (Floaters, Oxygenators and Water Lilies) are necessary for maintaining the correct balance, but Marginals are not essential. The Formal pond is nearly always at ground level, but there is no reason why it cannot be a **Raised pond** — page 63 describes several advantages for this type of structure. Raised ponds are useful where space is limited as on a patio — there are several types of **Minipond** for such situations.

With the **Informal pond** the outline is not clearly defined — it merges into the adjoining feature or features which may be a rock garden, waterfall or **Bog garden** (see page 64). The outline is irregular, as the object is to make the pond look like a natural stretch of water. Because of this Marginal plants are essential as they help to obscure the edges of the pond.

The recommended choice for a small garden or a large formal one is the Formal pond. Provided the surface is at least 40 sq.ft, there is no reason why this pond should not carry colourful fish and Water Lilies to make it a truly eye-catching feature for the compact garden of today. In formal surroundings a small Informal pond can look like a large puddle. The Informal pond needs both space and semi-natural surroundings, and in this environment it can be by far the better choice. There is a single exception — a small informal **Wildlife pond** can be accommodated in most gardens, as it is the natural population rather than the pond itself which is the main attraction.

SITE

For a worthwhile display of Water Lilies and other aquatic plants the site should be shade free for at least 5–6 hours a day. However, the location should not be exposed — protection is needed from the prevailing wind to avoid the scorching of young foliage and the toppling of tall Marginal plants. Overhanging trees are a serious problem. They cast shade, of course, but the hidden danger is that their leaves decompose to produce salts and gases which are harmful to fish and encourage green algae. Trees which are especially dangerous include Willow, Horse Chestnut, Poplar, Laburnum, Holly, Laurel and Rhododendron. Cherry and Plum are hosts to the Water Lily Aphid and tree roots can damage some pond linings.

Apart from avoiding danger spots there is a need for convenience and eye-appeal. Ideally the pond should be as near as practical to the source of electricity and water and also close enough to the house for the fountain or waterfall to be seen or heard. The reflection in the water should be attractive, and where feasible an Informal pond should be sited at the lowest part of the garden.

SAFETY

Ponds are attractive to visitors, wildlife ... and children. Crawling babies must be watched or a pond cover should be used — it is surprising that active toddlers can drown in a few inches of water. Remember that this means occasional visitors, such as grandchildren and the toddlers of friends. Some people prefer to have a fountain surrounded by pebbles rather than water whilst the children are small.

In addition, remember that water and electricity can make dangerous partners — do not undertake outdoor wiring as a DIY job unless you *really* know what you are doing. Instead of using mains voltage, it is a safer approach to have a transformer indoors and work with an outdoor supply of 24 V. There are many pumps which are powered by this low and safe voltage.

EARTH REMOVAL

It is true that pond-making has become a straightforward DIY job now that Rigid and Flexible liners have entered the scene. But this statement is only true if you ignore the arduous task of earth removal. For a small pond you can tackle this job if you are reasonably young and fit, but never try to excavate a hole for a pond by digging with a spade if you are not used to hard work of a similar nature. Make sure there are no cables or pipes in the area.

If the pond is large, then hiring an earth mover from your local plant hire company is the answer. The people there will advise you on the right type of equipment, and it may well be a good idea to obtain the services of an operator on an hourly basis.

Don't try to turn the mound of excavated earth into a 'rock garden' by sticking stones into it. The best plan is to separate the topsoil from the lighter-coloured subsoil. Spread the topsoil over beds, borders or use in rock garden construction — dump the subsoil.

SHAPE

Squares and rectangles can be made with concrete or building blocks, and are also available as Rigid liners. A wide variety of other shapes can be bought as Rigid liners — circles, ovals, oblongs, triangles and L-shapes as well as irregular forms.

With a Flexible liner it is best to stick to a simple shape with gentle curves. Avoid fussy shapes and sharp corners as they are not easy to produce with polythene, PVC or butyl sheeting.

Both vertical and gently sloping sides can pose problems — the usual advice is to aim for a 20° slope.

9

20°

3

CONSTRUCTION MATERIALS

The earliest construction material was **Puddled clay**. The excavated hole was lined with soot to deter worms and the surface was then plastered with wet clay. Not for you, unless you are devoted to ancient techniques. After Puddled clay came **Concrete** (page 62) and this was used to make the great and not-so-great ponds and pools of yesteryear. But its time has passed for the construction of home garden ponds — making a satisfactory concrete pond takes a good deal of skill and even more back-breaking labour.

There are now two basic materials for the gardener, and both are widely used. The **Rigid liner** (pages 60–61) makes pond construction a straightforward task, although not *quite* as easy as set out in the sales literature. It may be nice to see just what the finished pond will look like before you buy it, but remember it may look much smaller in your garden than it does in the garden centre. Mark out the size in your garden before you buy. With Rigid liners you get what you pay for. The cheap ones are not 'bargains' — they are vacuum-formed plastic which are only semi-rigid and have a life of a few years. In general terms, life expectancy is related to price — buy a Rigid liner with a life expectancy of 10 years or more if you want the pond to be a near-permanent feature.

The problems with the Rigid liner are that you are limited to the designs offered by the manufacturer and both depth and size are restricted to what can be carried on a lorry. To make a larger pond and/or one of your own design then you must use a **Flexible liner** (pages 58–59). This is a waterproof sheet which moulds itself exactly to the shape of the excavation. The major drawbacks are that marginal shelves have to be built and don't come ready made as with a Rigid liner, and sheeting is not really satisfactory for sharp-cornered ponds. As with the rigid type, you get what you pay for. At the bottom end of the scale there is polythene which lasts for a few years — at the top end there is butyl sheeting which will last for a lifetime.

With both Rigid and Flexible liners do be careful with colour. Pale blue or cream may seem a good idea and show up the fish, but it can look distinctly artificial. Black or brown is a better choice.

Finally, the miscellaneous construction materials. There are bricks and reconstituted stone blocks for raised ponds (page 63) — for miniponds (page 65) there are wooden tubs, glazed ceramic containers and old railway sleepers.

Flexible liner Pond

Using a Flexible liner (other name: Pool liner) is generally the most satisfactory way of creating a pond which is large enough to house numerous aquatic plants and a variety of fish. You are not limited to the range of sizes and shapes of Rigid liners offered in the catalogues and at the garden centre, and transport to and handling in your garden are much easier. And price is not a stumbling block — on an equal area basis, a top-quality Flexible liner is no more expensive than a fibreglass Rigid liner.

The drawback is that you cannot achieve the perfectly smooth surface and angles you find in a pre-formed pond. There will also be a few wrinkles, but this should not pose a serious problem.

Plan to start the work in the spring during a reasonably dry spell of weather. If the pond is to be permanent do buy butyl sheeting if you possibly can. It is the most expensive, but it will easily outlast other types and any tears can be repaired. Where money is a problem choose a good-quality PVC liner.

The position is quite different if you are building a temporary pond for breeding fish or holding the stock when you are cleaning out a permanent pond. Here cheap polythene sheeting is perfectly satisfactory.

A problem which occasionally arises when buying a Flexible liner is that some suppliers use trade names without stating in the catalogue just which construction material has been used. Make sure you ask before you buy, and do check the length of the guarantee.

POLYETHYLENE The use of ordinary polyethylene sheeting should be restricted to the construction of a temporary pond, as it is easily torn and cracks after long exposure to sunlight. Use a double layer of 500 gauge sheeting — anticipated life span 2–3 years. Some brands of polyethylene are durable — Toughliner has a 12 year guarantee.

PVC A strong and stretchable material which is about half the price of butyl sheeting. The simplest form is a single sheet — double sheeting is stronger and there is also a terylene netted version. The anticipated life span of PVC is 10–15 years, so it is worth considering if you cannot afford butyl. Look for a 10 year guarantee.

BUTYL This synthetic rubber sheeting is unquestionably the best material available. It is unaffected by sunlight and frost, stretches readily and is available in any size. The standard material is 0.03 in. thick and has an anticipated life span of 50 years. The usual guarantee is 10–20 years. The surface colour is dull black.

STEP 1:
MARK OUT THE POND
Mark out the shape
on the ground, using
a garden hose or thick
rope for curves and
string with pegs for
straight lines.
Measure the size of the
butyl sheeting required —
note the extra requirement
for the planned depth
of the pond.
Order the sheeting

STEP 2:
DIG OUT THE HOLE
Cut along the marked pond line
with a spade and remove soil to a
depth of about 1 ft — the level of
the planting shelf. Next, mark and
dig out the central area to leave
a 1 ft wide shelf. Check with a
board and spirit level to ensure
that the top is not sloping —
add or remove earth as necessary.
Remove stones and roots from the
hole and line the sides and base
with a 1 in. layer of wet sand

STEP 3:
INSTALL THE LINER
Place the sheet across (not inside)
the hole. Leave for a couple
of hours — warmth makes it more
flexible. Make sure the sheet is
centred and then weigh down the
edges with stones. Start to fill the
pond slowly with tap water —
the liner will stretch to the contours
of the hole. As the water level rises,
remove some of the stones to
allow the liner to move gradually
into the pond space

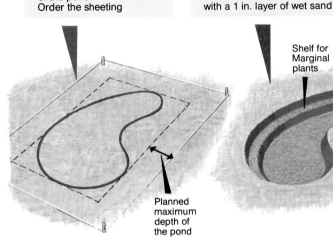

Shelf for
Marginal
plants

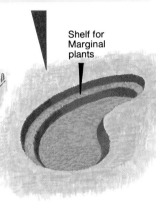

Planned
maximum
depth of
the pond

STEP 4:
TRIM THE LINER
Make neat folds as
necessary to cope with
corners — turn off the
water when the level is
about 2 in. below the soil
surface. Remove the
stones. Trim the edge
with scissors, leaving a
6 in. overlap all round.
Pleat the liner to form
a neat edge. Stretch and
peg down this liner edge

STEP 5:
FINISH THE POND
Lay paving stones (crazy
paving, slabs, natural stone etc)
around the edge, so that they
project about 2 in. over the
water. These stones should be
set on mortar and a board and
spirit level used to ensure that
the surround is level.
Break or cut stones to fill
any gaps between the paving —
make sure that all the surface
sheeting is covered

STEP 6:
STOCK THE POND
Be very careful not to
drop any mortar into the
pond — if you do then
emptying and refilling
will be necessary as lime
is harmful to fish. You
are now ready to stock
the pond, first with plants
and then with fish.
Read Chapter 7 for
guidance if you are new
to water gardening

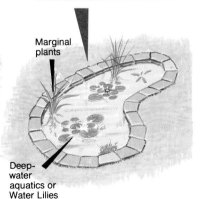

Marginal
plants

Deep-
water
aquatics or
Water Lilies

Rigid liner Pond

Using a Rigid liner (other names: Pre-formed pool, Moulded pool, Ready-formed pool, Pre-cast pool) is perhaps the simplest way of creating a small pond. It is worth considering if you want a pond for rearing fish, a small area of water for children who are past the toddler stage, a little wildlife pond or a minipond for a few aquatic plants and Goldfish. It is also a good way of lining a small raised pond.

Over the years most experts have warned against the use of a Rigid liner if you wanted a well-balanced pond for a range of aquatic plants and several types of fish in water which will not be green with algae. Until quite recently they were generally correct as there was a long list of drawbacks. The cheaper liners had an unacceptably short life span and were often garishly coloured, the depths were generally less than the critical 1½ ft and the usual shape was too small and too fussy.

Things have changed recently. There are now tough black plastic ponds with long-term guarantees — sizes over 40 sq.ft surface area and depths of more than 1½ ft are readily available, and straightforward geometrical shapes are offered alongside the convoluted ones. In addition shelving for Marginals has been improved and there is even a range with a planting area for Bog plants.

So a Rigid liner is a practical choice if you want a Formal pond of 40 sq.ft or more these days, but do choose carefully. Make sure the guarantee is for at least 10 years and choose a dark colour if the construction material is plastic. Check that the depth is at least 1½ ft and remember that a simple shape will give you more surface area for your money than a fussy one.

ORDINARY PLASTIC The least expensive liner and not a good buy if you are looking for permanence. It is made of vacuum-formed polythene in blue, grey, brown or green and is only semi-rigid. The surface, which is either smooth or simulated rock, is weakened by exposure to sunlight and the corners crack with age.

REINFORCED PLASTIC A much more practical proposition than the ordinary plastic liner. These smooth-walled shells have a high resistance to ultra-violet light and both corners and floor are reinforced. Marginal shelves are generally adequate and the usual depth is 1½ ft or more. Sizes up to 75 sq.ft are available. Guarantee 10–20 years.

FIBREGLASS Resin-bonded fibreglass is virtually indestructible by the elements, as it is completely resistant to water, frost and ultra-violet light. It is now recognised as the best construction material for a Rigid liner and is available in buff, black, grey, green or blue. The guarantee should be for at least 20 years.

STEP 1:
MARK OUT
THE POND
Mark out the perimeter
of the liner — make a
second line about 1 ft
out to mark the area
of excavation

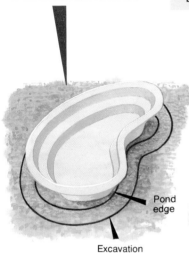

Pond
edge

Excavation
edge

STEP 2:
DIG OUT THE HOLE
Cut along the excavation edge with a
spade and remove soil. The bottom
of the pit should be about 2 in. lower
than the liner — measure the depth
using a ruler and straightedge.
Then make sure that the ledges and
base are horizontal

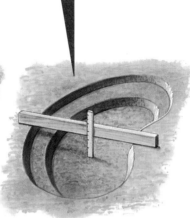

STEP 3:
INSTALL THE LINER
Compact the base — add a 2 in.
layer of sand. Lower the liner
into the pit and bed down firmly
into the sand. Check that it is
level. If not, take out the liner
and add or remove sand and/or
soil as necessary

STEP 4:
INFILL AROUND
THE LINER
Once the liner is level,
insert battens to hold it in
place. Start to fill with tap
water — at the same time
add sand or sifted soil to fill
the space. Make sure that no
gaps are left under the
shelves or around the sides

STEP 5:
FINISH THE POND
Lay paving stones (crazy
paving, slabs, natural stone
etc) around the edge, so that they
project about 2 in. over the water.
These stones should be set
on mortar and a board and
spirit level used to ensure
that the surround is level

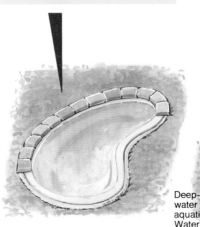

STEP 6:
STOCK THE POND
Be very careful not to drop any
mortar into the pond — if you
do then emptying and refilling
will be necessary as lime is
harmful to fish. You are now
ready to stock the pond, first
with plants and then with fish.
Read Chapter 7 if you are
new to water gardening

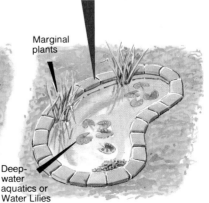

Marginal
plants

Deep-
water
aquatics or
Water Lilies

Concrete Pond

The traditional type of pond, and still regarded by some as the best. Concrete continues to be used where a large square or oblong pond or pool is to be built, but this is a job for the professional. It is possible to make a simple round or oval pond if you have some experience of concreting — follow the steps on the right and make sure you complete the job in a single day. When dry, paint the surface with a proprietary sealant such as Silglaze before filling and stocking — raw concrete is harmful to fish.

STEP 4:
ADD REINFORCEMENT
Press wire netting into the moist concrete lining the sides

STEP 5:
FINISH CONCRETING
Cover the wire netting with a 2 in. layer of concrete. Trowel the surface smooth

STEP 2:
LINE THE HOLE
Use heavy gauge builders' polythene sheeting

STEP 1:
DIG OUT THE HOLE
The slope of the sides should be about 45°. Ram down the soil very firmly

STEP 3:
ADD THE FIRST LAYER OF CONCRETE
Cover the base and sides with a 4 in. layer of concrete

Raised Pond

It is surprising that books and articles on pond construction say so little about raised ponds, bearing in mind the number of advantages they have over ground-level and sunken ponds:

- The fish and plants are brought closer to eye level, so that their beauty is enhanced.
- Routine maintenance is made easier — included here are dead-heading of spent blooms, planting, autumn clean-up, blanket-weed removal etc. This is especially important for the elderly and infirm.
- From a purely practical point of view, the labour of large scale excavation and earth removal is eliminated.
- Babies and toddlers are less likely to fall into the water, although care will still be necessary.
- Water can be easily siphoned out when the pond has to be cleaned.

A number of advantages, but there are also two important drawbacks. The small raised minipond on a patio looks attractive, but a large raised pond can look out of place in many gardens. Secondly, the superb insulating properties of the soil around a ground-level pond are lost — this means that freezing in winter and overheating in summer are more likely.

The smallest type is the half-barrel, deep trough or self-contained pool/fountain unit on the patio — see the minipond section on page 65. The simplest form of walling around the larger raised pond is an earth bank around a Rigid liner — easy perhaps but not appealing in most garden situations. For more suitable suggestions see the diagrams on the right.

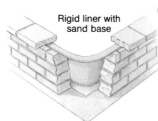

Rigid liner with sand base

Flexible liner folded at corner — polystyrene insulation

Blocks treated with pond paint on concrete base

RIGID LINER Use a fibreglass liner — choose a simple shape. Walls can be made of brick, blocks of concrete or reconstituted stone, or railway sleepers — the best choice depends on availability, personal taste and shape. Provide a firm foundation and remember that an inner wall is necessary to support the marginal shelf.

FLEXIBLE LINER Use butyl sheeting — choose a simple shape for the pond. Compared with the Rigid liner pond the walls will have to take a much greater strain from the weight of water and the thin liner has little insulating effect. For a pond of 40 sq.ft the wall should be two blocks thick. Use polystyrene slabs for insulation. Make sure mortar is set before folding in liner and filling with water.

NO LINER It is possible to dispense with a liner if the brick or block wall is well made with firm foundations and surrounds a strong concrete base. The inside can be rendered with cement to improve the appearance — this is optional but painting the inside with two coats of pond paint is absolutely essential. Follow the instructions on the tin exactly. A marginal shelf can be built in the same way.

Bog Garden

As noted at the beginning of this chapter, an Informal pond should look as natural as practical. One of the features of many low-lying natural ponds and lakes is a range of Bog plants growing in the moist soil surrounding the water's edge.

If the area around your pond is heavy and constantly damp then you can grow Bog plants without any further preparation. In nearly all cases, however, a bog garden has to be created. Follow the general guidelines shown on the right, bearing in mind the following points:

- Do not make your bog garden too wide — it is a difficult area to care for.
- It must not be waterlogged for long periods — drainage holes in the liner are essential.
- The compost should be free-draining and moisture-retentive — its surface should be below the pond edge.
- Water copiously and regularly during dry spells in spring and summer.

STEP 6:
COMPLETE THE GARDEN
Rake 2 oz Growmore or balanced organic fertilizer per sq. yard into surface.
Plant with varieties from pages 87–93

STEP 4:
ADD COMPOST LAYER
Compost mix of 3 parts topsoil, 3 parts peat and 1 part lime-free grit

STEP 5:
ADD STONE EDGING
Place pebbles along either side of the bog garden to hide liner

STEP 1:
LAY THE LINER
Use butyl sheeting — place under the Flexible or Rigid pond liner and on top of 2 in. sand layer

STEP 3:
ADD GRIT LAYER
Place 2 in. layer of lime-free grit or gravel at the base

STEP 2:
MAKE DRAINAGE HOLES
One ½ in. hole every 3 ft is necessary

Minipond & Minipool

There is no precise definition of a minipond — basically it is a miniature pond measuring 1½–4 ft across and is used to cultivate one or more aquatic plants. It may house a few fish but not a fountain — moving water is rarely practical in a tiny pond when plants are present. The fountain and water spout are features of the minipool (see below) rather than the minipond.

There are two reasons for choosing a minipond rather than a regular-sized one. Shortage of space is the usual reason, as a raised minipond can be put on a patio or balcony and both the raised and ground-level versions will fit into the smallest garden. The second reason is the undesirability of having a large stretch of water where active and unsupervised toddlers are present.

Any container which will hold at least 5 gallons of water can be used as a minipond as long as it is weatherproof, waterproof, non-corrosive and non-toxic. This rules out copper containers and wooden ones which have contained oil-based products. Half-barrels can be bought from your garden centre — varnish the outside and treat the inside with bitumen paint. Place in a sunny spot and plant with one or more compact Marginals and/or a dwarf Water Lily or two. Depending on the size of your minipond a few Goldfish can be kept, but in a thin-walled raised minipond they will not be happy as water temperature will fluctuate widely during the year. If the pond is very small and you do not have a water heater then move the fish to a larger pond in winter.

The minipool is a reservoir for a moving water feature such as a fountain or water spout. It may be self-contained or custom-built in the garden, and can be placed in sun or shade as there is no plant life to support. The water surface can be covered with pebbles etc, making it perfectly safe for small children.

RAISED MINIPOND An excellent feature for bringing life and interest to the patio. A raised pond made from bricks or blocks (see page 63) can be constructed, but it is more usual to use a ready-made container such as a half-barrel, sink, fibreglass tank or large plastic trough. Lack of insulation against summer heat and winter frost is the main drawback.

SURFACE MINIPOND Any of the containers recommended for a raised minipond can be set into the soil as a surface minipond, but it is more usual to start with a small Rigid or Flexible liner. Compared with the raised version, temperature fluctuation is reduced but it is still necessary to remove fish in winter if the minipond is very shallow.

MINIPOOL This may be raised or at ground level, and contains neither fish nor plants. It is the ornamental or purely practical catchment area for the water from a fountain or water spout and the water surface may be either uncovered or else concealed by large pebbles. The pebble fountain illustrated on the left has all the virtues of moving water with none of the hazards for toddlers.

Wildlife Pond

The purpose of an ornamental garden pond is to delight the eye with its blend of clear water, attractive fish close to the surface and range of aquatic plants. The wildlife which arrive (frogs, dragonflies etc) are a bonus.

The purpose of the wildlife pond is quite different. It provides a haven and in some cases a breeding ground for insects, amphibians, birds and small mammals — to do this it should be as natural as possible. Fish should be omitted or must be chosen with care — the native stickleback is acceptable but Goldfish and other exotics are not. The aquatic plants should all be native species. For the deep water part of the pond you can choose the Wild Water Lily (Nymphaea alba) if the area is large or Nymphoides and Aponogeton if the pond is small. For planting close to the margin there are Menyanthes, Typha, Eriophorum, Scirpus, Iris and so on — see Chapter 7 for details. The plants mentioned so far are grown in baskets rather than in the soil layer so as to limit their spread, but Oxygenators such as Myriophyllum or Ceratophyllum are usually planted in the mud. Finally there are the native Bog plants — Lychnis, Cardamine and Geum are examples.

Make an Informal pond with a Flexible liner by following the general rules set out on pages 56-59 — adapt to incorporate the special needs shown below. The benefits to be derived from a wildlife pond are the knowledge that you are providing a small habitat for our native fauna and flora, and the enjoyment of watching the pond's population in a 'natural' home. It will not be as visually attractive as an ornamental pond — exotic Water Lilies are not grown and there is a semi-wild look. Some algal growth is inevitable, but do scoop away excess blanketweed and duckweed to stop the pond from becoming choked.

It is sometimes recommended that you can get the best of both worlds by adapting an existing ornamental pond to support a large wildlife population. This is rarely successful and the outcome is often the worst of both worlds.

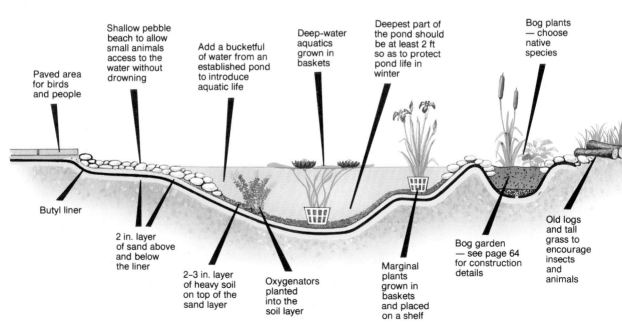

Paved area for birds and people

Shallow pebble beach to allow small animals access to the water without drowning

Add a bucketful of water from an established pond to introduce aquatic life

Deep-water aquatics grown in baskets

Deepest part of the pond should be at least 2 ft so as to protect pond life in winter

Bog plants — choose native species

Butyl liner

2 in. layer of sand above and below the liner

2-3 in. layer of heavy soil on top of the sand layer

Oxygenators planted into the soil layer

Marginal plants grown in baskets and placed on a shelf

Bog garden — see page 64 for construction details

Old logs and tall grass to encourage insects and animals

CHAPTER 7

STOCKING A WATER GARDEN

The selection of plants for a new bed or border which you have created in your garden is up to you. Bearing in mind the amount of light and soil type which are present you will have a vast range of plants from which to make your choice, depending only on your likes and dislikes. Roses on their own or mixed with other plants ... Bedding plants or Bamboo, it's up to you.

One of the basic rules for making a successful water garden is that stocking is not just up to you and your desire to have a beautiful pond. Stocking calls for bringing together a number of ingredients, both plant and animal, so that a healthy and stable balance is maintained. As noted in the Plants section below and on the following pages, it will be necessary to introduce some uninteresting plants without any ornamental value because they help to keep the water clear. You will also have to make sure that a certain amount of the water surface is covered by foliage, whether you like it or not.

In the Fish section (pages 95–98) of this chapter you will discover that choosing a specimen from your aquatic centre or catalogue merely because it looks the most attractive can be a serious mistake. The showiest fish will require a much larger than average pond or an ice-free environment in winter. Some fairly strict rules, then, for making the correct choice of stocking material.

In addition there are rules concerning the time for stocking. First of all, plants should be introduced during the growing season and you should wait a few days after the pond has been filled with fresh tap water — this allows the dissolved chlorine to disperse. The second rule is that you should leave 4 weeks between planting and the introduction of fish. The reason is that fish tug at submerged plants and nibble the leaves, so Water Lilies, Marginals, Oxygenators etc should be allowed to establish themselves before being exposed to Goldfish, Shubunkins or other fish.

Plants

One of the major practical purposes of putting plants in a pond is to provide surface cover. This blanket of leaves serves two functions. Firstly, the growth of algae is discouraged by the shading effect of the foliage and this helps to keep the water clear by contributing to 'balance' — see page 111. Secondly, the fish are provided with cooling shade during the hot days of summer. Fortunately the larger surface-covering plants are also ornamental as they bear attractive flowers. Pride of place goes to the **Water Lilies** — you can extend both the interest and the flowering season at the centre of the pond by also growing **Deep-water aquatics** which, like Water Lilies, produce foliage which floats on the surface.

Of course it would be quite wrong to overdo the use of plants with floating foliage — you should aim to cover about one half of the water surface. This is difficult to achieve with newly-planted Water Lilies and Deep-water aquatics, and so **Floaters** are often introduced at the early stage of pond development. Here the whole plant and not just the leaves float on the surface — some but not all Floaters bear flowers. Floaters are sometimes removed when the Water Lilies and Deep-water aquatics are fully established.

There is another practical job for plants to do in the pond. Foliage absorbs both minerals and carbon dioxide from the water and this helps to starve out the algae. The **Oxygenators** are especially effective here — the leaves of these useful but generally dull plants are totally submerged.

The plants in the four groups dealt with so far have a practical purpose in the pond and most but not all have an ornamental value as well — another common feature is that each group contains only a small number of genera. The fifth group is quite different — the **Marginals** are shallow-water plants which are grown close to the edge of the pond and have a purely ornamental function. There is a large number of genera and an extensive range of species and varieties from which to make your choice — a feature shared with the sixth and final group, the **Bog plants**. These moisture-loving plants which grow at the pondside require damp but not continually waterlogged soil in order to flourish.

Planting

Plant between May and September — not in the dormant season. It is much better to plant in open-sided plastic containers known as baskets (large size: Water Lily baskets) than in soil at the bottom of the pond. In this way growth is controlled and plants can be lifted for dividing and repotting after a few years.

STEP 1:
LINE THE BASKET
Use hessian — Finofil and louvred baskets do not need lining

STEP 2:
FILL THE BASKET
Use heavy loam from which twigs, roots etc have been removed. Do not add peat or compost — enrich with a little Bone Meal

STEP 4:
ADD GRIT LAYER
Place a 1 in. layer of pea shingle on top of the soil to prevent soil disturbance by fish

STEP 3:
PLANT UP
Firm planting is essential. Read Nymphaea section (page 70) before planting Water Lilies

planting depth

- Take the plant out of the plastic bag and put it in a bucket of water or plant up immediately — never let it become dry.
- Water the basket thoroughly before placing in the pond.
- If the pond is a large one and you are planting beyond your reach tie string to each of the four corners of the basket. Use the strings to lower the basket gently into the water — a 2-man (or woman) job.
- Deep-water aquatics and Water Lilies should be introduced to the pond gradually. Stand the basket on one or more bricks so that the crown is a couple of inches below the surface. Remove bricks as growth increases until the plant reaches its permanent base in deep water.

WATER LILIES

pages 70–73
Other names: None

Roots submerged, leaves on the surface and flowers on or above the surface
One genus only (Nymphaea) but there are many hardy species and varieties in nearly every colour. Not harmed by winter cold unless water is frozen solid. Tropical Water Lilies are not suitable for outdoors as year-round warm nights are necessary. Useful for keeping water clear and the fish cool in summer. Depending on the variety the recommended planting depth is 4 in.–3 ft — most flourish at 9 in.–1½ ft. Choose a spot in full sun and away from moving water produced by a fountain or waterfall.

DEEP-WATER AQUATICS

page 74
Other names: Deep Marginals,
Surfacing Plants

Roots submerged, leaves on the surface and flowers on or above the surface
Only a few varieties are available, but they are very useful where Water Lilies are absent or are not yet established — their leaves help to keep water clear and the fish cool in summer. The recommended planting depth is 1 ft or more depending on the variety — shallower planting may result in leaves held above the surface and an inferior floral display. Not as dramatic as Water Lilies, but there are Deep-water aquatics for partial shade, fountain-disturbed surfaces and very deep water.

The 6 Groups of Pond Plants

FLOATERS

pages 75–76
Other names: None

Roots submerged, leaves and stems free-floating on or just below the surface and flowers, if any, on or above the surface

Their main purpose is to provide surface cover where Water Lilies or Deep-water aquatics are sparse or absent, but a few are also ornamental. There are two basic types — the carpeters such as Lemna and Azolla which can cover the whole surface with tiny leaves, and the non-carpeters which have larger leaves and tend to be less invasive. Planting could not be simpler — Floaters are available between April and September, and you just drop the plants in the water. In a large pond use with care as control can be difficult. In winter most hardy Floaters sink to the bottom of the pond and survive as buds or seeds.

BOG PLANTS

pages 87–93
Other names: Poolside Plants, Waterside Plants, Moisture-loving Plants

Roots in moist soil but not permanently submerged in water, leaves and flowers clearly above the surface

These plants require damp humus-rich soil which is never allowed to dry out, but they will not survive in permanently waterlogged ground. The term 'Bog plant' is therefore not an accurate description and many experts prefer 'Poolside plant' for this group. Their home is in the bog garden constructed at the side of the pond — see page 64 for details. There is no clear-cut definition — some like Hemerocallis and Astilbe flourish in the herbaceous border, and there are Marginals such as Caltha and Mimulus which will grow in the bog garden. Follow the garden rules rather than the pond ones for Bog plants — divide every few years.

OXYGENATORS

pages 77–78
Other names: Submerged Aquatics, 'Water Weeds'

Roots and stems submerged, leaves almost always submerged and flowers, if any, on or above the surface

Extremely important for keeping the water clear and for providing both food and a spawning area for fish. The underwater leaves absorb both minerals and carbon dioxide which helps to starve the algae. Oxygen production is of much less importance, despite the common name. Nearly always sold in bunches — a group of cuttings held together at the base by a lead strip. Don't just drop into the water. In May or June plant several bunches into heavy soil in a shallow basket — cover the top with gravel and place the basket at the bottom of the pond. You will need about 1 bunch per 3 sq.ft. Some are temperamental — plant a mixture.

MARGINALS

pages 79–86
Other names: None

Roots submerged, leaves and flowers clearly above the surface

Their role is purely ornamental as they do not play a part in maintaining a satisfactory balance in the pond (see page 111). They serve two functions. The boundary between the water and the pondside is softened which is often desirable in a Formal pond and always essential in an Informal one, and they provide floral colour and/or interesting leaves during the growing season. Many types are available. The recommended planting depth is 0–6 in., depending on the variety — their home is on the marginal shelf or in the shallows of the pond. The traditional method of growing them is to plant in soil at the bottom of the shelf, but it is better to set them in baskets — see page 68. Do not mix different varieties in a single container.

Water Lilies

NYMPHAEA Water Lily

The Water Lily is the unchallenged Queen of aquatic plants, and every pond owner either has or wants one. The value of the hardy Water Lily lies not only in the beauty of its cup-shaped or star-shaped blooms — the round or heart-shaped leaves ('pads') help to keep the fish happy and the water clear.

It is a fascinating plant with a number of surprises for all and an equal number of pitfalls for the novice. The first surprise for the beginner is the enormous range of flower size, leaf size, leaf spread and planting depth. The Dwarfs (Miniatures) with 1 in. wide leaves covering about 1 sq.ft of pond surface and bearing medal-sized flowers are an excellent choice for a minipond made from a half-barrel. At the other end of the scale there are the Vigorous varieties with leaves measuring more than 8 in. across which blanket 50 sq.ft or more and produce blooms the size of dinner plates.

The golden rule is never to buy a Water Lily just because the picture looks nice and it costs less than the others on show. You should measure the size of your pond surface and then aim to buy one or more specimens with an anticipated total spread of no more than half of the pond surface. And never be guided by the price — the ones which are far too vigorous for the average pond actually cost less than the more compact ones which do not look value for money.

To make selection easier it is usual to group Water Lilies into a small number of Types — Dwarf, Medium etc. All you have to do is to choose the Type with the right planting depth and anticipated spread for your needs and then find a variety in that Type with a shape and colour which you find attractive. The time of flowering does not come into the selection as all Water Lilies behave more or less the same. Blooming starts in June and the flowers appear in succession until September. Each bloom opens from late morning to late afternoon and lasts for about four days.

Unfortunately this division into Types and the naming of Water Lilies are not as straightforward as they sound. The final spread depends on many factors and the figures given in the catalogue are only a guide — Water Lilies do not fall neatly into groups and so can't easily be pigeon-holed. There is also much confusion over naming — one man's so-called 'Sunrise' may be quite different to another supplier's offering! Bearing in mind the difficulties, the Type grouping given below is as good as any.

Now for one of the surprises. Most of the scores of varieties on offer today came from the breeding work of a Frenchman — M. Joseph Bory Latour-Marliac. The first one appeared in 1877 but unfortunately his secrets died with him in 1911. Because of this the majority of the Water Lily varieties in the catalogues are more than 80 years old! New American varieties are now beginning to appear, but Latour-Marliac hybrids still dominate.

Now for the planting rules. May and June are the best months and you will need a sunny spot and still water. Remove old leaves from the rootstock and trim back the fibrous roots. Plant firmly (see page 68) so that the crown is just protruding above the surface. Submerge the basket so that the young leaves float on the surface — gradually lower to the final depth as the leaves grow. This may take several months.

There are two reasons why leaves may grow well above the surface. The first cause is that the water is too shallow — the other cause is that the plant needs repotting in new soil and perhaps a larger basket. This is to be expected three or four years after planting. For details of propagation see page 94.

Type	Planting Depth	Spread	Cover	Flower Size
DWARF	4–10 in.	1–2 ft	1–3 sq.ft	2–4 in.
SMALL	6 in.–1½ ft	2–4 ft	3–12 sq.ft	4–6 in.
MEDIUM	1–2 ft	4–5 ft	12–20 sq.ft	6–7 in.
VIGOROUS	1½–3 ft	5–8 ft	20–50 sq.ft	7–10 in.

Colours: The colour range is large — only black, purple, pure blue and green are missing. The Changeables alter with age, deepening from cream or yellow to orange or red.

DWARF
N. 'Paul Hariot'

SMALL
N. 'Firecrest'

MEDIUM
N. 'Sunrise'

VIGOROUS
N. 'Gladstoniana'

Variety	Colour	Description
DWARF WATER LILIES		
N. 'AURORA'	Orange/red. Golden stamens	A Changeable variety which is compact enough (spread 1½–2 ft) for a half-barrel or other minipond. Colour changes from pinkish yellow to deep orange and then ruby red. Leaves splashed with brown
N. CANDIDA	White. Golden stamens	This native of N. Europe is a good choice if you want a white variety for a minipond. The cup-shaped flowers are held above the surface — in the heart of the blooms are bright red stigmas
N. 'GRAZIELLA'	Orange. Orange-red stamens	Dwarf or Small, the catalogues can't agree. They do agree, however, that this is a good variety for a small pond or minipond — very free-flowering with attractive purple-splashed leaves
N. LAYDEKERI 'LILACEA'	Pale pink — darkens with age. Yellow stamens	The fragrant blooms are cup-shaped with the pointed petals arranged above the dark green sepals. Leaves are blotched with brown. A smaller variety than N. laydekeri 'Fulgens' and 'Purpurata'
N. ODORATA MINOR	White. Yellow stamens	A good one for small ponds — spread is no more than 2 ft and the star-shaped fragrant blooms appear quite freely if the site is in full sun. The pale green leaves are red below
N. 'PAUL HARIOT'	Yellow, shaded coppery red. Golden stamens	Blooms are large (4–5 in.) for a Dwarf. One of the Changeables — flower colour alters from yellow to orange-pink and finally red. Free-flowering. Leaves spotted with brown
N. PYGMAEA ALBA	White. Yellow stamens	The smallest of the whites. Tiny 1 in. starry flowers are borne freely above the purple-backed leaves. An excellent choice for tubs, sinks and other miniponds. Some frost protection is advised
N. PYGMAEA 'HELVOLA'	Pale yellow. Golden stamens	The smallest of the yellows — perhaps the most popular Dwarf. The star-shaped flowers are borne above the surface and the brown-mottled leaves. Blooms appear all summer long
SMALL WATER LILIES		
N. 'FIRECREST'	Pink, streaked orange and red. Red-tipped stamens	You will find this fragrant American hybrid in a number of catalogues but not in the bestseller lists. It is an eye-catching flower with bright petals and stamens. Worth considering
N. 'FROEBELI'	Deep blood red. Orange stamens	An excellent choice for a small pond — this German-bred variety is both reliable and prolific. The flowers are upright and are borne on or just above the surface. Dull olive-green leaves
N. 'JAMES BRYDON'	Carmine red. Orange stamens	Few Water Lilies are praised so highly. The reason is that it is adaptable — it will stand a partly-shaded spot better than others. Paeony-shaped flowers — purplish leaves
N. LAYDEKERI 'FULGENS'	Red — darkens with age. Orange-red stamens	One of the brightest of the reds. Like other N. laydekeri varieties this one is suitable for a minipond — leaves are few but flowers are plentiful. Foliage is long-stemmed with purple undersides
N. LAYDEKERI 'PURPURATA'	Deep pink — darkens with age. Orange stamens	Another of the N. laydekeri varieties which is suitable for the little garden pond or minipond. Petals are pointed and the flowers are plentiful. Leaves are blotched with brown — undersides are purple
N. ODORATA 'SULPHUREA'	Canary yellow. Orange-yellow stamens	Popular, but not a good choice as it needs above-average temperatures to bloom freely. Star-shaped slightly fragrant flowers are borne above the surface. Petals are narrow and leaves are mottled
N. 'SIOUX'	Orange. Golden stamens	One of the Changeables — the pointed petals are at first buff yellow and then change to orange-pink and finally to coppery red. The leaves are spotted with brown or purple
MEDIUM WATER LILIES		
N. 'CONQUEROR'	Crimson — outer petals paler than inner ones. Yellow stamens	The large, cup-shaped blooms are eye-catching — red incurved petals above white sepals. The young foliage is purple. An attractive free-flowering variety
N. 'GONNERE'	White. Yellow stamens	Appropriately called 'Snowball' in the U.S — the multi-petalled flower looks like a snowball on the water before it opens to reveal the golden centre. Leaf spread is quite modest
N. MARLIACEA 'ALBIDA'	Pure white. Yellow stamens. Back flushed pale pink	Probably the most popular of all Water Lilies. Reliable and free-flowering with brown-edged leaves and 6 in. wide fragrant blooms borne just above the water surface
N. MARLIACEA 'ROSEA'	Pale pink. Golden stamens. Colour darkens when plants mature	Similar to N. marliacea 'Carnea' but growth is rather more restrained and the large fragrant blooms are deeper pink. Young leaves are purplish-green. Not for a small pond

WATER LILIES

Variety	Colour	Description
MEDIUM WATER LILIES *continued*		
N. 'MASANIELLO'	Rose-pink — outer petals paler than inner ones. Orange stamens	A strong and reliable grower which needs space. The Paeony-like flowers have white sepals and stand above the water surface. This free-flowering Latour-Marliac hybrid has long been a favourite
N. 'MME WILFRON GONNERE'	Pink flushed with white. Deep rose centre	If you have space for a Medium Water Lily and like blooms which are double and filled with petals then this one is a good choice. Flowers are cup-shaped — leaves are plain green
N. 'MOOREI'	Primrose yellow. Yellow stamens	An Australian variety which looks rather like N. marliacea 'Chromatella' but growth is more restrained, the green leaves bear brown spots and it is less free-flowering
N. ODORATA ALBA	White. Yellow stamens	A free-flowering U.S variety with 5–6 in. cup-shaped flowers bearing numerous pointed petals. The spread is about 5 ft, but it will flourish in shallow water with a planting depth of 9–12 in.
N. ODORATA ROSEA	Pale pink. Yellow stamens	There are a number of pink varieties of N. odorata — this is the basic one. Like its parent the foliage spreads for about 5 ft but it will adapt to a planting depth of 9 in.–2 ft. Flower size 5 in.
N. 'PETER SLOCUM'	Pink. Golden stamens	One of several new hybrids ('Perry's Fire Opal', 'Perry's Pink' etc) from the Perry Slocum Nursery in the U.S. The many-petalled blooms are double. You may have to search for it
N. 'RENE GERARD'	Rose red — outer petals paler than inner ones. Golden stamens	The 8 in. flowers are upright and star-shaped with petals which are oval and pointed. It is a free-flowering variety which needs a planting depth of about 1½ ft. Leaves are round and plain green
N. 'ROSE AREY'	Rose pink. Yellow stamens	The star-shaped blooms are large (7–8 in.) and the long pointed petals make up one of the most elegant of all Water Lily flowers. Fragrant and free-flowering. Young foliage is crimson
N. 'SUNRISE'	Canary yellow. Golden stamens	The 8 in. blooms are considered by some experts to be the best of the yellows. Each flower is made up of narrow incurved petals and it is borne above the surface. Leaves red underneath
N. 'WILLIAM FALCONER'	Deep red. Orange stamens	Choose this one or N. 'Atropurpurea' if you want a blood red Water Lily with a Medium growth habit. The cup-shaped blooms bear upright petals. Young leaves are purple
VIGOROUS WATER LILIES		
N. ALBA	White. Yellow stamens	This is the Wild Water Lily which grows in lakes and sluggish rivers, and there it should remain. Buy one only if you need a plant for a deep and very large pond. Blooms are cup-shaped and the leaves are large
N. 'ATTRACTION'	Red flecked with white. Golden stamens	Wide-spreading, so this free-flowering Water Lily needs a large pond. The flowers on a young plant may be quite small and pale pink, but on a mature specimen they are 9 in. rich red beauties
N. 'CHARLES DE MEURVILLE'	Wine red — darkens with age. Golden stamens	A very vigorous variety noted for its enormous leaves and its early flowering habit. The 9–10 in. blooms open flat, each red petal being tipped and streaked with white
N. 'COLOSSEA'	Blush pink — fades to white with age. Golden stamens	The most vigorous pink Water Lily which will grow in ponds or lakes 5–6 ft deep. The 9 in. fragrant blooms are borne over a long period. The leaves are large and dark green
N. 'ESCARBOUCLE'	Rich red — outer petals paler than inner ones. Golden stamens	The experts will tell you that this is probably the best red of all, but it does need plenty of space and a planting depth of at least 2 ft. Flowers up to 1 ft across — prolific, reliable and fragrant
N. 'GLADSTONIANA'	White. Golden stamens	Strictly one for the large pond or lake — a planting depth of 2 ft is necessary and so is an extensive water surface. Broad-petalled flowers are up to 1 ft across. Wavy-edged leaves
N. MARLIACEA 'CARNEA'	Pale pink. Golden stamens. May appear almost white	The most widely-grown pink Water Lily. Easy and free-flowering with large (8 in.) fragrant blooms. Sometimes classed as 'Medium', but not a plant for average-sized ponds. Spread 6 ft
N. MARLIACEA 'CHROMATELLA'	Canary yellow. Yellow stamens. Outermost petals sometimes tinged pink	The 7 in. wide flowers are bowl-shaped with incurved broad petals — the common name 'Golden Cup' is appropriate. Leaves are splashed with brown. Reliable and free-flowering. Very popular
N. 'MRS RICHMOND'	Pink — inner petals turn red with age. Golden stamens	The globular blooms are large (9 in.) with broad petals — the sepals at the base are white. Leaves are pale green. A free-flowering and spreading variety suited only to a large pond
N. TUBEROSA 'RICHARDSONII'	White. Yellow stamens	A giant which needs to be in about 3 ft of water or more — a plant to admire in lakes but not one for the home pond. The globular flowers appear unusually early in the season

Nymphaea pygmaea 'Helvola'

Nymphaea 'James Brydon'

Nymphaea 'Sioux'

Nymphaea 'Froebeli'

Nymphaea 'Peter Slocum'

Nymphaea 'Moorei'

Nymphaea Marliacea 'Rosea'

Nymphaea 'Escarboucle'

Nymphaea tuberosa 'Richardsonii'

Deep~water Aquatics

APONOGETON Water Hawthorn

Aponogeton distachyos is one of the best Deep-water aquatics — it is an easy plant to grow with leaves which are often evergreen and flowers which appear for months on end. These curious flowers are borne on spikes which float on the surface — each flower has waxy white petals and black anthers. The fragrance is strong, variously described as 'vanilla' and 'Hawthorn-like'. The oblong leaves are often blotched with brown and the eventual spread is about 2 ft. Unlike a Water Lily it will flourish in partial shade and moving water, but make sure that it is deep enough for the tubers to be below the ice in winter.

PLANTING DEPTH: 1–2 ft.

HEIGHT ABOVE SURFACE: Floating.

FLOWERING PERIOD: Spring and autumn.

PROPAGATION: Divide clumps in late spring or sow fresh seeds under glass.

Aponogeton distachyos

NUPHAR Pond Lily

This relative of the Water Lily is not as attractive as its illustrious cousin — the flowers are small, rather plain and are carried on thick stems above the water. There are, however, a few distinct advantages — light shade is no problem and neither is moving water. For an average-sized pond choose **Nuphar minima** (**N. pumila**). The yellow flowers are about 1 in. across and the underwater foliage is translucent. Unfortunately the types on offer are often the giants such as **N. lutea** (Brandy Bottle) with its 3 in. bottle-shaped yellow flowers which smell strongly of alcohol. Like **N. japonica** and **N. advena** it is a plant for a large pond or lake.

PLANTING DEPTH: 1–2 ft (small species); 2–6 ft (large species).

HEIGHT ABOVE SURFACE: 3 in.

FLOWERING PERIOD: June–September.

PROPAGATION: Divide clumps in late spring or summer.

Nuphar minima

NYMPHOIDES Water Fringe

There is just one basic species — **Nymphoides peltata** commonly known as Water Fringe or Floating Heart. In the catalogues you may find it listed as **Villarsia bennettii** or **Limnanthemum nymphoides**. The miniature Water Lily-like leaves measure about 2 in. across and are often crinkly-edged and blotched or spotted with brown. The 1½ in. yellow flower is more like a Buttercup than a Water Lily, and the petal edges are fringed. The blooms are borne in small clusters. A useful plant for giving rapid surface cover before Water Lilies have become established, but it can get out of hand.

PLANTING DEPTH: 1–2 ft.

HEIGHT ABOVE SURFACE: 2–3 in.

FLOWERING PERIOD: July–September.

PROPAGATION: Divide clumps in late spring or summer.

Nymphoides peltata

ORONTIUM Golden Club

Orontium aquaticum is a trouble-free and non-invasive plant with only one fussy requirement — it does need a lot of soil, so plant it in a deep Water Lily basket. It will grow in shallow water, but it needs a planting depth of at least 1 ft if you want the leaves to float on the water rather than stand erect. This foliage is attractive — blue-green above and silvery below. The most outstanding feature of this member of the Arum family is the unusual flower-head. This stands above the water like a pure white pencil with a tip which is coloured gold by a mass of tiny yellow florets. Highly recommended.

PLANTING DEPTH: 1–1½ ft.

HEIGHT ABOVE SURFACE: 1 ft.

FLOWERING PERIOD: April–May.

PROPAGATION: Sow fresh seeds in summer.

Orontium aquaticum

Floaters

AZOLLA   Fairy Moss

This is the most widely available of all the Floaters, and the one you will almost certainly be offered is **Azolla caroliniana**. It is a tiny fern with fronds which measure about ½ in. across. The dense mats of pale green 'leaves' spread rapidly — if left unchecked the whole surface may be covered, so only introduce this plant where the pond is small enough for you to remove excess growth by netting. In summer the fronds turn red and in winter much of the growth is cut back by frost and ice. It is a good idea to overwinter some of the fern in a jam jar filled with water and soil — reintroduce in April.

HARDINESS: Hardy — survives average winter.

FLOWER HEIGHT ABOVE SURFACE: —

FLOWERING PERIOD: —

PROPAGATION: Divide clumps of fronds in summer.

Azolla caroliniana

EICHORNIA   Water Hyacinth

Eichornia crassipes is a menace to waterways in frost-free countries but is a colourful Floater for outdoor ponds in Britain between June and September. The leaves are dark and shiny with swollen stems. The late summer flowers are extremely attractive — strong spikes bear Orchid-like blooms in blue, lavender and yellow. However, the catalogues sometimes forget to mention that the flowers fail to appear in a cool summer. Plant in June and take them indoors before the first frosts.

HARDINESS: Tender — killed by frost.

FLOWER HEIGHT ABOVE SURFACE: 1 ft.

FLOWERING PERIOD: August–September.

PROPAGATION: Remove young plants in September. Keep indoors in wet mud until June — need a well-lit spot.

Eichornia crassipes

HYDROCHARIS   Frog-bit

Hydrocharis morsus-ranae is a good choice for a small garden pond or a minipond — growth is restrained and a succession of small and short-lived white flowers appear in summer. In autumn the foliage starts to die away and the plant survives at the bottom of the pond in the form of dormant buds. In early summer these rise to the surface and growth begins again. When not in flower Hydrocharis looks like a tiny Water Lily — the green kidney-shaped leaves measure 1–2 in. across. Overwinter some buds in a jam jar filled with water and soil — put back in the pond in April.

HARDINESS: Hardy — survives average winter.

FLOWER HEIGHT ABOVE SURFACE: 1–2 in.

FLOWERING PERIOD: July–August.

PROPAGATION: Divide clumps in summer.

Hydrocharis morsus-ranae

LEMNA   Duckweed

Duckweed is in the catalogues, but do take care. You will see **Lemna minor** in stagnant ponds everywhere — a bright green blanket covering the surface. The usual pattern is a tiny leaf with a root below, and a rapid rate of reproduction. Several types may be offered by your supplier and they do provide food for the fish and shade for the water surface. In addition there are **L. gibba** (Thick Duckweed) and **L. polyrhiza** (Greater Duckweed). Avoid them like the plague — the only one to consider is the much less invasive **L. trisulca**.

HARDINESS: Hardy — survives winter.

FLOWER HEIGHT ABOVE SURFACE: —

FLOWERING PERIOD: —

PROPAGATION: Divide green mat in spring or summer.

Lemna minor

FLOATERS

PISTIA   Water Lettuce

An easy plant to recognise but a difficult one to grow. It does not thrive in summer if the temperature is below average and it is rapidly killed by frost in winter. **Pistia stratiotes** is the one you will find — not really worth the trouble unless you like to collect uncommon plants. The Lettuce-like leaves are felted and form a floating rosette on the surface of the pond. The roots are feathery and are a haven for spawning fish, and the small greenish flowers have no ornamental significance. Before the first frosts of autumn the plants have to be lifted and moved indoors. Put back at the end of May.

HARDINESS: Tender — killed by frost.

FLOWER HEIGHT ABOVE SURFACE: —

FLOWERING PERIOD: —

PROPAGATION: Divide clumps in summer.

Pistia stratiotes

STRATIOTES   Water Soldier

Stratiotes aloides is a native plant which looks rather like a Pineapple top floating on the water. The sword-like leaves have serrated edges and it comes to the surface only at flowering time when white three-petalled blooms appear. When flowering is over the plant sinks to the bottom of the pond and it overwinters as dormant buds. In late spring the young plants move upwards, but remain below the surface when not in flower. Male flowers are borne in clusters — female ones are solitary. An interesting plant, but it can be invasive where conditions are favourable.

HARDINESS: Hardy — survives winter.

FLOWER HEIGHT ABOVE SURFACE: 1–2 in.

FLOWERING PERIOD: July.

PROPAGATION: Divide clumps in summer.

Stratiotes aloides

TRAPA   Water Chestnut

Trapa natans bears dark green serrated leaves at the ends of swollen stems, each of the rosettes producing small white flowers in summer. The novel feature of this plant is that the flowers are followed by 1 in. wide spiny fruits. These black 'nuts' fall to the bottom of the pond where they overwinter and produce new plants in spring — the plants are annuals and do not survive the late frosts of autumn. At least that is what some of the catalogues say — in actual fact the plant only flowers in a warm summer and the fruits are rarely produced in our climate.

HARDINESS: Tender — killed by frost.

FLOWER HEIGHT ABOVE SURFACE: Floating.

FLOWERING PERIOD: July–August.

PROPAGATION: Drop fruits into the water in spring.

Trapa natans

UTRICULARIA   Bladderwort

The Bladderworts are unusual plants — they are not easy to find as few suppliers offer them and they are carnivorous. The finely-divided foliage floats just below the surface and the bladders on the leaves and stems capture minute aquatic animals. This microscopic fauna dies and is digested. Yellow flowers appear in late summer and the plant then dies down, surviving over winter as dormant buds at the bottom of the pond. In the spring these develop into young plants which rise and the cycle begins again. **Utricularia vulgaris** is the one to look for — the Antirrhinum-like flowers are deep yellow.

HARDINESS: Both U. vulgaris and U. minor are hardy.

FLOWER HEIGHT ABOVE SURFACE: 9 in.

FLOWERING PERIOD: July–August.

PROPAGATION: Divide clumps in summer.

Utricularia vulgaris

Oxygenators

CALLITRICHE
Water Starwort

Some species produce a star-shaped leafy rosette on the surface — hence the common name. An example is **Callitriche verna** which is suitable for shallow ponds — the green leaves die back in winter. The best one is **C. autumnalis** with masses of pale cress-like foliage which is evergreen — the leaves are entirely submerged and remain active in winter. A good choice, especially if Goldfish are present, but it can be temperamental. Take cuttings in spring or summer.

Callitriche verna

CERATOPHYLLUM
Hornwort

Ceratophyllum demersum is at or near the top of every expert's recommendation list. It will grow in sun or shade and is easily kept under control as it does not root. Planting could not be simpler — just drop the weighted cuttings into the water. The branched stems bear crowded whorls of dark green bristly foliage, giving a bottle-brush effect. In late autumn the stems sink to the bottom and the plant overwinters as dormant buds — these produce new stems in spring. Take cuttings or divide clumps in summer.

Ceratophyllum demersum

CHARA
Stonewort

A native plant with bristly stems and bristly leaves which may find its way into your pond whether you like it or not. A useful feature is that it helps to remove lime from the water — the stems become encrusted with a chalky deposit. There are several species, including the slender **Chara aspera** which is almost white, and the grey-coloured **C. vulgaris**. The problem with Chara is that it can spread very rapidly, and is generally not recommended, which is why it is almost impossible to find a supplier.

Chara aspera

ELEOCHARIS
Hairgrass

Eleocharis acicularis is something of a novelty — it is purchased in the form of small clumps and after planting it covers the basket or soil at the bottom of the pond with dense tufts of grass-like leaves. This mat is generally only a few inches high and so an underwater lawn is produced. Propagation is easy — all you have to do is to break away clumps and plant in spring or summer, but it is generally recommended for large aquaria rather than outdoor ponds.

Eleocharis acicularis

ELODEA
Canadian Pondweed

Everybody agrees that **Elodea canadensis** is one of the most efficient of all oxygenating plants, and everybody agrees that it can be very invasive and get out of control. There is disagreement, however, on whether you should ever plant it. The best advice seems to be to avoid Elodea if your pond is large, but to try it if other Oxygenators fail to thrive in a small pond. Lance-shaped dark green leaves are borne on long stems. Take cuttings in spring or summer.

Elodea canadensis

FONTINALIS
Willow Moss

Fontinalis antipyretica is the popular one — a native plant which bears dark green oval leaves on narrow stems. It has a number of virtues — it is evergreen, slow-growing, thrives in sun or shade and bears all sorts of aquatic wildlife on its leaves and stems. Unlike many aquatics it prefers moving to still water. It is an effective Oxygenator and excellent for spawning fish — the smaller species **F. gracilis** is a rarity. Propagate by dividing the mossy clumps in spring or summer.

Fontinalis antipyretica

OXYGENATORS

HOTTONIA
Water Violet

Hottonia palustris is one of the few flowering Oxygenators. The bright green foliage below the surface is finely divided into feathery leaves, and in early summer the flower-stalks appear. These branching stems grow about 9 in. above the water level and bear whorls of pale lavender flowers. In autumn the foliage dies down and the plant overwinters as dormant buds. It is not an easy plant to establish — it needs still and soft water. **H. inflata** is a white-flowering species. Take cuttings in summer.

Hottonia palustris

LAGAROSIPHON
Goldfish Weed

Lagarosiphon major is the correct name for the plant often sold as **Elodea crispa**. The long stems bear tightly-packed whorls of curled leaves and it is widely sold for aquaria. It is a good Oxygenator which is easy to establish outdoors, but it can be invasive and get out of hand. Some experts recommend Lagarosiphon provided that the pond is small enough for the plants to be reached for thinning or removal, but others advise against it under all circumstances. Lagarosiphon tends to deteriorate with age — replace with cuttings every few years.

Lagarosiphon major

MYRIOPHYLLUM
Water Milfoil

The Water Milfoils have long trailing stems which are clothed with very fine feathery foliage. A recommended Oxygenator as it is effective and suitable for a small pond. The leaves are green or brownish, depending on the species, and some produce flowers which are borne above the surface. **Myriophyllum spicatum** produces red-petalled flowers about 1 in. above the water level — another popular species is **M. verticillatum**. Take cuttings in spring or summer. Remember that some species are not hardy, so check before buying.

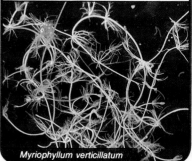
Myriophyllum verticillatum

POTAMOGETON
Pondweed

Potamogeton crispus (Curled Pondweed) is a large-leaved Oxygenator which is quite restrained and does not become an invasive weed. The long wiry stems bear strap-like reddish leaves which are wavy-edged and look rather like seaweed. In poor light the foliage remains green rather than turning red or bronze. Small pinky-white flowers appear just above the water in early summer. It is happier in moving water than in a still pond. **P. densus** is an unusual and hard to find species. Take cuttings in spring or summer.

Potamogeton crispus

RANUNCULUS
Water Buttercup

Ranunculus aquatilis has two types of foliage. Below the water the green leaves are finely cut into hair-like segments — on the surface float the Clover-like leaves. In early summer branched stems carrying white Buttercups appear — these flowers are held about 1 in. above the surface. After flowering the plant dies back. A good choice for ponds of all sizes as it does not get out of hand, and flowering Oxygenators are uncommon. Take cuttings in spring or summer.

Ranunculus aquatilis

TILLAEA
Swamp Stonecrop

Tillaea recurva (Crassula helmsii) is an Australian aquatic which has been grown in Britain for over 60 years, but the experts still can't make up their minds. Some say it is far too vigorous for a garden pond — others claim it to be "one of the finest Oxygenators available". The stems and fleshy leaves form a dense evergreen mass which is easily propagated from cuttings in spring or summer. The best plan appears to be to use it in a new pond but to remove the plants when more desirable types take over.

Tillaea recurva

Marginals

ACORUS Sweet Flag

There are two distinct species. **Acorus calamus** is the large one — an Iris-like plant with erect sword-shaped leaves which emit a tangerine odour when crushed. The tiny horn-like flower-heads are insignificant. The variety **'Variegatus'** is more striking — the green leaves are boldly striped with cream, and also with rose at the start of the season. Height is 2–3 ft, planting depth 3–6 in. These two plants are highly recommended, and so is the much smaller species (Japanese Rush) for small ponds and tubs — the leaves of the basic type (**A. gramineus**) grow about 6–9 in. high, planting depth 0–1 in. They are dark and evergreen, but there are doubts about the plant's hardiness in a severe winter. The variety **'Variegatus'** grows to the same height — the dark green leaves are edged with pale yellow.

PROPAGATION: Divide clumps in spring or summer.

Acorus calamus 'Variegatus'

ALISMA Water Plantain

A Plantain-like aquatic with attractive foliage — deeply ribbed and borne on long stalks. Throughout the summer months the tiny three-petalled flowers appear in whorls on the upright flower-stalks. A good choice for the larger pond, but there is one point of caution. Seeds germinate quickly and self-sown seedlings can be a nuisance, so dead-head spent blooms. **Alisma plantago-aquatica** is our native species with ovate leaves, pale pink flowers and flower-stalks which reach 2–3 ft. Planting depth 2–6 in. **A. parviflora** is an American species which has round rather than oval leaves and the flowers are usually white rather than pink. The flower-stalks grow 1½–2 ft high and the recommended planting depth is 3–5 in. The dwarf **A. ranunculoides** (6 in.) is sometimes offered.

PROPAGATION: Sow seeds or divide clumps in summer.

Alisma plantago-aquatica

BUTOMUS Flowering Rush

Butomus umbellatus is one of the most attractive of our native aquatics and is highly recommended as a Marginal plant for ponds everywhere. The long grass-like leaves are triangular in section — they are purplish-green when young but this purple tinge soon disappears. In summer the smooth and tall flower-stalks appear, reaching 2½–4 ft. The top of each of these stalks is crowned by 20–30 rose-pink flowers in July and August. The recommended planting depth is 3–5 in., but it will grow reasonably well in boggy land at the edge of the pond. The creeping rootstock produces numerous bulbils at the edges and these can be used for propagation. It is necessary to divide the rootstock every two or three years or the number of flowering heads will decline.

PROPAGATION: Plant bulbils or divide clumps in spring.

Butomus umbellatus

CALLA Bog Arum

Calla palustris is a creeping plant with long and fleshy rhizomes which spread below the surface and up the side of the pond. It is highly recommended for hiding the edges of a Rigid liner pond, the camouflage being the 8 in. long glossy and heart-shaped leaves which are abundant if the site is sunny and the water is still. In May and June the small white flowers appear, similar in shape but not in size to the familiar Arum Lily. These blooms are pollinated by water snails and in late summer the clusters of bright red berries appear — more showy than the flowers. The height of C. palustris is 6–9 in. and the recommended planting depth is 2–4 in. Collect the berries if you wish to raise more plants.

PROPAGATION: Sow seeds in autumn or divide rhizomes in spring.

Calla palustris

MARGINALS

CALTHA Marsh Marigold

The Marsh Marigolds are perhaps the most popular of all Marginal plants, and quite rightly so. The size of the smaller types makes them suitable for small ponds and they are reliable under a wide range of conditions. The recommended planting depth is no problem — they need very little water above the crowns and will grow quite happily in the bog garden. Their greatest advantage is the time of flowering — the Buttercup-like flowers appear above the round or heart-shaped leaves in spring. These April blooms herald in the start of the floral year. Grow Marsh Marigolds in groups in full sun or partial shade. The basic and most popular species is the Kingcup **Caltha palustris**. In April the bright yellow waxy flowers are borne on branching stems above the dark green leaves. Height 1–1½ ft, planting depth 0–2 in. The best Caltha of all is **C. palustris 'Plena'** — double yellow flowers which look like small pompon Chrysanthemums appear in April. The leafy mounds are small (6 in.–1 ft) and are often completely covered by the blooms. The white variety **alba** produces its blooms in May — height 6–9 in., planting depth 0–1 in. It is often disappointing as a Marginal — grow it as a Bog plant. **C. leptosepala** is a more attractive white-flowered Caltha, but it is not easy to find. **C. polypetala** is the giant — height 2–3 ft, planting depth 2–5 in. The leaves and the yellow blooms are large — not one for a small pond.

PROPAGATION: Sow fresh seeds or divide clumps in late summer.

Caltha palustris 'Plena'

Caltha palustris alba

CAREX Sedge

The Sedges are included here as they are generally found in the Marginal plant section of the catalogues, but these grassy perennials are generally happier growing in wet soil rather than within the pond. Planting depth when grown as a Marginal is 0–2 in. There is nothing special about these plants, but the yellow-leaved **Carex stricta 'Bowles Golden'** (1½ ft) has become quite popular in recent years. **C. riparia variegata** (1–2 ft) has green and white variegated leaves. **C. pendula** and **C. pseudocyperus** are the giant 3–4 ft species which in summer bear drooping spikes of catkin-like flowers. These tall Sedges can look attractive at the water's edge of a large pond, but they have no place in the average-sized one. For the ordinary garden pond there are more interesting Marginals than Carex.

PROPAGATION: Divide clumps in spring.

Carex stricta 'Bowles Golden'

COTULA Golden Buttons

A useful Marginal, especially for the edge of small ponds. The spreading leafy clumps are no more than 6 in. high and are covered all summer long with small yellow button-like flowers. The foliage is aromatic. **Cotula coronopifolia** is an annual and that means that it dies once the flowering season is over. This generally does not pose a problem as the plant readily sets seed and a flush of self-sown seedlings in spring replaces last year's specimens. You can save seeds and raise plants in the same way as annual bedding plants for the garden — sow the seeds in spring and transplant into containers which are set out on the marginal shelf in late spring. The recommended planting depth for Cotula is 0–5 in.

PROPAGATION: Sow seeds in spring.

Cotula coronopifolia

CYPERUS   Umbrella Grass

These graceful members of the Sedge family are foliage plants which bear lance-shaped leaves which radiate from the tops of the stems like the ribs of an umbrella. The summer flower-heads are branching spikes of tiny brown or reddish flowers. The popular one is the Sweet Garlingale **Cyperus longus** which is used to consolidate the banks of natural ponds and is cut for flower arranging. An invasive plant growing about 3 ft high — planting depth 3–5 in. The dark green leaves are rough and spiky. **C. vegetus** is more compact and therefore more suitable for the average garden pond. The leaves are broader than those of C. longus but the stems are only 1–2 ft high. The recommended planting depth is 0–4 in. — it can be grown in a bog garden.

PROPAGATION: Sow seeds or divide clumps in spring or summer.

Cyperus longus

ERIOPHORUM   Cotton Grass

A plant for shallow water at the edge of the pond or in the bog garden. It is an easy one to recognise — between June and August silky cottonwool-like seed-heads appear above the thin upright stems and the grassy foliage. Don't bother to grow Eriophorum unless you can provide the acid soil and acid water of its native moorland home. The popular species is **Eriophorum angustifolium** which grows 1–1½ ft high and has a recommended planting depth of 0–2 in. In some catalogues you will find **E. latifolium** as an alternative — it is very similar to E. angustifolium but it has broader and less attractive leaves, and is also short-lived. Stick with the popular one, but beware of its invasive nature.

PROPAGATION: Divide clumps in spring.

Eriophorum angustifolium

GLYCERIA   Water Grass

Yet another grassy Marginal, and one with a bad reputation for being invasive and for swamping more delicate plants. **Glyceria spectabilis variegatus** (Manna Grass) is a striking plant growing 2–3 ft high, with green leaves which are boldly variegated with yellow and white stripes. The young spring foliage has a distinctly rosy hue. The wide-spreading grass flower-heads are of little ornamental value and should be removed. The planting depth is 0–6 in., and it can be grown in the bog garden. Unless Glyceria is used to stabilise the bank of a lake or large pond, it should always be grown in a container to restrict its sideways spread. It is an easy plant to grow even in partial shade and it quickly becomes established and starts to spread, which is its problem.

PROPAGATION: Divide clumps in spring.

Glyceria spectabilis variegatus

HOUTTUYNIA   Houttuynia

An easy-to-grow carpeter for planting between taller specimens, but you must grow it in a container to keep its invasive nature in check. The stems are red and the bluish-green leaves are distinctly heart-shaped. It grows 6 in.–1 ft high and in early summer the cone-shaped flowers appear, each one surrounded by four white bracts. **Houttuynia cordata** bears single flowers — the double-flowered variety **'Plena'** is preferred. **'Variegata'** has the most colourful foliage — reddish-green splashed with yellow and cream but with few flowers. The recommended planting depth is 2–4 in. — it will grow quite happily at the surface or even in damp soil, but the roots are damaged in winter if they are exposed to frost or ice.

PROPAGATION: Divide clumps in spring.

Houttuynia cordata

MARGINALS

HYPERICUM   Marsh St John's Wort

There is just one species — **Hypericum elodes**. This lowly relative of the well-known Rose of Sharon which grows in shrub borders everywhere thrives happily in mud or an inch or two of water. Its creeping stems and mass of small rounded and woolly leaves make it a useful carpeter for growing between taller plants such as Iris or for disguising the edges of a Rigid liner pond. It spreads about 1½ ft, and in July and August small yellow bowl-shaped flowers are borne at the tips of the stems. It grows about 9 in.-1 ft high and the recommended planting depth is 0–2 in.

PROPAGATION: Divide clumps in spring or take cuttings in summer.

Hypericum elodes

JUNCUS   Rush

The Rushes appear here because one or two varieties are listed in most books and catalogues, but they are of no special value as pond plants. The slim cylindrical leaves and tiny flowers are generally uninteresting and the various species are often invasive. There are three which you can try. **Juncus effusus 'Spiralis'** is the Corkscrew Rush and is by far the most popular one. Height 1½ ft, planting depth 3–5 in. and stems contorted in corkscrew fashion — unusual rather than attractive. **J. effusus 'Aureostriatus'** has green and gold variegated leaves — height 1½ ft, planting depth 2–4 in. Remove all-green leaves immediately or the plant will revert. **J. ensifolius** is perhaps the most interesting one — the foliage is more like that of an Iris rather than the standard Rush and in summer brown globular flower-heads appear — height 1½ ft, planting depth 0–3 in.

PROPAGATION: Divide clumps in spring.

Juncus effusus 'Spiralis'

IRIS   Iris

There are three species of Iris which can be considered to be true aquatics for growing year round in the shallows of the pond, and it would be unthinkable to have a collection of Marginals without at least one of them. The most important species for the ordinary garden pond is **Iris laevigata** (Japanese Water Iris). The three-petalled blooms are about 5 in. across and are borne on 2 ft high stems — the first flowers open in June and are clear blue with a yellow line down the centre of each petal. A second flush may appear in September. There are a number of varieties — choose from **'Snowdrift'** (white, six petals), **'Colchesteri'** (white mottled with blue, six petals), **'Dorothy'** (blue with white line down the centre of each petal), **'Variegata'** (blue, leaves variegated yellow and green) and the hybrid **I. 'Rose Queen'** (rose-pink). The planting depth for I. laevigata and its varieties is 0–3 in. **I. pseudacorus** (Yellow Flag or Yellow Water Iris) is more vigorous and taller than I. laevigata — the foliage is 3–4 ft long and the yellow flowers are on 3 ft stems. The species is too coarse for ordinary garden ponds but the variety **'Variegata'** (2–2½ ft) with its more restrained growth habit and cream leaves edged with green makes an outstanding choice. Other varieties include **'Sulphur Queen'** and **'Bastardii'**. The planting depth for I. pseudacorus and its varieties is 2–10 in. The third aquatic species is **I. versicolor** (American Blue Flag). This is a restrained plant for the smaller pond — its leaves are 2 ft long and the flower-stalks 1½–2 ft high. The violet blue flowers appear in June or July and have narrow petals blotched with gold at the base. The popular variety is **'Kermesina'** — claret-red flowers flecked with white. The planting depth for I. versicolor and its varieties is 2–4 in.

PROPAGATION: Divide clumps as soon as flowering has finished.

Iris laevigata 'Colchesteri'

Iris pseudacorus

LOBELIA Lobelia

The Cardinal Flower (**Lobelia cardinalis**) will grow in the shallow water at the pond edge or in the damp soil of a bog garden, and the experts can't agree whether it should be treated as a Marginal or a Bog plant. It thrives in rich soil which suggests it should be planted outside the pond, but here it is susceptible to slug damage and usually needs winter protection. Do plant it in the pond if you don't have a bog garden — the 3 ft stems are topped by bright red flowers in late summer and early autumn. Recommended planting depth is 2–6 in. **L. fulgens** is a larger but less hardy plant, but both giant and compact hybrids are available. Look for **L. 'Queen Victoria'** (5 ft, scarlet), **L. 'Russian Princess'** (3 ft, pink) and **L. 'Dark Crusader'** (2½ ft, dark red).

PROPAGATION: Divide clumps in spring or take cuttings in summer.

Lobelia cardinalis

MENTHA Water Mint

Water Mint (**Mentha aquatica**) is a useful creeping plant which can be used to cover the edge of the pond. It is easy to grow and spreads rapidly, which can be a problem if you have small choice specimens growing nearby. The rule is to grow it in a basket and trim back stems which are becoming invasive. The rounded leaves are hairy and often take on a purplish tinge — as you would expect, the foliage is aromatic when crushed. In mid and late summer it becomes an attractive flowering plant — the tiny lavender flowers are grouped together in miniature powder-puffs which are borne in whorls along the stems. These flowers are especially attractive to bees. Water Mint grows 1–1½ ft high and the recommended planting depth is 0–3 in.

PROPAGATION: Divide clumps in spring.

Mentha aquatica

MENYANTHES Bog Bean

A sprawling plant with a creeping rootstock, **Menyanthes trifoliata** can be used to disguise the pond edge — grow it in a container to stop it getting out of hand. The leaves have three lobes like a Broad Bean — hence the latin species and common names. The main feature is the display of starry flowers which appears in May and June. They are borne in upright spikes and are quite distinctive. The buds which are pink open into white flowers with fringed edges to the petals. Height is about 9 in. when in flower and the planting depth is 1–3 in. The Bog Bean is recommended in situations where a taller plant would block the view of the water and the Water Lilies, and also for underplanting between tall and upright Marginals.

PROPAGATION: Divide clumps in spring.

Menyanthes trifoliata

MIMULUS Monkey Flower

There are numerous species, varieties and hybrids — most of them can be grown in either shallow water or wet soil to give a bright display of Snapdragon-like flowers during the summer months. Unfortunately some of them such as **M. cupreus** and **M. cardinalis** do not survive the winter under water and so belong in the bog garden. There is, however, a true aquatic species — **Mimulus ringens**. The branched slender stems are about 2 ft high, which is different from the low-growing mound of leaves usually associated with Mimulus. Small lavender flowers appear between June and August — planting depth 2–4 in. **M. luteus** can be grown as a Marginal — height 9 in., planting depth 0–2 in., yellow flowers with red-blotched petals appear throughout the summer.

PROPAGATION: Sow seeds or divide clumps in spring, take cuttings in summer.

Mimulus ringens

MARGINALS

MYOSOTIS Water Forget-me-not

Myosotis scorpioides (**M. palustris**) is a perennial Marginal which will creep over the edge of the pond and root in surrounding wet soil. An untidy sprawling plant, perhaps, but highly recommended by all the experts. It grows no more than 6–9 in. high and its free-flowering nature means that there are abundant blooms from May until August. These flowers have a typical Forget-me-not shape — sky-blue with yellow centres. Planting depth 0–3 in. The species is a reliable and easy-to-grow plant for sun or partial shade, but there are improved varieties. **'Mermaid'** and **'Semperflorens'** are claimed to be even more free-flowering and the blooms are a little larger. For white flowers grow the variety **alba**.

PROPAGATION: Sow seeds or divide clumps in spring.

Myosotis scorpioides 'Mermaid'

MYRIOPHYLLUM Parrot's Feather

The hardy Myriophyllums (Water Milfoils) are used as Oxygenators in the pond — see page 78. These species have underwater leaves, but there is one species which can be grown as a Marginal plant. **Myriophyllum proserpinacoides** (**M. aquaticum**) or Parrot's Feather has sprawling pinkish stems which float on the surface and also rise about 6 in. above the water to display the attractive feathery foliage. The flowers are insignificant. Winter hardiness is a problem, as the stems exposed to the air are killed by frost. The plant can be overwintered by lifting the container and keeping it indoors before returning it to the marginal shelf in spring. That's a lot of trouble, and it is easier to keep the crown below the ice level and let it overwinter in the pond — use a planting depth of 4–6 in.

PROPAGATION: Divide clumps in summer.

Myriophyllum proserpinacoides

PELTANDRA Arrow Arum

The best-known species is **Peltandra virginica**, the Green Arrow Arum. The large arrow-shaped leaves are glossy and deeply ribbed, and in June the flowers appear — pale green Arum-like blooms which look rather like large Callas. These flowers are followed by green berries — hence the common name. This Peltandra grows about 1½–2 ft high and the recommended planting depth is 3–5 in. You should be able to find a supplier without much trouble — harder to find is the more showy species **P. alba** (White Arrow Arum). The spathe of the flowers which appear in June is almost pure white rather than green and the berries are an eye-catching red instead of dull green. The planting depth is 3–5 in.

PROPAGATION: Divide clumps in spring.

Peltandra alba

PONTEDERIA Pickerel Weed

A Marginal for which there is nothing but praise — the bold glossy leaves form attractive clumps which do not spread to nuisance-sized proportions, and the flowers appear when most Marginals have stopped blooming. The popular species is **Pontederia cordata** which has heart-shaped leaves and between July and September it bears cylindrical spikes of pale blue flowers. The height of the flower-stalks bearing these terminal spikes is 2–2½ ft. Planting depth is 3–5 in. — note that it is important to cover the crown with at least 3 in. of water to avoid winter frost damage. There is a white variety (**alba**) which is hard to find. Equally difficult to find is the tall **P. lanceolata** (3–4 ft) which has lance-shaped leaves and bright blue flowers.

PROPAGATION: Divide clumps in late spring.

Pontederia cordata

RANUNCULUS   Water Buttercup

The Greater Spearwort (**Ranunculus lingua grandiflora**) is a tall (2–3 ft) and vigorous plant for the larger pond or lake. The pinkish leaves appear in spring and 2 in. yellow Buttercup flowers appear all summer long. It is widely available, but the experts can't quite agree whether you should grow this one. The plant is indeed very invasive and not right for a tiny pond, but it can be kept in check by growing it in a container and cutting back unwanted growth. The recommended planting depth is 2–6 in. **R. flammula** is the Lesser Spearwort — much less invasive and much less showy. The 1 ft spreading stems are useful for hiding the pond edge but the pale yellow Buttercup flowers are small and not very numerous. Planting depth 0–3 in.

PROPAGATION: Divide clumps in spring.

Ranunculus lingua grandiflora

SAGITTARIA   Arrowhead

The common name indicates the most distinctive feature of this plant — large leaves which are sharply and distinctly arrow-like. Three types are grown as Marginals — the recommended planting depth is 3–5 in. and the flowering period is July and August. **Sagittaria japonica** produces white three-petalled flowers with yellow centres — they are borne in whorls on 2 ft stems. An attractive plant, but it is the double form **'Flore Pleno'** which is the most popular and most highly praised Sagittaria. The flowers are a mass of white petals like a double Stock and the stamens are completely hidden. A somewhat smaller plant is the 1½ ft native species **S. sagittifolia** which is more invasive than the others and its white flowers have black and dark red centres.

PROPAGATION: Divide clumps in summer.

Sagittaria japonica 'Flore Pleno'

SAURURUS   Lizard's Tail

The only species you are likely to find is **Saururus cernuus**, the American Swamp Lily. The heart-shaped leaves are quite attractive, but the primary reason for growing this plant is the display of unusual flower-heads which appears between June and August at the top of slender stems. The small creamy-white blooms are slightly fragrant and are clustered to form a long cylindrical spike which curls at the end (the 'lizard's tail'). Height is 1–1½ ft and the recommended planting depth is 1–4 in. It appears in most of the catalogues but rarely in the 'highly recommended' lists of the experts. It is an invasive aquatic, so grow it in a container rather than soil lining the marginal shelf. There is an Asian species (**S. chinensis**) which is very similar but rarely seen.

PROPAGATION: Divide clumps in spring.

Saururus cernuus

SCIRPUS   Bulrush

There are many species of Scirpus but only two or three are suitable as garden aquatics. **Scirpus lacustris** is the True Bulrush, which is worth growing if you want to show your friends that you do know the difference between a real Bulrush and the incorrectly-named one (Typha latifolia). This Scirpus has stiff, needle-like leaves 2–4 ft tall and hanging tassels of tiny brown flowers in late summer. Planting depth is 2–4 in. The variegated types are a much better choice. **S. 'Albescens'** has pale yellow Rush-like stalks (3–5 ft) with thin vertical stripes of green — planting depth 3–5 in. Even more popular is the Zebra Rush **S. 'Zebrinus'** with 2–3 ft high quill-like stalks which are horizontally banded in green and white. Planting depth 3–5 in. — divide every two years.

PROPAGATION: Divide clumps in spring.

Scirpus 'Zebrinus'

MARGINALS

SPARGANIUM Bur-reed

Nearly all of the plants in this Marginals section make a welcome addition to the pond, although there is sometimes a precautionary note that a plant may be too large, too invasive or perhaps too dull for the ordinary garden pond. With this one, however, there is a definite warning — the sharp-pointed rhizomes growing out from the container can readily puncture a Flexible liner. The common one is **Sparganium ramosum (S. erectus)** — a Rush-like plant with 2–3 ft high leaves and round prickly seed heads. The recommended planting depth is 3–5 in. It is very invasive, and so is the lowly **S. minimum** with its sprawling stems and floating leaves. You will find Sparganium offered in many catalogues — leave it alone.

PROPAGATION: Divide clumps in spring.

Sparganium ramosum

TYPHA Reedmace

Typha is one of the most widespread of all our native aquatics. The giant is the Great Reedmace **Typha latifolia** — popularly but incorrectly known as 'Bulrush' (see Scirpus). This familiar plant has broad leaves and 5–7 ft stalks which in summer bear the familiar brown 'pokers' or 'cats-tails'. Planting depth is 3–10 in., but this is one for large lakes only. Equally unsuitable for the home garden pond is **T. angustifolia** which has slender green leaves and stalks which grow 3–5 ft high. For the larger garden pond pick **T. laxmanii** (**T. stenophylla**) with its grey-green leaves and small pokers between June and October — height 3 ft, planting depth 1–6 in. For a small pond the only choice is **T. minima** — 1–1½ ft high and a planting depth of 1–4 in. Rush-like foliage, squat flowerheads.

PROPAGATION: Divide clumps in spring.

Typha minima

VERONICA Brooklime

A large genus of herbaceous plants which contains just one aquatic species, **Veronica beccabunga** — a lowly plant with untidy creeping stems and glossy olive green foliage. It grows about 6–9 in. high and can be used to hide the pond edge — its other virtue is the abundance of white-eyed bright blue flowers which are borne all summer long. The recommended planting depth is 0–4 in. The only problem is that Brooklime starts to look weedy after a season or two — cut back the stems if they become too straggly and take cuttings by pushing non-flowering stem tips into the mud of the container. The plant can be left to spread into the soil surrounding the pond as it readily roots along the length of the stems.

PROPAGATION: Take cuttings in summer.

Veronica beccabunga

ZANTEDESCHIA White Arum Lily

This plant is usually regarded as a greenhouse plant, and yet you will find it in various sections of the aquatic plant catalogues, ranging from the Bog plant lists to the Deepwater aquatics. The truth of the matter is that **Zantedeschia aethiopica** will survive the winter in most areas, provided the crown is 6 in. below the surface. Choose the variety **'Crowborough'** which is hardier than the species. It is well worth the slight risk involved — above the glossy arrow-shaped leaves the 2 ft high flower-stalks arise from July to September, and the blooms are truly eye-catching. Around each yellow poker-shaped spadix is a large white spathe — after a few weeks yellow berries appear.

PROPAGATION: Divide clumps in spring.

Zantedeschia aethiopica

Bog Plants

ARUNCUS Goat's Beard

There is a single species — **Aruncus dioicus**, usually sold as **A. sylvester**. It may take a year or two to become established, but given the right conditions will reach 6 ft or more. For a few weeks in June or July the tall stems are crowned with large fluffy flower-heads. Each flower-head is about 8 in. long and bears a multitude of tiny creamy-white flowers. It needs plenty of space — set plants 2½ ft apart and cut the stems down to an inch or two above ground level in late autumn. Choose a spot which receives some shade during the day. A. dioicus is too large for most bog gardens and the lobed leaves cast a lot of shade — pick the variety **'Kneiffii'** (2 ft) where space is limited. Flowers creamy-white — looks rather like an Astilbe.

PROPAGATION: Divide clumps in autumn.

Aruncus dioicus

ASTILBE Astilbe

Astilbe is one of the most widely grown and best Bog plants available, and no sizeable bog garden is complete without one. The foliage is deeply cut and often coppery in spring, and the flowers are tiny. What the blooms lack in size they make up for in quantity — between June and August large feathery plumes appear which are clothed with a multitude of flowers. The popular varieties belong to **Astilbe arendsii** — height 2–3 ft, spread 1½ ft. Look for **'Bressingham Beauty'** (pink), **'Fire'** (red) and **'Deutschland'** (white). Others include **'Fanal'** (deep red) and **'White Gloria'**. The plumes are not always erect — **'Ostrich Plume'** (pink) bears pendant flower-heads. For dwarf plants grow **A. simplicifolia 'Sprite'** (1 ft, pink) or **A. crispa 'Lilliput'** (6 in., pink).

PROPAGATION: Divide clumps every 2–3 years in spring.

Astilbe arendsii

CARDAMINE Cuckoo Flower

Cardamine pratensis (Lady's Smock) is a native plant which will flourish in sun or partial shade in the bog garden. The mounds of pale green ferny foliage quickly spread and may have to be kept in check — in April and May the 1 ft flower-stalks appear. The single blooms are pale lilac and are borne in great numbers. Most people choose the variety **'Flore Pleno'** which is rather shorter and less invasive. The flowers are fully double and the plant can be propagated only by division. Much less common is **C. latifolia** which has Watercress-like leaves and bears its lilac flowers in May or June. It is a larger plant than C. pratensis — the stems of this evergreen grow about 1 ft high and the spread is 2 ft.

PROPAGATION: Sow seeds of the species in spring or divide clumps in late autumn.

Cardamine pratensis

EUPATORIUM Boneset

Several species and varieties are available for the bog garden — but plant with care as most are large with coarse leaves and out of place in a small plot. **Eupatorium cannabinum** is our native Hemp Agrimony, a downy plant with stems growing 2–4 ft tall and bearing clusters of reddish-purple flowers at the tops in late summer or autumn. It self-seeds very freely — cut down to nearly ground level after flowering. **E. purpureum** (Joe Pye Weed) is even larger, reaching 6 ft or more and with large flat heads of rose-purple flowers in late summer. The dark green leaves are borne in whorls — for purple leaves choose the variety **'Atropurpureum'**. One of the smallest species is **E. fraseri** (2 ft, white flowers).

PROPAGATION: Divide clumps in early spring.

Eupatorium cannabinum

FILIPENDULA Dropwort

The leaves are often fern-like and the stems bear terminal clusters of small flowers. With some types the foliage is the main attraction and the flowers are removed — with others the blooms are attractive enough for garden display. **Filipendula ulmaria** is the Meadowsweet which grows wild along streams and in ditches. It grows about 3 ft high and bears feathery spires of fragrant creamy-white flowers in June–August. The variety **'Aurea'** is grown for its yellow foliage — remove flowers as they form. **F. palmata** (2–3 ft) produces large flat heads of rosy flowers in midsummer. **F. rubra 'Magnifica'** is the giant — 5–6 ft high with wide heads of pink feathery flowers.

PROPAGATION: Divide clumps in autumn or spring.

Filipendula ulmaria 'Aurea'

GEUM Water Avens

Geum is a very popular plant in the herbaceous border, but it is much less common in the bog garden. The reason may be that there is not much variety — there is just one species. **Geum rivale** is a native plant with feathery foliage, but with flowers in late spring and early summer which are quite different from the popular garden varieties. These nodding blooms are bell-shaped and the pink petals are backed by prominent purple sepals. Water Avens grows about 1–1½ ft high and has a spread of about 1½ ft. Choose a variety — **'Jeannie Ross'** is pink and **'Leonard's Variety'** has large orange-pink flowers. **'Lionel Cox'** is golden yellow. All varieties thrive in sun or light shade. Divide every few years.

PROPAGATION: Divide clumps in autumn or spring.

Geum rivale 'Lionel Cox'

GUNNERA Prickly Rhubarb

With **Gunnera manicata** it is a matter of once seen never forgotten, but it is not for you unless you have a large tract of unoccupied boggy land next to a lake or stream. It is our largest hardy herbaceous plant, with vast Rhubarb-like leaves which are 5 ft or more across and grow 8 ft high. In late summer the 3 ft high cone-like flower-head appears, and in autumn it is necessary to protect the crown against winter's frosts by bending the old leaves over a straw or bracken covering. **G. scabra** is a somewhat smaller plant, but the real novelty for the garden pond is **G. magellanica**, a miniature species which grows no more than 3 in. high and bears rounded leaves and reddish florets on a 3 in. flower-head. It is only semi-hardy.

PROPAGATION: Divide crowns in early spring.

Gunnera manicata

HEMEROCALLIS Day Lily

Day Lilies make excellent Bog plants with a long flowering season and thriving in sun or partial shade. No longer is the gardener restricted to dull yellow and orange shades — modern hybrids are available in colours from palest yellow to richest red. Clumps of arching strap-like leaves give rise to branching stalks which bear trumpet-shaped blooms from June to August. Each bloom lasts a single day, but new buds appear continually during the flowering season. There are 1½ ft dwarfs and 4 ft giants — examples are **Hemerocallis 'Pink Damask'** (pure pink) and **H. 'Stafford'** (yellow-eyed red). Others include **H. 'Luxury Lace'** (green-throated lavender) and **H. 'Canary Glow'** (velvety yellow).

PROPAGATION: Divide clumps in autumn or spring.

Hemerocallis 'Stafford'

HOSTA   Plantain Lily

A dual purpose plant, grown for its spikes of trumpet-shaped flowers as well as its attractively-shaped leaves which are often variegated or distinctly coloured. It is a popular subject for a shady spot in the bog garden and it has just one drawback — slugs find the young foliage irresistible. You will find a large selection in catalogues and garden centres, with leaves varying from near-blue to almost pure yellow. Basic details are height 1½–3 ft, spread 2 ft, flowering period July–August. Some popular ones include **Hosta 'Royal Standard'** (glossy green leaves, white flowers), **H. fortunei 'Aureomarginata'** (gold-edged dark green leaves), **H. sieboldiana 'Elegans'** (large bluish-green leaves, purple-tinged white flowers), **H. ventricosa** (dark green leaves, lilac flowers) and **H. undulata** (white-splashed green leaves).

PROPAGATION: Divide clumps in spring.

Hosta undulata

IRIS   Bog Iris

There are several species which will flourish in the damp soil of a bog garden, but only two are really popular and neither of them likes over-wet soil in winter. **Iris kaempferi** is the delightful Japanese Clematis Iris sometimes listed as **I. ensata**. Basic details are height 2–2½ ft, flowering period June-July, acid soil essential. The foliage is broad and the flowers large and flattened — varieties are available in purple, blue, mauve and white. **I. sibirica** is an easier plant to grow which does not demand lime-free conditions. The leaves are narrower and the flowers are smaller, but there is a host of beautiful varieties in a range of sizes from **'Perry's Pygmy'** (1½ ft, violet) to **'Perry's Blue'** (3 ft, sky-blue). If the ground remains very wet in winter, grow **I. ochroleuca** (white and gold flowers).

PROPAGATION: Divide clumps immediately after flowering.

Iris kaempferi

LIGULARIA   Golden Rays

The large leaves of this plant cover the ground and effectively smother weeds, and in summer the flower-heads appear. Each individual bloom is a yellow or orange Daisy, but the size and arrangement depend on the variety. Choose a shady spot, cut back the stems when flowering is over and divide the clumps every three years. The popular species is **Ligularia dentata** (**L. clivorum**), sometimes listed under 'Senecio'. The 3–4 ft stems bear large, spreading heads of flowers between July and September and the heart-shaped leaves are purplish (**'Desdemona'**) or red (**'Othello'**) underneath. **L. stenocephala** (**L. przewalskii**) **'The Rocket'** (5 ft) bears its small yellow flowers on erect spikes rather than wide heads — **L. veitchiana** is another spike-bearing species.

PROPAGATION: Divide clumps in autumn or spring.

Ligularia dentata 'Desdemona'

LOBELIA   Lobelia

The Marginals Lobelia cardinalis and fulgens have already been described on page 83 — both of them can be grown in the bog garden. There are a few other varieties which are readily available for bog garden use only — they cannot tolerate waterlogged soil for long periods. The most popular one is the unfortunately-named **Lobelia syphilitica** — a shade-loving plant with green leaves and spires of blue flowers in late summer. It grows about 2½ ft high and is rather short-lived — for white flowers choose the variety **alba**. **L. vedrariensis** grows a little taller (3–4 ft) — its leaves are flushed with purple and the long spires of violet flowers appear in late summer. The hybrid **L. gerardii** is not easy to find — violet-purple flowers on strong 4 ft stems.

PROPAGATION: Sow seeds under glass in spring.

Lobelia syphilitica

LYCHNIS Ragged Robin

The rockery types of Lychnis are described on page 35 — small plants for sunny spots in rock gardens, sinks and between paving stones. There is just one species which can be grown in the bog garden — the Ragged Robin (**Lychnis flos-cuculi**) which grows wild in wet areas throughout Europe. It is not a choice plant and it is described in very few books on water gardening, but you will find it in many catalogues and it is an excellent subject for the area surrounding a wildlife pond. The stems grow about 2 ft high, clothed with narrow leaves and in summer with a crown of numerous pink flowers. Several varieties are available, including the low-growing **'Nana'**, white-flowered **'Alba'** and the double pink **'Rosea Plena'**.

PROPAGATION: Divide clumps in autumn.

Lychnis flos-cuculi

LYSICHITON Skunk Cabbage

Lysichiton (also known as Lysichitum) is not difficult to grow in either the bog garden or covered with an inch or two of water on the marginal shelf. It is a bold and eye-catching plant, and so it is surprising that you will have to search for a supplier. This lack of popularity may be due to its size or unpleasant smell — hence the common name. **Lysichiton americanum** produces 1 ft high Arum-like flowers with a yellow spathe in April — these blooms are followed by 3 ft long leaves. The seeds germinate readily so self-sown seedlings can be a problem. Where space is limited it is better to grow the Oriental variety **L. camtschatcense**. The flowers are smaller and the spathes are white — it grows about 2 ft high. With both species you may have to wait several years before flowers appear.

PROPAGATION: Sow fresh seeds in late spring.

Lysichiton americanum

LYSIMACHIA Loosestrife

The old favourite Creeping Jenny (**Lysimachia nummularia**) has already been described on page 35 under Rock Garden Plants — it is equally suitable in the bog garden. Choose the yellow-leaved variety **'Aurea'**. This is a sprawling plant for use below taller specimens — an upright Loosestrife for the bog garden is **L. punctata** which grows up to 3 ft high. From June to August the leafy stems bear whorls of yellow, starry flowers which have a reddish tinge at the base of the petals. **L. vulgaris** has a similar appearance, but is too invasive for the average bog garden. **L. clethroides** (Chinese Loosestrife) is quite different — it bears curved spikes of tiny white flowers and lance-shaped leaves which give it the appearance of a small Buddleia. Height 2 ft, spread 2 ft, flowering period August–September.

PROPAGATION: Divide clumps in autumn or spring.

Lysimachia clethroides

LYTHRUM Purple Loosestrife

A good choice. The leaves are dark green and elongated — above them rise the narrow flower spikes, densely packed with pink, red or purple starry blooms from July to September. These spikes are colourful, prolific and long-lasting. The basic species is **L. salicaria** — a 4–5 ft high wild flower which grows along streams. The hybrids are shorter and more attractive — popular ones include **'The Beacon'** (3 ft, crimson), **'Lady Sackville'** (4 ft, rose-pink), **'Robert'** (2½ ft, clear pink) and **'Firecandle'** (3 ft, rose-red). For an average-sized bog garden it is better to grow the more restrained **L. virgatum** which has daintier spikes and grows 1½–2 ft high. Choose one of the popular named varieties — look for **'The Rocket'** (deep pink), **'Dropmore Purple'** (rose-purple) and **'Rose Queen'** (rose-pink).

PROPAGATION: Divide clumps in autumn.

Lythrum salicaria 'Firecandle'

MATTEUCCIA Ostrich Feather Fern

As any garden designer will tell you, ferns have an important part to play in a large bog garden, but use them in moderation to add occasional points of interest amongst the flowering plants. **Matteuccia struthiopteris** is one of the most attractive — green feathery fronds are arranged around the woody crown like the feathers of a shuttlecock. The outer 'feathers' are sterile — the shorter fertile fronds appear later to produce an inner ring. It is an upright plant, growing about 3 ft high but only 1½ ft wide, the rather delicate appearance belying the fact that it is extra hardy and extremely tough. It spreads by means of underground rhizomes. The rare variety **pennsylvanica** grows 6–8 ft high.

PROPAGATION: Divide crowns in spring.

Matteuccia struthiopteris

MIMULUS Monkey Flower

Mimulus appears in several places in this book. The low-growing ones are described in the Rockery section on page 36 as they are widely used in the rock garden and peat bed — they are also an excellent choice for the bog garden. The 6–9 in. mounds of **Mimulus cupreus** varieties flower from June to September and most come true from seed. Bronze and red are the usual flower colours — the dwarf **M. 'Whitecroft Scarlet'** (4 in.) is a popular choice. Mimulus is also found amongst the Marginals and one of them (**M. luteus**) will thrive in wet soil. The most popular Bog Mimulus is **M. cardinalis** — an erect plant with 1½–2 ft stems and spires of orange-red blooms between July and September. **M. bartonianus** is rather similar and **M. lewisii** is a popular rose-pink species. **M. 'Hose-in-Hose'** (1 ft) has one flower within another.

PROPAGATION: Divide clumps or sow seeds under glass in spring — take cuttings in autumn.

Mimulus 'Whitecroft Scarlet'

ONOCLEA Sensitive Fern

Onoclea sensibilis is one of the few ferns which can be grown either in the bog garden or the shallow water at the edge of the pond. Below ground it spreads by means of black rhizomes — above ground the foliage changes colour with the seasons. In spring the new fronds appear — pink at first and then changing to pale green as spring turns into summer. The triangular fronds grow 2 ft high — the toothed leaflets (pinnae) arranged in herringbone fashion. In autumn the fronds turn russet brown, completing the round of colour changes. These brown fronds are sometimes cut for flower arranging. Onoclea is offered by some but not by the majority of aquatic plant suppliers — if you buy one then remember that it can spread very rapidly in its favourite situation of shade and very wet soil.

PROPAGATION: Divide clumps in spring.

Onoclea sensibilis

OSMUNDA Royal Fern

There is common agreement that Osmunda is the most impressive of the hardy ferns. **Osmunda regalis** grows 4–6 ft high, its tall lime-green fronds changing to bronze with the onset of autumn. The spore-bearing fronds are quite different — they are smaller, greenish-brown and are borne on stalks, giving a rather flower-like appearance. Cover the crown with its dead leaves and straw during winter and early spring. For something rather different choose the purple-tinged variety **'Purpurascens'**. Both these plants need plenty of space and they will not tolerate lime in the soil. Where space is limited you can consider the smaller varieties. **'Cristata'** grows 3–4 ft high and bears twisted fronds with curiously tasselled ends. **O. undulata** (3–4 ft) has fronds with cockscomb-like tips.

PROPAGATION: Divide crowns in spring.

Osmunda regalis

BOG PLANTS

PELTIPHYLLUM   Umbrella Plant

Peltiphyllum peltatum is a good plant to choose if you have a bare area of rich wet soil to cover — it grows 3–4 ft high so plenty of space is needed. In early spring the 2 ft high leafless flower-stalks appear, topped with globular heads of small pink blooms in April and May. These Saxifrage-like flowers are followed by the umbrella-like leaves in summer — tall green stalks bearing 1 ft wide round leaves which are serrated and lobed around the edges. During the growing season the foliage has a bronzy-green colour but this changes to reds and browns in autumn. A good choice as it provides spring flowers and autumn tints, but too large for the average bog garden. Choose the variety **'Nanum'** (1½ ft) where space is limited.

PROPAGATION: Divide rhizomes in spring.

Peltiphyllum peltatum

POLYGONUM   Knotweed

You will find the Knotweeds on offer as Bog plants at garden centres and in catalogues, but experienced pond gardeners know that you have to choose with care. Nearly all types are invasive and many can quickly become weeds. The most popular ones are **Polygonum affine** and its varieties such as **'Donald Lowndes'** and **'Dimity'**. Long-lasting poker-like heads of tiny flowers are produced on 6 in.–1 ft stems — pretty but invasive. **P. milletii** (1 ft, bright red flowers) is not invasive — another Knotweed which is easy to keep under control in the bog garden is **P. bistorta 'Superbum'** (3 ft) which bears 6 in. long spikes of pink flowers in early summer. **P. campanulatum** (pink, late summer) grows to a similar height.

PROPAGATION: Divide clumps in autumn or spring.

Polygonum bistorta 'Superbum'

PRIMULA   Bog Primula

Primula is considered by many gardeners to be the queen of the bog garden plants. There is a large range of species which will flourish in rich and moist ground but not in constantly wet soil, and by choosing wisely you can have flowers from early spring to late summer in a wide variety of colours. The general height range is 6 in.–2½ ft and most will grow in sun or shade. Mulch in spring, dead-head faded blooms and divide the clumps every two or three years. The flowering year begins in March with **Primula rosea** (6 in.), a Primrose-like plant with rose-pink flowers. A month later the Drumstick Primrose (**P. denticulata**) is in bloom — small yellow-eyed lavender flowers crowded on 3 in. wide globular heads. White, blue and pale purple varieties are available. Between May and July the largest Primula group is in bloom — the Candelabra Primroses. The flowers are borne as a series of whorls up the stem — some of the more popular species are listed below. **P. japonica** (2 ft, red, pink or white) is noted for its reliability and **P. 'Inverewe'** is the showiest one — bright orange flowers and 2 ft high white stems. **P. aurantiaca** bears orange-red flowers on 1½ ft stems in June. **P. pulverulenta** is a tall-growing Candelabra species, growing 2–3 ft tall with red flowers on white mealy stems. **P. helodoxa** (Glory of the Marsh) is noted for the brightness of its yellow flowers and **P. chungensis** (2 ft) bears bold orange blooms. **P. beesiana** is a vigorous species (2–2½ ft) with yellow-eyed rosy-purple flowers — **P. burmanica** is another variety which has yellow-eyed purplish blooms. Several Bog Primulas belong to the Cowslip group — the bell-like flowers are pendant and often fragrant. **P. sikkimensis** (2 ft, yellow) blooms in May — **P. florindae** (3 ft, yellow) blooms in July–August.

PROPAGATION: Sow seeds under glass or divide clumps of named varieties in spring.

Primula denticulata

Primula florindae

RHEUM   Ornamental Rhubarb

The most popular and successful species is **Rheum palmatum**. It needs plenty of space, as its large and wide-spreading foliage can reach 6 ft or more. In May and June the plumes of small flowers appear on top of the stout stalks. The two varieties **'Atrosanguineum'** (**'Rubrum'**) and **'Bowles Crimson'** are even more colourful — the leaves which are red when young have a purplish cast when mature, and the flowers are crimson. **'Tanguticum'** is another red-flowered variety, but with this one the foliage is deeply cut. Rheum is not a difficult plant to grow in either sun or light shade — it is hardy and it will grow under drier conditions than Gunnera. It has to be used as a specimen plant, however, as little will grow under its leaves — where space is limited grow the 2 ft high variety **'Ace of Hearts'**.

PROPAGATION: Divide crowns in spring.

Rheum palmatum

RODGERSIA   Rodgersia

These plants from China and Japan are grown as ground cover, their large crinkled leaves carpeting a wide area when the plant is fully established. In midsummer plumes of small flowers are borne on top of 3–5 ft high stems. Rodgersia thrives best in a sheltered and partially shaded part of the bog garden. Leaf form and flower colour depend on the species. The most popular one is **Rodgersia tabularis** — the circular leaves are up to 2 ft across and the flowers are creamy white. **R. pinnata** is quite different — the foliage is made up of paired leaflets and the flowers are pink or white. **R. aesculifolia** is another bronze-leaved species, but the foliage is Horse Chestnut-shaped and the white flowers are followed by red seed heads.

PROPAGATION: Divide clumps in autumn or spring.

Rodgersia pinnata

SCHIZOSTYLIS   Kaffir Lily

This South African plant has flowers which have been described as similar to a Freesia, miniature Gladiolus or small Hemerocallis. They appear above grassy foliage remarkably late in the season, the first buds opening in October and the last blooms fading in December. Despite this ability to extend the floral display in the bog garden, Schizostylis appears in none of the bestseller lists and is missing from many catalogues. The problem is that it is not fully hardy, and should therefore be grown in a sheltered sunny spot. Mulch in winter. The basic species is **Schizostylis coccinea** which grows 1–2 ft high. A number of varieties are available. **'Grandiflorus'** produces red flowers like the species but they are larger — **'Mrs Hegarty'** is rose-pink and **'Viscountess Byng'** is pale pink.

PROPAGATION: Divide clumps in spring.

Schizostylis coccinea

TROLLIUS   Globe Flower

Trollius is deservedly a favourite plant for the bog garden. The mounds of dark green lobed leaves are not invasive and the wiry stems which grow about 1½–2 ft high bear large globular Buttercups in May and June. Mulch in spring and divide the plants every three years. The usual choice is a variety of the hybrid **Trollius cultorum** — a plant which produces showy yellow or orange blooms in great profusion. **'Earliest of All'** (bright yellow) is the first to bloom, and the flower colour of the other varieties is usually obvious from their names — **'Alabaster'** is cream, the yellow ones include **'Canary Bird'**, **'Golden Queen'** and **'Gold Cup'** and orange blooms are produced by **'Fire Globe'**, **'Orange Globe'** and **'Orange Princess'**. **T. asiaticus** is a bronze-leaved species — the dwarf Trollius is **T. pumilus** (6 in., yellow).

PROPAGATION: Divide clumps in autumn.

Trollius cultorum 'Golden Queen'

Propagation

Raising garden plants at home is a popular and money-saving task as there are so many beds, borders and containers to fill, but the propagation of aquatic plants is a much less common practice. It sounds like a difficult concept as the plants have to be kept in water — in addition the need for fresh material for the water garden is limited. After all, the average-sized garden pond can only hold a handful of plants.

Propagation is, however, an important technique in the water garden if you have a sizeable collection of plants. As noted on the previous pages, many aquatics have to be lifted every few years and divided — the old exhausted parts are discarded and the young vigorous sections are repotted.

For the enthusiast there are additional techniques — cuttings can be taken and seeds sown for the propagation of some aquatics. There are a number of basic differences from the standard techniques used for ordinary garden plants. For example, soil is used rather than a seed or cutting compost and the leaves, roots and soil must be kept constantly wet. Still, all you will need is a large washing-up bowl and perhaps a cold frame, so it cannot be all that difficult.

WATER LILIES

Lift the plant in early summer and take it out of the basket. Remember that it will have to be replanted at the same angle, so note whether it is growing vertically or horizontally.

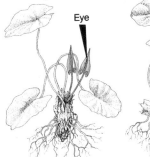 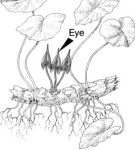

Vertical Rhizome
Most Water Lily varieties

Stump-like rhizome — roots form a ring below crown

Horizontal Rhizome
Varieties of N. odorata and N. tuberosa

Long, fleshy rhizome — roots in groups along length of rhizome

Wash the mud off the rhizome and remove all old leaves and some of the thick roots. Place on a polythene sheet and make sure the plant never dries out — sprinkle occasionally with a watering can.

Use a sharp knife to remove eyes (tiny plants with small leaves) — dust cut surfaces with sulphur. Plant eyes in small pots filled with loam — place the pots in a bowl and fill with water so that the soil surface is about 1 in. below the water level. Leave outdoors during summer and place in a greenhouse or cold frame over winter.

Next spring the young Water Lilies will be ready for planting in baskets and then transferring to the pond — see page 68. You will have to wait another year before the new plants reach flowering size.

The lifted plant from which the eyes were taken can also be used for propagation. Break off or cut away young and vigorous rooted segments which should be 4–8 in. long. Plant these cuttings as instructed on page 68 — vertically or horizontally as appropriate.

FLOATERS

Nothing could be simpler — lift the plant in summer, cut or tear off one or more clumps and then return the plant and the clumps to the pond. Just one (Trapa) is propagated from spring-sown seed.

OXYGENATORS

Another easy group to propagate. In spring or summer take 6 in. long cuttings from the tips of healthy stems and fasten about eight together by winding wire around the bottom of the clump. Plant this clump in a new or original container so that the wire is below the soil level. Renewal by taking cuttings every few years is recommended for most types — a few are propagated by division.

DEEP-WATER AQUATICS & MARGINALS

These aquatics are raised from seeds, cuttings or by division — the right technique depending on the plant in question.

CUTTINGS are taken during the growing season. Trim off 3 in. long non-flowering stem cuttings and plant in a tray filled with loam. Place this tray in a bowl — add water so that the soil surface is kept permanently wet. Place the bowl in a cold frame and plant the rooted cuttings into pots before transferring to planting baskets.

DIVISION is easier. Lift the planting basket and remove the plant. Trim back old roots and cut back some of the foliage — do not cut back hollow stems to below the old waterline mark. Cut or break up the clump into sections, retaining the young and vigorous ones for replanting. Discard the old, worn-out part of the plant. Keep the stems, leaves and roots wet at all times while you are dividing up the clump. Plant up the divisions as instructed on page 68.

SOWING SEEDS is for the enthusiast — it certainly isn't as easy as raising ordinary garden plants from seed and it may be two or more years before the flowering stage is reached. The first rule is to use fresh seeds which should not have been left to dry out. Next, the planting medium and seedlings must be kept constantly wet.

Put 3 in. of sifted loam in a bowl and place the seeds on the surface. Cover with a thin layer of loam and soak using a watering can with a fine rose. Finally, gently add more water until the soil surface is about 1 in. under water. Place the bowl in a frost-free spot and when the seedlings are large enough to handle they should be transplanted into small pots filled with loam which again are kept under water. The final stage is their transfer to planting baskets which are placed in the pond — see page 68.

BOG PLANTS

All the Bog plants are treated as ordinary garden plants and not as aquatics for propagation. Follow the standard rules outlined on page 52 and described in more detail in The Flower Expert.

Fish & Wildlife

Fish bring life to a pond — they add both interest and charm, and they work for their living. Their value for changing the oxygen/carbon dioxide balance is often overrated, but they are extremely effective in keeping down both the midge and mosquito populations. They do not play a part in maintaining the balance in the pond which keeps the water clear — this means that fish are highly desirable but they are not essential.

TYPES
The main factor which should govern your choice is the size of your pond. If money is no object then you might want to pick the expensive and beautiful Koi. Unfortunately these fish demand special provisions — in order to flourish they need a surface area of at least 80 sq.ft and a depth of 4 ft, for other requirements see page 97. At the other end of the scale are the hardy and accommodating Goldfish and Shubunkin which are at home in a pocket-sized pond if there is protection from a prolonged ice cover in winter. Between the Koi and the Goldfish is the Golden Orfe, which needs a minimum surface area of about 40 sq.ft.

Another key factor is visibility. Multicoloured Shubunkins and black Moors may look quite spectacular in an aquarium, but in a pond they can look dull or invisible. As a general rule it is best to stick to the light and bright colours — white, yellow, orange and red. Here the Goldfish and the more active Golden Orfe are an excellent choice as they stay close to the surface.

BUYING
You can obtain your fish by mail order or by going to a garden centre with an aquatic section. Look at the tanks and make your choice, and remember that good health and freedom from disease are what you are looking for — one diseased fish can infect the others in your pond. Bright coloration is attractive but not a sign of good health — it may mean that the fish has been recently imported. The experts look for a dorsal fin which is erect and upright, eyes which are bright, no sign of missing scales and no sign of sluggishness. Never buy any fish which have white spots along their bodies.

The time to buy is between late spring and summer when the water in your pond is at least 50°F. Buy medium-sized fish (3–5 in.) as smaller ones are susceptible to a number of problems and larger ones are expensive and often not freely adaptable to new conditions. Buy several rather than just one as loneliness is linked to nervousness.

Always buy from reputable suppliers — they will ensure that the fish are properly packed in polythene bags which contain water and have been inflated with air or oxygen. Large fish should be packed singly. This packaging will ensure that the specimens will stay alive for at least 36 hours if kept cool.

THE NUMBER TO BUY
The controlling factor is the amount of oxygen in the water, and this is linked to the surface area. The usual rule is 1 in. of fish body length (mouth to tip of tail) for every sq.ft of water surface when first stocking your pond. This will give them the space and air supply to grow. This first stage stocking should be with the old reliables such as Goldfish and Shubunkins — later on you can add a few other fish. Koi have their own rules — one fish per 25 sq.ft.

STOCKING THE POND
A pond is ready for stocking with fish about one month after planting. Keep the polythene bag cool and dark during the journey home, and then float it (covered with newspaper if the sun is shining) in the water. After an hour gently open the bag and add some water from the pond — leave the bag in the water for another ten minutes. The final stage is to slip the fish into their new home — don't just tip them in. It is quite normal for them to hide amid the foliage for a few days — don't try to coax them out.

FEEDING
Fish get most of their food from their environment, but supplementary feeding in spring and summer when they are active will make them larger and friendlier — Koi can be trained to eat out of your hand. Don't overdo it — feed only once or twice a day and use a floating form of fish food. Remove any which remains after 5 minutes. Don't worry about holidays — the fish will happily fend for themselves while you are away.

WILDLIFE
You may want more than fish in your pond — you may want wildlife such as newts, toads, frogs and dragonflies. Read page 99 for more information about this fascinating aspect of water gardening.

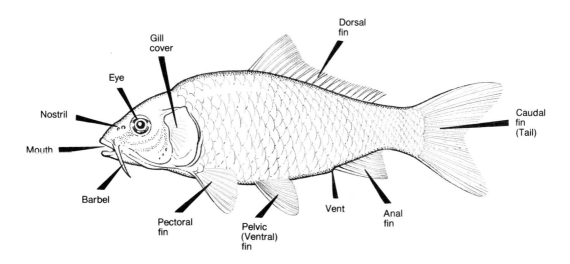

GOLDFISH & SHUBUNKIN

Goldfish were first bred about 1000 years ago in China, but it was not until 300 years ago that they came to Europe. There are now many varieties and all sorts of intermediate hybrids, but for convenience they can be divided into two groups. The Pond Types can be left outdoors in winter, with the proviso that if a thick sheet of ice is allowed to cover the whole of the surface for a prolonged period then the fish may be harmed. The Fancy Types have split and ornate tails, and must be brought indoors before the icy weather arrives — some of the more exotic varieties cannot be housed in an outdoor pond even in a frost-free locality.

Common Goldfish

POND TYPES
The great favourite is the **Common Goldfish** — reliable, inexpensive and colourful. The fins are short and the caudal fin has rounded ends. The appearance is shiny and metallic, and the usual colour is reddish-gold. There are other colours — yellow 'Canaries', matt cream-white 'Pearls' and spotted 'Orioles'. Under good conditions and with plenty of space they can reach 15 in. and live for 20 years. They become sexually mature when they are 5–6 in., and in the spawning season (April–July) the males develop small white lumps ('tubercles') on their gills and fins. A much more obvious sign of spawning is the sight of a group of males chasing and pushing the egg-bearing female.

London Shubunkin

The **Shubunkin** was developed from the Goldfish — its scales are almost transparent and its body appears smooth and multicoloured — a selection of white, yellow, red, blue, violet and black. The most popular specimens have a blue background. There are two basic sorts of the Common Shubunkin — the **London Shubunkin** has the shape of the Common Goldfish, and the **Bristol Shubunkin** which has a larger caudal fin.

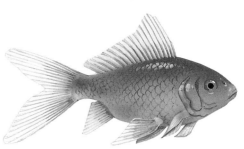

Comet Goldfish

The **Comet** is a Goldfish or Shubunkin which has large fins and a long caudal fin which is deeply forked. It moves faster than the common forms and is often sleeker. The white and red one is known as the **Sarasa Comet**.

FANCY TYPES
These beautiful and sometimes bizarre fish have egg-shaped bodies and complex tails. The **Fantail** has forked twin tails — the black form with bulging eyes is known as the **Moor**. The **Veiltail** is even more showy and there are several others — **Oranda**, **Lionhead**, **Ranchu**, **Pompon**, **Celestial** etc. They are poor pond fish — keep them in the aquarium.

Sarasa Comet

Moor

Comet Shubunkin

KOI

Koi (or Goi) is the Japanese word for all Carp. The ornamental forms which have become so popular during this century are properly called Nishikigoi (Brocaded or Fancy Carp) ... or just Koi for short.

They are the most impressive of all pond fish — large, long-lived, frequently highly coloured and patterned, and tame enough to eat out of your hand. Under ideal conditions they can reach 2½–3 ft, but it is not only their habit of continuing to grow even under cramped conditions which makes them unsuitable for a small or average-sized pond. They stir up mud from the bottom of the pond, eat soft leaves of underwater plants and require a good filtration system. Despite all of this, you can put one or two Koi at the 4–8 in. stage into your pond if it has a surface area of 50 sq.ft or more. You may have to put a net over the top for the first few days to stop them jumping out and if the pond is quite small you must be prepared to pass them on to the owner of a larger pond when the fish reach 1 ft or more.

If you wish to take up Koi-keeping seriously then you will need a special Koi pond which will have a bottom drain, a depth of at least 4 ft and a filter. You will also need a good text-book to explain their bewildering classification and how to look after them. The major colour types are shown on this page, but there are also variations in surface texture. Most Koi have a non-metallic body, but the Ohgon has a metallic lustre and has become very popular — there are both gold and silver (Platinum Ohgon) forms. The Gin rin varieties have shiny sequin-like scales but the Doitsu (German) Koi are scaleless apart from lines of large and prominent scales which may be present along their backs and sides. The Ghost Koi is a rather plain brown or grey variety.

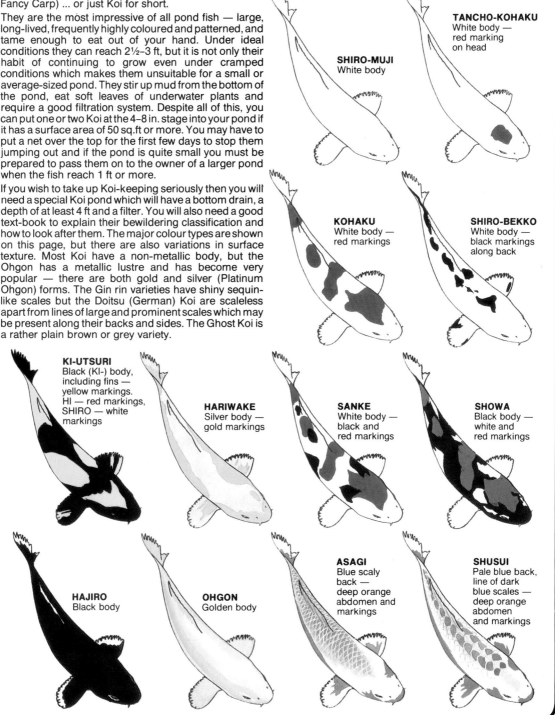

SHIRO-MUJI
White body

TANCHO-KOHAKU
White body —
red marking
on head

KOHAKU
White body —
red markings

SHIRO-BEKKO
White body —
black markings
along back

KI-UTSURI
Black (KI-) body,
including fins —
yellow markings.
HI — red markings,
SHIRO — white
markings

HARIWAKE
Silver body —
gold markings

SANKE
White body —
black and
red markings

SHOWA
Black body —
white and
red markings

HAJIRO
Black body

OHGON
Golden body

ASAGI
Blue scaly
back —
deep orange
abdomen and
markings

SHUSUI
Pale blue back,
line of dark
blue scales —
deep orange
abdomen
and markings

OTHER FISH

If you have a lake or really large pond there are numerous coldwater fish from which to choose. There are the Carp varieties such as Mirror, Leather, Prussian and Crucian. There are also Trout, Roach, Gudgeon and so on, but predators such as Catfish, Perch and Pike should be avoided.

The choice is much more limited for the garden pond where you want something other than Goldfish and Shubunkin. The best choice is probably the **Golden Orfe** if your pond is 40 sq.ft or more — these slender golden or salmon-coloured fish move rapidly and stay close to the surface. The trick is not to buy just one or two as they are timid fish and will hide amongst the plants — introduce six or more and they will quickly adapt and move as a shoal. In time they can grow up to 1½ ft and are extremely useful as scavengers of insects on or just below the surface — the only problems are that they do not readily breed and they need moving water to satisfy their high oxygen requirement. The **Blue Orfe**, a slower-growing form with pale blue scales, is becoming popular.

The **Golden Rudd** is rather similar but it has duller colouring and its silvery scales are large and coarse. The key recognition feature is the reddish colour of the fins. It is less visible in the pond than the Golden Orfe but it is a tough fish which can put up with less oxygen and higher temperatures than most other types. It rarely grows larger than 6–9 in.

The Tench is often sold as a scavenger fish which will remove waste material from the bottom of the pond, but it is no more effective than a Goldfish. It is also reputed to be a 'doctor' fish with surface mucus which cures various ailments, but there is no real evidence for this. In truth it is a bottom-dwelling fish which rarely comes to the surface. Not a good choice — if you want one pick the pale orange **Golden Tench** rather than the **Green Tench** as it is much more visible. Both have a maximum size of about 1½ ft.

Space is not a problem for the **Minnow**, the silvery 'tiddler' which moves in shoals and rarely exceeds 3 in. in length. In the breeding season the males develop a bright red colouring. The usual variety sold is the American **Rosy Minnow**. Another small fish well suited to the wildlife pond is the **Three-spined Stickleback**.

Golden Orfe

Golden Rudd

Minnow

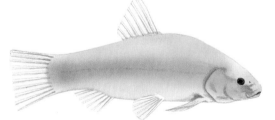

Golden Tench

Three-spined Stickleback

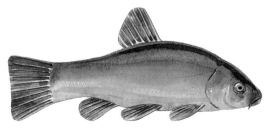

Green Tench

Mirror Carp

WILDLIFE

Within a short time your new pond will be teeming with animal life, and their numbers will increase with time as eggs hatch and frogs, newts and toads return. The greatest influx of animals occurs in the wildlife pond (page 66) with its stock of native plants and fish.

Most of this animal life cannot be seen — there is a vast collection of microscopic animals in every drop of pond water. The insects can be seen — none more so than the **Dragonflies** and the smaller **Damselflies** which flit and hover above the surface in summer. But their adult life lasts for only a few weeks — for a year or more they will have been active crawling larvae below the surface, eating a variety of living and dead material. On the surface you will see the **Pond Skater** with its long, thin legs, the **Water Cricket**, **Water Measurer** and **Whirligig Beetle**. A few underwater insects are pests — the **Water Boatman** and **Great Diving Beetle** are large enough to attack small fish.

Snails will no doubt appear, and some are harmful to aquatic plants. Never introduce the **Great Pond Snail** which can shred Water Lily leaves — the only safe one to buy is the Catherine wheel-like **Ram's Horn Snail**, but its beneficial effect in keeping down algae is overrated. The **Swan Mussel** is sometimes sold to filter out microscopic algae, but it is of little value in a mud-free pond.

Frogs and other amphibians come to the pond to breed, and once established will return in future years. The **Common Frog** is a welcome sight, laying its lumpy mass of spawn in spring followed by tadpoles which hatch out about a week later. The tadpoles live in the pond for about 4 months, eating small creatures and smaller tadpoles. The **Common Toad** has a drier, warty skin and is much less attractive but is more useful, devouring large quantities of slugs and snails. The eggs are borne in long ropes of jelly and these hopping (not leaping) amphibians prefer larger ponds than those chosen by frogs. Newts are small lizard-like creatures which spend part of their life in the water. Look for the **Common Newt** and the strange courtship 'dance' of the male in spring — the largest species is the 6 in. long **Great Crested Newt**.

It would be quite impossible to do more on this page than touch on some of the more notable examples of animal life which dwell within the pond or its surroundings. The **Water Shrew** and the **Vole**, the **Kingfisher** and the **Grass Snake**, the **Heron** and the **Mayfly** ... a strange and fascinating world.

Common Frog

Common Toad

Smooth Newt

Ram's Horn Snail

Water Vole

Hawker Dragonfly

Pond Skater

CHAPTER 8
WATER GARDEN FEATURES

A properly constructed and well-stocked pond does not demand the presence of other features. There is smooth water with fish below, Marginals above and Water Lilies on the surface — if aquatic plants are your first love then this may well be sufficient. But Formal ponds in a prominent position can look distinctly dull in the winter months when fish are inactive and the pond plants have been cut down. A water garden feature or two can be helpful here, but the golden rule is not to overdo it.

These features are of two basic types. Firstly there is the non-electrical group — here you will find **Statuary**, ranging from the humble garden gnome at the edge of the pond to the glorious marble goddess at the end of a long canal in a Grand Garden. Then there are the **Ornaments** for the pondside — sundials, Japanese lanterns, urns, etc. These may have limited appeal, but **Containers** have become extremely popular. A planted-up tub can break the monotony of a paving-stone edging running right round a Formal pond, but containers like all other water garden features have their set of good design rules. Pots and other planting containers generally fit in much better in the Formal rather than the Informal water garden, and the construction material should be in keeping with the environment — a garish plastic pot would be an eyesore at the side of an old world pond. But in the end the choice must be up to you, even if it is a large plastic heron which may drive away the neighbours if not other herons.

By far the most important features belong to the electrical group, and so this chapter begins with the basics of electricity in the garden. This current is nearly always used to drive a pump which may be inside or outside the pond, and the basic purpose of this pump is to provide moving water.

Nobody is indifferent to moving water, but the effect may be good or bad, depending on whether you are a human being, fish or plant. For humans the sight and sound of moving water have a calming influence and are prominently featured on relaxation tapes.

Nobody can explain just why, but for many people a pond is not complete without moving water.

For most of the year fish are quite unconcerned whether the water in the pond is moving or not, but things are different in thundery weather or on warm still nights in summer. Under these conditions the water can be seriously deficient in oxygen and over-rich in carbon dioxide, and here moving water can literally be a life-saver by changing the balance of these gases.

Moving water is always beneficial for humans and sometimes extremely helpful for fish, but Water Lilies and some Deep-water aquatics are not so lucky. They dislike rapid currents below the surface and the effect of droplets constantly raining down on them can be disastrous. Water Lily pads often rot and the flower buds refuse to open.

There are two ways to create water movement and the **Fountain** is the easier one to install. The experts will tell you that it is much better suited to a Formal pond rather than an Informal one, but this is not a strict rule. For Informal ponds which have been created to have a natural look the preferred moving water feature is the **Waterfall** or **Cascade**. Not for Formal ponds, say many of the text-books, but a series of square or round pools can be effectively linked together by strictly geometrical cascades. Another point from the professional designers — although you can easily run both a fountain and waterfall from a single pump, these two features rarely look comfortable in the same pond.

The strainer on the pump is designed to stop suspended solid matter from reaching the moving parts, but it is not designed to remove algae. Where there is a persistent green water problem it is useful to run an underwater **Filter** from the pump (see page 110) — in the over-stocked pond or Koi pond it is essential rather than useful. Another use for the electric circuit leading to the pond is to run the **Pool Heater** which replaces the submersible pump in autumn or winter, as described on page 112.

One of the most spectacular ways of using the electric cable leading to the pond is to install **Lighting**. No other part of the garden can be as dramatically brought to life by lighting as a fountain or waterfall.

ELECTRICITY

At the heart of the fountain or waterfall is the pump, and this is driven by electricity. The key requirement is for a buried cable and a waterproof connector to join the electricity supply to the lead from the pump.

There is a basic choice to make — you can have either a mains or low-voltage system. Drawing electricity directly from the mains has a few advantages. Firstly, it will give you all the power you need if you want a number of lights to give indoor-type brightness or a pump to operate a 5 ft high waterfall or a spray jet shooting 4 ft or more into the air. Both lights and the pump can work off the same circuit, and a mains pump is usually cheaper than the equivalent low-voltage one. But the advantages end there if your moving water requirements are modest. A low-voltage circuit does not require a qualified electrician for its installation and cables need not be protected — you simply draw 12 V or 24 V current from the transformer which is plugged into an indoor socket.

The introduction of the circuit breaker has made electricity much safer to use in the garden, but there are still rules to follow:

- All equipment must be specifically designed for outdoor use.
- Maintain all equipment properly.
- Never use mains electricity without a Residual Current Device ('circuit breaker').
- Keep a record of where the underground cables are located.

Low-voltage — Submersible Pump — Fountain Arrangement

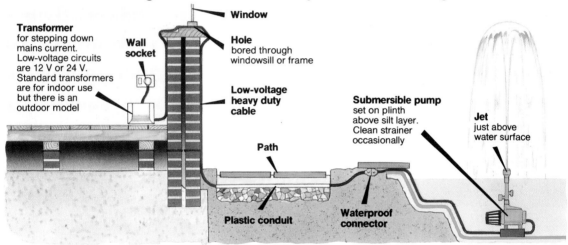

Transformer for stepping down mains current. Low-voltage circuits are 12 V or 24 V. Standard transformers are for indoor use but there is an outdoor model

Wall socket

Window

Hole bored through windowsill or frame

Low-voltage heavy duty cable

Submersible pump set on plinth above silt layer. Clean strainer occasionally

Jet just above water surface

Path

Plastic conduit

Waterproof connector

Mains — Surface Pump — Waterfall Arrangement

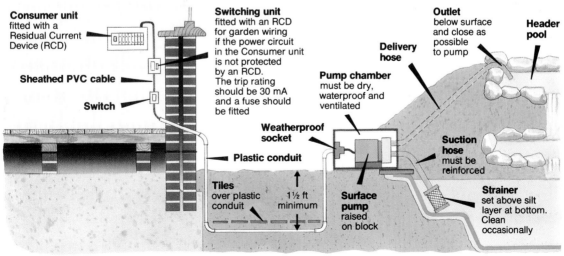

Consumer unit fitted with a Residual Current Device (RCD)

Sheathed PVC cable

Switch

Switching unit fitted with an RCD for garden wiring if the power circuit in the Consumer unit is not protected by an RCD. The trip rating should be 30 mA and a fuse should be fitted

Plastic conduit

Tiles over plastic conduit

1½ ft minimum

Weatherproof socket

Surface pump raised on block

Delivery hose

Pump chamber must be dry, waterproof and ventilated

Outlet below surface and close as possible to pump

Header pool

Suction hose must be reinforced

Strainer set above silt layer at bottom. Clean occasionally

WATERFALL

A waterfall has a more limited use than a fountain in the average home garden, and there are two basic reasons. A cascade of tumbling water only looks right when it is in an informal setting — an apparently natural pond backed by a sloping bank with stones and rockery plants. It can be quite small, but it should never look obviously artificial — a shiny plastic waterfall set in a cone of earth can be an eyesore. Secondly, compared to a fountain it does need a lot of time and money to buy the liner, create a sloping support of soil and then set it correctly so that it both looks attractive and works satisfactorily.

Despite these difficulties, a waterfall in the right situation is a splendid feature. Three construction materials are readily available — the same three used for ponds and with the same advantages and disadvantages. Do not be too ambitious — for most situations the 'head' (distance from the pond surface up to the outlet) should be 3 ft or less and the sill (area over which the water flows) should be 4–6 in. wide. The distance from one tier to the one below should be 3 in.–1 ft. Paint all concrete and reconstituted stone surfaces with a proprietary sealant.

RIGID LINER Two types are available — the waterfall unit which is a complete structure with a header pool and one or more linked pools, and the cascade units (header pools, reservoir pools etc) which are set one above the other to form the waterfall. Fibreglass and reconstituted stone are the best materials — polythene is the cheapest but not recommended.

CONCRETE Formerly the standard way to build a waterfall, but now replaced by the liner methods. The work is heavy and cracks often develop after a few years. Stones should be bedded in the moist concrete to relieve the stark effect.

FLEXIBLE LINER Butyl sheeting allows you to build a natural-looking waterfall to your own design. Use separate sheets for each tier, overlapping as necessary. Each level should slope backwards to form a pool — a projecting stone at the front will form a weir. Bed stones and pebbles in mortar at the sides and bottom to remove artificial look.

Flow rate is the amount of water flowing through the system. The output of the pump is governed by the 'head' — the higher the head, the lower the output:

Head	Pump Output (gallons/hour)		
	Pump rating: 180	Pump rating: 400	Pump rating: 650
3 ft	180	400	650
5 ft	110	240	530
7 ft	0	70	400

These outputs are reduced if there are long lengths or kinks in the tubing.

The right pump to choose will have sufficient output to satisfy the following two requirements:

● The flow rate should be between 100–150% of the volume of the pond — for example, a 300 gallon pond will need 300–450 gallons/hour.

● The flow rate should produce a sheet of water right across the sill ('lip') at the front of the cascade. This will require at least 50 gallons/hour per 1 in. width — for example, a 6 in. sill will need a minimum of 300 gallons/hour.

Making a Cascade Unit Waterfall

STEP 1:
DIG OUT THE HOLES
Mark the outline — the holes should be a few inches wider than the units. Remove soil with a spade, beginning at the lowest level. Make sure the bases for the units are horizontal. Put in the tubing for the pump at this stage

STEP 2:
INSTALL THE UNITS
Firm the soil in the holes — add a layer of sand. Put in each unit, making sure that the sill overlaps the unit below. Do not fix permanently at this stage — use a hose pipe to ensure that flow is satisfactory

STEP 3:
FINISH THE WATERFALL
Use blobs of mortar to secure each unit, beginning with the lowest one. When set fill the gap between the units and the earth with sand — now switch on the water. If the flow is insufficient most suppliers will allow you to return and upgrade the pump. Hide the unit edges and outlet with stones and plants

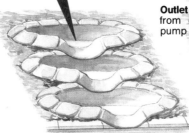

Outlet
from
pump

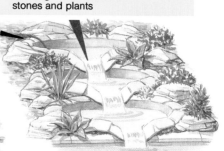

Waterfalls Illustrated

This natural-looking waterfall ▷
shows the effect that can be achieved
with carefully placed stones above
butyl sheeting. Using a few bold plants
rather than a carpet of small ones has
improved the effect.

◁ A waterfall need not be an imitation
of a natural stream falling over a rocky
outcrop. This cascade linking one Formal
pond with another is obviously artificial,
but that does not make it less attractive.

△ A waterfall constructed using fibreglass cascade units. This type is easier
to build than ones made with flexible sheeting, but it can look somewhat
artificial if the edges are not hidden by rocks and well-placed shrubs.

FOUNTAIN

Many people feel that a fountain in the centre of a round, square or rectangular pond is essential, and the large range of moderately-priced submersible pumps which is available these days makes this possible for the average gardener.

The simplest and most popular way to introduce a fountain is to buy a kit. This will contain a submersible pump, a T-piece with a fitted flow adjuster and a fountain jet. These are put together as shown on page 107 and the electricity supply is either joined to the mains or a low-voltage system by means of a waterproof connector. Place the pump on a block or brick to keep it off the bottom of the pond and make sure that the tube holding the fountain jet is truly vertical. Switch on and your pond now has a fountain — it may be necessary to turn down the flow adjuster if the spray is too high or too wide.

It is sometimes necessary to have a rather more complicated arrangement. In a larger pond it would not be possible to reach a centrally-placed fountain as shown on page 101 and described above by just stretching out one's arm. To avoid

having to wade through the water every time you have to clean the strainer or remove the pump for servicing, it is necessary to use the remote jet arrangement shown below. A further variation is to have a fountain ornament rather than the simple underwater tube to support the jet. You will find a wide variety of these ornaments in the catalogues and garden centres — reconstituted stone is the favourite material but you can find lead, stone, bronze, terracotta, fibreglass etc. Make sure the one you buy is frost-proof and mount it firmly on an underwater base if the ornament is not designed to sit on the bottom of the pond. The jet is screwed on to the brass-threaded connector at the top of the fountain ornament.

As stated on page 100 it is generally felt by garden designers that the upward water move-ment of a standard fountain and the downward movement of a waterfall do not blend well in most situations. However, a simple poolside ornament fitted with a water spout (see page 105) can often be a pleasant feature for a pond which has a waterfall.

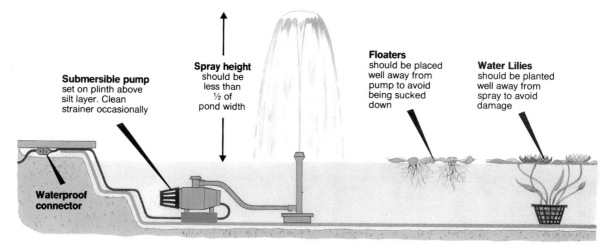

Submersible pump set on plinth above silt layer. Clean strainer occasionally

Spray height should be less than ½ of pond width

Floaters should be placed well away from pump to avoid being sucked down

Water Lilies should be planted well away from spray to avoid damage

Waterproof connector

Fountain Notes

- Jets producing a very fine spray are not a good idea — the plume cannot be seen from a distance and the droplets are easily blown away. In addition the fine holes are easily clogged by particles, but on the credit side fine drop-lets are less harmful to Water Lilies than coarse ones.

- Make sure that the size of both the fountain spray and any ornament are in keeping with the size of the pond. A large and ornate figure and wide-spreading spray pattern can look out of place in a small pond.

- Where the pond is quite small and you want to grow Water Lilies it is a good idea to consider a bell or geyser jet (see page 105) which does not produce small droplets and results in a restricted area of water disturbance.

- Make sure that the pump you buy is the right one for the fountain you have in mind — remember that there will be a serious loss of power if you run a secondary feature (waterfall, filter or second fountain), or use a long length of narrow-bore tubing for connecting a remote jet to the pump.

Spray height	Suitable pump
Up to 4 ft	LV submersible pump
Up to 7 ft	Mains submersible pump
Over 7 ft or multiple fountains	Mains surface pump

Fountain Types

Pebble Fountain   **Millstone Fountain**   **Poolside Ornament**   **Surface Jet**   **Fountain Ornament**

Jet Types

Water Spout   **Single Spray**   **Multi-tiered Spray**   **Whirling Spray**

Fishtail   **Geyser**   **Tulip**   **Ring**

Bell   **Hemisphere**   **Tiffany**

Fountains Illustrated

Not all fountains produce a spray of
droplets. This bell jet forms a
hemispherical film of water and is effective
in the right setting. Little disturbance
of the overall pond surface is involved,
which is helpful for Water Lilies. ▷

◁ A Pebble Fountain — the maximum
sound of water with the minimum risk
of drowning for little children.
The geyser jet produces a column of
milky-white aerated water which splashes
down on to the pebbles below.

△ The Poolside Ornament with a water spout need not be the traditional terracotta
lion's head, dolphin or little boy with a jug. This unusual stainless steel
clown's head provides a striking feature for a Formal minipool.

PUMP

As stated in the introduction to this chapter, there are two types of pump for operating fountains and waterfalls — the **submersible** pump which is kept totally submerged and would be damaged if used above ground, and the **surface** (or **external**) pump which is operated above ground and would be damaged if submerged in the pond. This is not strictly true, as there are a few submersibles which can be adapted for use as surface pumps.

A simple start to this introduction, but the range of pumps available within these two groups is complex and bewildering. It is easy to choose the wrong one — the notes on this page should help you to avoid the pitfalls. As a starting point, if you want a pump to operate an ordinary fountain with or without a waterfall in the garden, then you will need a submersible pump. The surface ones do have a few good points as noted on the right, but these are greatly outweighed unless you have a series of fountains and/or tall waterfalls needing more than 1000 gallons of water per hour.

The submersible pump is stood on one or more bricks to keep it off the bottom and is positioned below the surface. Water is drawn in through a strainer and pumped out through a fountain jet or along a piece of tubing to a fountain elsewhere in the pond. A T-piece is usually present and this carries a flow adjuster to cut down the flow to the fountain if necessary, and an outlet for tubing for a waterfall. Always buy a pump with this T-piece — even if you do not plan on a waterfall the side outlet will be required when pumping out the pond for maintenance and perhaps for a filter. Wherever possible the pump should be removed and cleaned at the end of the season and then stored indoors until the spring. If this is not possible then switch on for a short time every two weeks during the winter when the pond is not frozen.

If you intend to have a small fountain with a spray no more than 4 ft high or a 2 or 3 ft high waterfall with a water face which is no more than a few inches wide, then you can manage with a low-voltage (24 V) pump. Otherwise you will need a mains-operated one. A number of factors can reduce the output of the pump — one of them is the use of narrow-bore tubing. The smaller pumps will run satisfactorily with ½ in. hose, but larger pumps require ¾ in. or 1 in. hose.

If you do decide on a surface pump then you will have to erect a suitable chamber for it, as shown on page 101. This should be as close as possible to the pond and tubing lengths should be kept as short as practical. A footvalve will be needed for priming if the housing is above the water level in the pond.

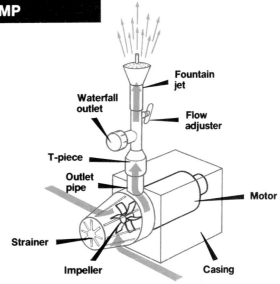

Submersible Pump Advantages

- **Convenient** — no plumbing or housing is required as it is simply put into the pond.
- **Inexpensive** — low and medium output models are available for the ordinary garden.
- **Low-voltage models** are available if a high flow rate is not needed.
- **Self-priming** — no need to fill with water before use.
- **Silent** — no constant hum as with a surface pump.

Surface Pump Advantages

- **High output** — a number of fountains and impressive waterfalls can be operated.
- **Continuous running** will not burn out the motor if an induction-driven model is chosen.
- **Pump can be examined or removed** without having to lift it out of the water.

Choosing a Pump

The section on waterfalls (page 102) will give you a rough idea of the rating of the pump you require. With a fountain a 180 rated pump will give you a 4 ft high spray — a 400 pump will give a 5 ft spray.

These are, however, approximate figures and actual performance is affected by length of tubing, bore, presence of bends or kinks, fountain jet, height of waterfall etc. For most home garden purposes a pump which produces 350–650 gallons/hour will be suitable and should give you power to spare, but the best course of action is to seek advice from a qualified supplier. Give him or her all the necessary information:

- Head — height of outlet of waterfall above the pond.
- Fountain jet — type and height of spray required.
- Sill width of waterfall.
- Dimensions of pond.
- Tubing details — length and bore.
- Use — fountain, waterfall and/or filter.
- Continuous or intermittent operation.

LIGHTING

It has been said many times that well-placed lighting can turn an ordinary garden into a magical place at night. There are several practical uses for illumination after dark — security, safety near steps, an extension of outdoor living time etc, but the most important purpose of putting lights in the garden is to add a dramatic touch of beauty.

Nowhere is this dramatic effect more spectacular than in the water garden. Above-ground lighting brings ornaments and surrounding plants to life — in-pond lighting turns a fountain, waterfall or the water surface with the fish below into glittering features.

Of course there is a right and wrong way to light up the pond area, and to place a few floodlights here and there around the water's edge is a missed opportunity. All that happens is the whole site is illuminated with an even glow. The secret of good lighting is to highlight certain areas and features whilst leaving other parts in darkness — to do this effectively there are a number of lessons to learn.

To begin with, you must know the difference between floodlighting and spotlighting. It is nothing to do with the power of the illumination — the effect may be brilliant or quite subdued with either type, and both are available in mains and low-voltage form. The essential difference is that floodlighting produces a diffuse pool of light which covers a wide area rather than an individual plant or feature, whereas spotlighting produces a beam which lights up a specific plant, group of plants or an attractive feature. This spotlight effect is due to the type of bulb or the use of a holder which constricts the beam to 10°–30°.

Next, there is the question of mains versus low-voltage. For powerful lighting (80–150 watts) you will need mains electricity. Low-voltage bulbs are much less dazzling — typically 11–25 watts running off a 12 V or less frequently a 24 V circuit. A transformer is used to step down the mains supply (see page 101) and 2–6 lights can be included in the circuit — check before you buy a kit.

Several types of bulbs are available. There are ordinary tungsten ones, which are widely used in LV circuits. The halogen bulb has now become popular as a replacement, as it gives about three times the light intensity for the same wattage. For mains fixtures without a shade the right choice is a PAR 38 bulb which has a built-in reflector. Colour is a matter of taste — white or amber is the safest choice, but you can try green (restful) or blue (dramatic).

Finally, the lamp holders. For pondside use there are Spiked and Surface-mounted models for floodlighting or spotlighting — for general illumination there are the Globe and Searchlight styles and for downlighting there are Mushroom and Tiered shades.

For in-pond lighting there are a number of exciting models. Simplest of all are the round Water Lights which float on the surface or are weighted down to provide light from below the surface — do not submerge too deeply or much of the power will be lost. Check whether the Water Lights you buy are for surface or underwater use. An important rule to remember is that a waterfall or fountain should be lit from directly below the jet or cascade. You can buy Underwater Floodlights for powerful illumination or a Light Fountain where the jet is actually set into the lens. Most dramatic of all is the Rainbow — a colour-changing illuminated fountain. A four-colour disc is rotated by water pressure and the bulb at the bottom of the fountain provides the illumination. This changes the spray at regular intervals from red to blue, amber and green. Brilliant, but a little too garish for some people. As with so many other garden features, lighting must be in keeping with the size and style of the pond.

PONDSIDE LIGHTING

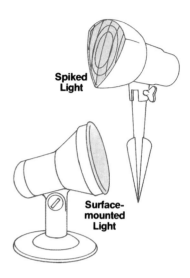

Spiked Light

Surface-mounted Light

IN-POND LIGHTING

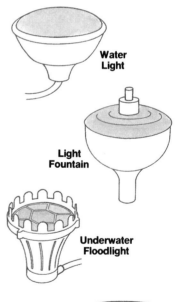

Water Light

Light Fountain

Underwater Floodlight

Colour-changing Illuminated Fountain

Pond Lighting Illustrated

Pondside and in-pond lighting combine ▷
to transform this pond, waterfall and
rock garden into a kaleidoscope of
colour. Nobody could deny the effect is
dramatic, but some gardeners prefer
a more subdued use of colour.

◁ A middle-ground approach to the use of coloured
lighting. The fountain ornament is illuminated
with an overall pink glow by the use of in-pond
lights, with the tracery of the screen wall
picked out in green by pondside floodlights.

△ A spectacular demonstration that you do not need a wide range of colours
to create a dramatic effect. The beauty at night of this ring fountain
and its central elegant ornament may well have been reduced if
a variety of coloured lights had been used.

FILTER

Most ponds do not have a filter. In some cases the water area is large enough, the planting adequate enough and the number of fish small enough to avoid excessive algal growth, toxic gases and undesirable waste products. With small ponds the owners may either use algicides or just put up with cloudy or green-tinged water. The strainer on the pump is not a filter — its job is to stop solid material from getting into the working parts.

The idea of water filtration in the garden pond is relatively new and is highly desirable or essential in a number of cases. The owner of a small pond may want clear water, and the gardener with a pond overstocked with fish may not want to change the water regularly in order to get rid of toxic material. A filter is an excellent answer. It is the *only* answer to pollution if you want a successful Koi pond.

There are two basic types of filtration — mechanical and biological. The purpose of the mechanical filter is to sieve out dirt, solid waste and algae — it is effective immediately when switched on and can be run intermittently. The purpose of the biological filter is quite different — waste products (dead organic matter, uneaten pellets, fish excreta etc) and the fish-harming ammonia gas are all turned into harmless materials by the bacteria and tiny organisms which flourish on the filter medium. The filter must be run continuously as the bacteria will die in a few hours if the pump is switched off, and the full effect of a biological filter will not be seen for several weeks after switching on. All filters must be cleaned regularly, following the maker's instructions.

● **MECHANICAL FILTRATION** is the simpler type — inexpensive and usually installed in the pond. The Simple and In-pond models below are examples — water is drawn through foam, coarse sand, gravel and/or filter granules by the action of a submersible pump, the outlet of the pump feeding a fountain or waterfall. Suspended grit, waste products and algae are collected in the filter medium — there is some biological action but this stops if the pump is switched off when the fountain or waterfall is not in use.

● **BIOLOGICAL FILTRATION** is the more complex type and is suitable for large as well as small ponds. The unit is housed outside the pond, usually hidden by shrubs at a location close to the top of a waterfall. A surface or submersible pump is used to push or draw water through the inlet pipe — the water is then aerated through jets or holes in a spray bar and passes through one or more layers of filter medium. Several types of medium are available — rough-surfaced gravel, open-cell foam, resin-bonded fibre matting, Lytag granules, coarse sand etc. The clarified and purified water is returned to the pond through the outlet pipe.

SIMPLE FILTER

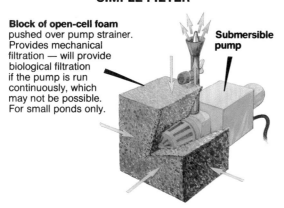

Block of open-cell foam pushed over pump strainer. Provides mechanical filtration — will provide biological filtration if the pump is run continuously, which may not be possible. For small ponds only.

Submersible pump

IN-POND FILTER

Mechanical filtration occurs in granule or gravel layer. Biological filtration takes place throughout all the filtration media (granules, gravel and foam) if pump is run continuously.

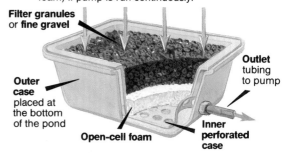

Filter granules or fine gravel

Outer case placed at the bottom of the pond

Open-cell foam

Outlet tubing to pump

Inner perforated case

EXTERNAL FILTER

Mechanical filtration occurs in matting or foam layer. Biological filtration takes place throughout all the filtration media. Pump is run continuously. Multi-chambered models are available.

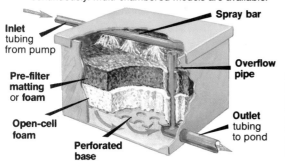

Inlet tubing from pump

Pre-filter matting or foam

Open-cell foam

Perforated base

Spray bar

Overflow pipe

Outlet tubing to pond

UV CLARIFIER

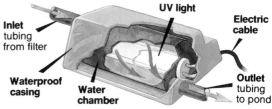

UV light

Electric cable

Inlet tubing from filter

Waterproof casing

Water chamber

Outlet tubing to pond

Sometimes water remains green even though a filter has been fitted — some species of algae are so fine that they can pass through virtually any filter medium. The UV (ultra-violet) clarifier such as the Lotus Clearpond is the latest form of defence in the green water battle. Water from the external filter is passed into the water chamber of the unit where UV light kills the algal cells. It is also claimed that many harmful bacteria are killed at the same time.

CHAPTER 9
WATER GARDEN MAINTENANCE

It has been stressed several times in this book that the secret of successful water gardening begins with building a satisfactory pond on the right site. The fabric must be sound enough to carry a minimum 20 year guarantee and it should be large enough for the correct balance (see below) to be sustained.

The second vital feature of successful water gardening is a regular maintenance programme. Few of the jobs are particularly back-breaking or time-consuming. The plants do not need watering and all the fish require is a daily feed when they are active. But the jobs which have to be done must be performed promptly and not left until problems arise. Dead and dying plants, fallen leaves, blanketing weeds and dead fish must be removed immediately, a hole in the ice should be created before the fish are harmed and pumps should be serviced at the end of the season rather than waiting until they break down.

Buy some basic water garden tools. You will need a net for lifting out fish and removing surface pond weeds, a pool heater for protecting fish in winter and a long pond rake or forked stick for removing blanket weed. A pool-covering net may be necessary and there are of course all sorts of optional extras, ranging from spawning mops to silt-sucking vacuum cleaners.

The maintenance programme will vary with the seasons, and the basic work involved is set out on the following four pages. Occasionally something may be seen which is a problem and disturbs the orderly routine. Fish may be gasping for air, Water Lily leaves may be shredded or the water level may have started to fall alarmingly. Don't guess at an answer unless you are an experienced pond owner. Look up the symptoms in the Water Garden Troubles chapter beginning on page 116 — carry out the recommended remedy without delay.

After several years you may find that the plants have become hopelessly overgrown, the bottom of the pond has become full of sediment or the edges loose and unstable. The time has come for a major overhaul, and this calls for emptying, cleaning and restocking. Read page 119 before you begin.

A Question of Balance

There are a number of components in the pond — water, aquatic plants, wildlife, soil, fish, dead organic matter and the dreaded enemy — algae. These primitive plants are either microscopic organisms or long thread-like strands which quickly appear in any stretch of water. At first the pond turns cloudy and then green if they are allowed to develop unimpeded. The balance between the components for which the pond owner aims is a very one-sided sort of balance — what we try to create is a set of conditions in which plants and fish flourish but in which algal growth is reduced to a minimum. We aim for the *pond keeper's* balance of aquatic plants and decorative fish in clear water, rather than a *natural* balance.

The first need is to keep down the amount of unwanted organic matter. Dead plants and fallen leaves should be removed at once — when they rot down various minerals are produced which harm fish, discolour water and encourage algal growth. Do not incorporate peat, compost, soluble fertilizers or manure when potting up aquatic plants and do not give more food to the fish than they can eat in a short time.

Next, provide some shade — algae thrive in sunlight. This calls for growing Water Lilies so that their floating leaves (pads) cover about half the surface. If these pads provide insufficient cover then introduce Deep-water aquatics and/or Floaters. The third basic need is to deprive the algae of the carbon dioxide and minerals which are so essential for their development. This task is performed by the Oxygenators — the lowly underwater plants which play such a vital role in keeping the water clear. They also supply oxygen which is utilised by the fish.

Proper balance is not achieved immediately. The water in a new pond will turn murky and green at first, but it should clear in two or three months if the right plants are introduced in the right quantity. Your pond will also turn cloudy and slightly green each spring, but this should soon clear once active plant growth begins.

Pond size is a critical factor — even if you do all the things recommended above, it will still be difficult or impossible to achieve balance in a small pond. We then have to turn to artificial aids, such as biological filters or algicides. See page 118 if green water remains a persistent problem.

Pond Care Round the Year

Doing the right thing at the right time is the secret of successful pond care. It is perhaps even more important than in the world of ordinary gardening, where we can plant container-grown specimens at almost any time, and where green weeds unlike green algae can be pulled up or hoed during any season of the year. There are a number of important seasonal jobs in the water garden and these are listed below and on the following pages. Some of these tasks are mentioned elsewhere in this book, but no apology is made for this repetition. It is better to be told twice that April is too early to start planting Marginals and October is too late for dividing them than not to be reminded at all of these facts and all the other key seasonal jobs which have to be done.

WINTER

Provided you have carried out the tasks set out for autumn, there is little or nothing to do during the winter months. The fish are now semi-dormant and so they should not be fed — the established plants have been cut down and this season is quite unsuitable for planting aquatics. Container-grown Bog plants, however, can be planted during a mild spell if the ground is reasonably dry.

The only occasion when the pond will need attention is when a really cold snap arrives. Obviously a very small and shallow pond can be turned into a block of ice, which means death for the fish and most plants, including the Water Lilies. You can cover a tiny pond with boards and sacking for a short time if arctic weather is forecast, but the flora and fauna should not be left in the dark for too long.

In a larger pond neither plants nor fish are directly killed by the presence of an ice sheet above them, but there can still be a serious problem. If a sheet of ice covers the whole of the surface for more than a couple of days, the gases which are produced by decaying organic matter ('marsh gas') build up to toxic levels which can kill the fish. Obviously an air-hole must be created to let these vapours escape.

This cannot be done by breaking the ice with a hammer — the shock waves will concuss the fish. A simple method is to stand a pan of hot water on the surface until it melts through and then if possible remove some of the pond water to lower the level by about ½ in. The problem of course is that rain or snow brings the water back to the original level and prolonged cold weather results in the hole freezing over again. The only real answer is to fit an electric pool heater — mains and low-voltage models are now available. Connect it to the electricity supply which was used for the pump — install it before the icy weather arrives, and that may be in autumn.

In a concrete pond float a plank in the water to take some of the pressure of the ice sheet. When not frozen run the pump every fortnight for half an hour if it has been left in the pond. One final point — use the quiet time of the year to look through the catalogues for new ideas and new plants for next year's pond.

SPRING

In March the first Primulas and early bulbs bloom in the bog garden, but you will have to wait until April for the start of the water garden year. Caltha will then be in full flower and the fish will slowly become active again. New Water Lily pads appear and so does frog spawn — this awakening means that there are jobs for you to do.

Begin feeding when fish start to come to the surface — just a little every couple of days will do. Disease resistance is at its lowest ebb at this time of year and a mixed diet helps — provide a few chopped-up worms and Daphnia as well as standard floating food. Check the electric wiring and equipment and make sure that the stored pump is in working order — send it off for servicing if there is a problem. Remove any leaves from netting which may still cover the pond and clean up the bog garden. April is a good month for putting in Bog plants because next month will be a busy time — the start of the aquatic planting season.

As soon as the danger of a prolonged spell of icy weather has passed, remove the pool heater, clean and store away. This may be in April or May depending on where you live — reconnect the submersible pump for the fountain or waterfall. May is a time of peak activity — this is the best month for restocking your pond with plants which will provide a summer or autumn display. Overcrowded Water Lilies and other aquatics will need to be lifted and divided — it is usually required after 3–4 years and is a late spring or early summer job. This is a simple task if the plants are grown in baskets rather than in a layer of soil at the bottom or on the shelves of the pond — see page 94. Feeding established aquatic plants is another job which takes place in May and needs some care. Never sprinkle plant food in the water or on top of the baskets — it will feed the algae more than the plants. Use sachets or pellets of special aquatic plant fertilizer — push into each basket to below the gravel layer.

Remove any dead leaves and rotting organic matter with a rake and net. Do not panic if the water turns rather green and murky in spring — this is because the algae start into growth earlier than the plants which ensure good balance. If the water does not clear by early summer, read the recommendations on page 118.

The problem may be more serious than the temporary and unavoidable greening of the water which occurs every spring. The pond may turn black, oily and evil-smelling, indicating that vegetable and other organic matter has been allowed to rot in the water. If the problem is relatively mild, all you will have to do is carry out a partial water change as described in the Polluted Water paragraph on page 119. This is quite an undemanding job provided that you have a convenient place to serve as a soakaway for the removed water. But sometimes the pollution is too severe for such a simple solution — the pond has to be cleaned out as described on page 119. Hard work, but the result is a pond restored to tip-top condition.

SUMMER

The main job in summer is to enjoy your pond — standing and staring are just as important as the many active jobs you have to do in spring and autumn. There are the fish and wildlife to watch and the aquatic flowers to admire — the Irises in June, the Water Lilies at their best in July and the Lobelias in August. But also watch for the arrival of pests, as early action often saves a lot of time and trouble later on. Occasionally spray the leaves of Marginals with water from a hose pipe in order to knock off insects which will then serve as food for the fish.

Continue feeding the fish with floating food in flake or pellet form — remember that they appreciate an occasional change of diet. Once a day should be enough, sprinkled on the surface at noon or early afternoon — evening meals are hard to digest. Remove any uneaten food after about 5 minutes.

Do all the spring jobs you forgot to do before late summer arrives — plant aquatics, introduce new fish, clean out the pond if necessary. In hot and dry weather the water level can drop up to 2 in. in a week. Replace the loss regularly by trickling in water through a hose — don't wait until the level is low enough to lead to damage to the liner, fish and plants. Thundery weather poses its own problems for fish — you will see them gulping for air at the surface. To increase the oxygen and lower the carbon dioxide content of the water, turn on the fountain or spray the surface with droplets from a garden hose.

The established plants generally require little attention at this time of year, but over-vigorous Marginals may need trimming back. A job which is often neglected is the removal of faded flower-heads before they set seed. Failure to do this task with Marginals results in a reduction in the strength of the plant and the appearance of unwanted seedlings in the pond.

A common midsummer problem is blanket weed, sometimes appearing and spreading very quickly. Remove by winding round a stick and disposing of it well away from the water garden. This weed together with floating matter such as algae can block the pump strainer — clean out if a blockage occurs.

There is work to do in the bog garden during the summer months — weed regularly, cut back invasive growth and apply an organic mulch around the plants before the hot midsummer days arrive.

Tiny fish (fry) will appear if there are both males and females in the pond. Unfortunately motherly love is not a feature of the fish world and parents will happily gobble up their own brood. Some fry will survive, but if you want to breed fish it is necessary to place the fry in a small holding pool or large bucket filled with pond water until they are big enough to be safely returned to the pond.

AUTUMN

Far too many pond owners believe that once the Water Lilies have stopped blooming and the Marginals start to die down then the pond, like the rose bed, can be left to await a spring clean up. This is dangerously wrong — one of the major causes of pond deterioration is autumn neglect.

During September the Water Lilies will still be in flower and unless the weather turns abnormally cold you can continue planting. But with the arrival of October the planting season is over and there are a number of autumn jobs to be done. The prime task is the removal of as much unwanted organic matter as possible — leaving it to fall and rot in the pond will lead to serious pollution.

The first plant group to deal with are the Oxygenators — cut back these underwater plants early in the month. It is important to cut back the Marginals once the leaves and stems have turned brown, as fallen leaves would pollute the pond and overwintering stems would provide a haven for pests. Cut these stems down so that several inches remain above the water — this is especially important with hollow-stemmed plants. In a large pond the Water Lilies and Deep-water aquatics may be out of reach, but do remove faded flowers and dead leaves if you can. Floaters must be left to form their overwintering buds which sink to the bottom, but it is a good idea to keep some of these buds in a jar of water indoors. They will germinate early in the spring and if then returned to the pond will provide surface cover much more quickly than the buds left in the pond — an important factor in the fight against spring algae.

If deciduous trees are nearby it is essential to put a fine mesh net over the surface to prevent leaves falling into the water. The net must be secured around the edges to stop cats and stray dead leaves getting in, and it should only be removed when all the leaves have fallen from the trees. It is a good idea to leave it until the spring if herons are a problem.

The proper feeding of fish in early autumn is important as it is necessary to build up their reserves for winter — use a high-protein food. Some experts believe that in a small, heavily-stocked pond it is a good idea to make a partial water change (page 119) in early autumn every year.

A number of tasks must be carried out before the onset of frosty weather. Remove non-hardy aquatics such as Water Lettuce and Water Chestnut and leave them to overwinter indoors in water-filled containers — do the same with the Fancy Goldfish (page 96). Remove, clean and store the submersible pump and replace with a pool heater. Drain the surface pump if one is installed. If herons are a nuisance and a net is not fitted it is a good idea to put a few 4 in. drainpipes on the pond bottom to serve as a hideaway for fish.

CHAPTER 10

WATER GARDEN TROUBLES

In the garden, as in any complex living system, there is a whole host of things that can go wrong. In a bed or border there are two basic sites of trouble — there are the plant problems (pests, diseases, frost damage, water deficiency etc) and the soil problems (impeded drainage, poor structure, weed growth and so on). With the water garden the number of potential trouble spots is doubled to four — Structural defects, Water problems, Plant pests and diseases and Fish complaints.

This may seem like a fearsome prospect as keeping pests and diseases at bay in the bed and border can sometimes be a time-(and money-) consuming task. The idea of having to do double the amount of that work to keep a pond healthy may be a worrying thought if you are about to make a pond for the first time.

Fortunately, double the number of trouble sites compared to gardening in soil does not mean double the amount of trouble. It has been said many times that a pond poses fewer problems than caring for an allotment or fruit garden. There are two reasons for this:

● **The number of different troubles is limited** The range of pests and diseases which can attack flowers, fruit and vegetables is vast. In addition the effect of the worst of them can be devastating — we have all seen rows of plants defoliated by slugs or caterpillars. In the water environment there are few serious plant pests and even fewer diseases. With proper care fish pests and diseases are unlikely to be serious.

● **There are friends on your side** Fish, frogs, toads and newts devour a wide range of insects. An additional friend is the water itself — for the plants there are no watering problems, few root pests to worry about and no need for a hoe to keep down the weeds.

All this means that owning a pond does not involve spending a lot of time tackling problems. There is, however, a fundamental proviso — you will only avoid serious problems if you do the right things at the start and then carry out a routine care programme as outlined in this book. By following the six golden rules you will prevent most serious troubles before they start.

1 Build your pond properly Read Chapter 6. Don't make a concrete pond unless you have the necessary skill and equipment. Buy a Flexible liner with a minimum 20 year guarantee. Site the pond in a suitable spot.

2 Choose wisely Read Chapter 7 — make sure that the plants and fish are suitable for the location. Buy healthy stock — this is much more important when selecting fish than when choosing plants. A newly-introduced diseased fish can infect your whole collection.

3 Stock your pond correctly Read pages 67, 68, 69 and 95. Add fish and plants in the right numbers, in the right way and at the right time.

4 Carry out routine maintenance Read Chapter 9 — the heavy work is over once you have built your pond, but there are a number of essential tasks which have to be dealt with at regular intervals.

5 Inspect your stock regularly Keep watch for trouble and look up the cause in the following pages. Once you have put a name to the problem, act quickly — most pests and diseases can be checked if treated promptly, but may be impossible to control if left to get out of hand. But don't assume that every insect or fish blemish is an enemy — you are unlikely to see more than a few real enemies in your pond.

6 Use chemicals very sparingly Never spray aquatic plants unless there is a specific recommendation to do so, and make sure the product is safe to fish. Fish medicines and algicides should only be used after you have carefully studied the instructions and precautions.

WATER GARDEN TROUBLES

STRUCTURE	*page 117*
WATER	*pages 118–119*
PLANTS	*pages 120–121*
FISH	*pages 122–124*

WATER GARDEN TROUBLES — STRUCTURE

Don't assume your pond is cracked if the water level falls in summer — a drop of ½ in. a week is quite normal and in hot and dry weather the weekly fall may be more than 1 in. Just trickle in tap water to make up the loss — see page 114 or 118. Evaporation is not the only cause of a drop in water level in a sound pond — apart from leaks in the pond or waterfall there may be splashing from a fountain or waterfall on to the surrounding area, and water can be drawn out of the pond by Marginals or spreading Bog plants.

Leaks, however, can occur. If the water continues to fall in cool weather when the pump is switched off, then there is a hole or crack in the structure — causes vary from ice damage to the careless use of garden secateurs when cutting back unwanted growth below the surface. You will have to let the water level fall to the source of the problem before carrying out the necessary repair. If the crack or hole is near the bottom of the pond it will be necessary to empty it before you can begin — see page 119 for instructions.

● CONCRETE

Concrete ponds leak because the mix was wrong for the purpose, the foundations were insufficient or subsidence has disturbed the foundations. The first basic problem is the surface made porous by the use of a concrete mixture with too much or the wrong type of sand, or the presence of a large number of tiny cracks. The recommendation here is to thoroughly clean the surface and then paint it with a couple of coats of pond sealant, carefully following the instructions. This repair should last for a few years.

The second type of problem is a distinct crack which is ½ in. or more wide. Undercut the crack with a cold chisel and club hammer — the prepared crack should be wider below than at the surface. Remove all dust and fill with a waterproof mastic cement and then paint the affected area with a proprietary sealing paint. The problem with all concrete pond repairs is that water loss is likely to recur — it is usually better to fill large cracks with mortar and then install a Flexible liner (see page 59). Whichever method is used, read page 67 before restocking the pond.

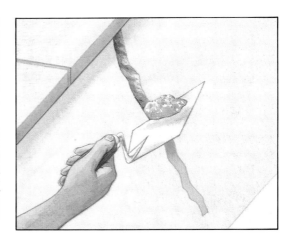

● RIGID LINER

You should never buy a Rigid liner made out of vacuum-formed polythene if you want a permanent feature. The surface tends to crack after a few years due to the effect of sunlight. Look for a liner with a guarantee of at least 20 years, but even here cracks will occur if you try to build a rockery on an unsupported edge. Cracks are not always easy to locate — try tapping the surface and listening for a different note. Repair kits are available.

● FLEXIBLE LINER

There is no point in trying to top up at frequent intervals if a leak has developed — the water will be constantly green and the surrounding soil will become very boggy. Locating a crack or hole is not always easy. Press the surface after emptying — an unusually soft spot generally indicates a hole or tear in the liner.

Flexible liners have a limited life span, but this varies from just a few years for cheap polythene to 50 years for top quality butyl sheeting. It is not worth trying to repair a cracked polythene-lined pond — remove it and replace with PVC or butyl sheeting.

If one of these better quality materials becomes torn or cracked, buy a repair kit from your garden centre or other supplier. Empty the pond to a level below the damaged area. Cut a piece of the repair sheet from the kit — it should be at least twice as long and wide as the tear or hole. Clean this patch and the area of the damage with methylated spirits and apply the waterproof adhesive to both the patch and the area around the tear. When the adhesive feels dry to the touch, press the patch over the damaged area and smooth it to drive out any air bubbles. Place a weight on the repair, as described in the kit instructions, and do not refill before the specified time. Follow the instructions on page 67 if restocking is necessary.

WATER GARDEN TROUBLES   WATER

Tap water is a satisfactory medium for the housing and breeding of pond fish provided you bear several points in mind. Our domestic water supply contains a disinfectant — this is generally chlorine and will disperse in a few days. For this reason it is necessary to wait several days before introducing fish to a large amount of fresh water. It is wise to check with your local water authority that chlorine is the agent used — there are other materials which take longer to disperse.

Water from the mains should be trickled in slowly through a hose pipe when topping up during a dry spell in summer. Adding a large amount suddenly to a small pond can result in an abrupt change in temperature and a harmful level of chlorine. Apart from this chlorine factor there is the pH factor — the acidity or alkalinity of the water. Fish can thrive over quite a large range, but occasionally the water can be too acid or too alkaline — see page 119.

The final point about water, whether from the tap or from rainfall, is that it becomes polluted in time and some form of treatment may be necessary. You may be able to avoid contamination from the surrounding soil and you may live in a clean air zone, but the fish waste and dead organisms lead to undesirable changes in the chemistry of the water. In a small, well-stocked pond you will occasionally have to do something about it, as noted on the next page.

● GREEN WATER

Green water is caused by the presence of a vast population of microscopic algae which float on or below the surface. These minute plants are not harmful to fish, but the water is rendered opaque, varying from a haze to 'pea soup'.

In any new pond the presence of these algae will be seen in a couple of weeks and if nothing is done about it matters will get steadily worse. If the surface is unprotected from sunlight and the water contains minerals and organic matter then the growth of algae will be greatly stimulated. The basic answer is to aim for 'balance' as described on page 111 — a set of conditions which inhibits the growth of the green water organisms. The surface area should be large enough (at least 40 sq.ft) and various plants are grown to shade the surface and to absorb the minerals from the water. In addition there are other jobs to do — remove dead leaves, avoid leaving uneaten fish food on the surface, etc.

Unfortunately defeating the green water problem is not always so straightforward and it may persist even though you have followed all the instructions laid down in the Question of Balance section on page 111. One of the major causes is the constant stirring up of the silt and waste products at the bottom of the pond by scavenging fish or by strong currents from an oversized pump.

For many gardeners it is not possible to satisfy all the conditions for a correct balance. The surface may be too small (less than 40 sq.ft) or the depth may be too shallow (less than 18 in. at the deepest part). Surface water carrying minerals and organic matter may run in from the surrounding land or paving, or there may be an absence or shortage of plants as in the Koi pond or free-standing fountain. Here it is necessary to adopt one or more anti-algal measures. There are several from which to make your choice, and their costs differ widely. You can place a bag of barley straw or pond peat at the bottom of the pond, but the benefit is usually limited. You can introduce Daphnia (Water Flea), but fish will eat them as quickly as they gobble up the algae. Chemical algicides are an obvious answer, and many different brands are available. The basic ones are toxic to algae but much less so to plants and fish — follow the instructions very carefully and do treat before the 'pea soup' stage. The effect is only temporary — you will have to repeat the treatment in 1–4 months. Another type of algicide is the flocculant which aggregates suspended material (algae, waste material etc) and deposits it on the bottom. The third type is often the most successful — a harmless dye which filters out the light which algae need for growth. None of these treatments provides a permanent solution — for that you will need a filter (see page 110).

WEEDS

There are several types of weeds which can spoil the appearance of the water, choke the plants and hide the fish from view. At the top of the list are the blanket weeds, also known as silkweed and thread algae. The long and silky green threads are attached to the sides and bottom of the pond, and may also appear as floating masses of tangled strands. Creating the conditions for a satisfactory balance (see page 111) will control these algae as well as the microscopic ones, but installing a filter will remove the free-floating algae and actually encourage the blanket weeds. Tackle the problem by removing as much as possible by means of a net and also by using a pond rake or forked stick. Twirl the rake or stick so that the blanket weed is wound on to it — dispose of the weed on the compost heap. An algicide recommended for the control of blanket weed can be used after this physical removal. A second group of troublesome weeds are the Floaters which may get out of hand — the Duckweeds (Lemna species) can invade the pond and cover the surface with their tiny green leaves. Remove as much as possible with a net before the problem becomes serious. The third group of weeds are invasive Marginals which are planted in soil on the marginal shelf. Cut back vigorously if growth starts to swamp more delicate plants.

POLLUTED WATER

Polluted water may or may not be discoloured or smelly — the key feature is that it is harmful in some way to plants and/or fish. There are several forms of pollution. An oily film may develop on the surface due to the decomposition of Water Lily and Deep-water aquatic foliage — this can cut down the oxygenation of the water and should be removed by pulling a sheet of newspaper over the surface. Black water indicates decomposition of fallen leaves or dead fish — if the problem is severe you will have to drain, clean and refill the pond. This drastic treatment will also be necessary if the pollutant is paint, weedkiller or other harmful chemical. The final type of pollutant occurs in small ponds which are well-stocked with fish. After a few years the waste products from the fish, old fish food, dead organisms etc produce water which can be moderately toxic. A partial water change in spring or early autumn is the answer — pump out a quarter of the water from the pond and then trickle in tap water very slowly until the original level is reached.

DIRTY WATER

Brown muddy water is harmless to both fish and plants, but it is unsightly. There are two major causes — scavenging fish may stir up soil from planting baskets on the bottom of the pond, or a powerful pump may create strong currents which drag sediment up to the surface. Obviously prevention is better than cure — always line planting baskets with hessian or buy soil-proof ones, cover the soil surface with gravel and site the pump so that water disturbance below the surface is reduced. You can temporarily relieve the problem by using a flocculating chemical which takes the muddy suspension to the bottom of the pond — this silt layer should be removed by a pond vacuum or some other means. Unfortunately the problem will return if you fail to cure the basic cause.

ACID & ALKALINE WATER

You can buy a simple kit to test the pH (acidity or alkalinity) of the water. There is no problem if the reading is between 6.5 and 8.5 — water outside this range means that both fish and plants are suffering. A pH of 9.0 or above indicates that it is too alkaline — water running into the pond from concrete or reconstituted stone paving is a common cause. Seal all concrete surfaces with pond paint, remove as much algae as you can and add a pH buffering agent which you can buy from your aquatics supplier. Acid water (pH 6.0 or below) is much less frequent — the usual cause is water running into the pond from nearby peaty land. A partial water change will help, and so will adding some limestone or a pH buffering agent.

Cleaning out the Pond

It may be necessary to clear out the pond because it is leaking, a deep layer of silt has accumulated at the bottom or the water has become polluted. Choose a mild day in late spring or summer. Remove the Marginal plants first and then the Deep-water aquatics. Store in a temporary pool if possible — otherwise keep constantly wet by hosing down frequently. Make a temporary pool out of plastic or butyl sheeting in a shaded spot — fill with pond water and have separate holding pools for the fish and the plants. Remove Floaters and Oxygenators and keep in water-filled plastic containers. Begin to pump out the water — when shallow enough net the fish and place in the temporary pool. Check that fish are healthy and cover the pool with fine netting.

Complete draining the pond and remove the silt layer at the bottom. Scrub the walls, taking care not to damage the surface. Refill the pond, using tap water and some retained pond water if it is not polluted. Return the plants after dividing them and cleaning the baskets as necessary, add pool conditioner to the water and finally gently transfer the fish back to the pond.

WATER GARDEN TROUBLES   PLANTS

Aquatic plants are less likely to be attacked by pests and diseases than those growing outside the pond. This is fortunate because chemical sprays should not be used — the effect on fish, beneficial insects and other forms of wildlife can be disastrous. The basic control technique is to remove the affected leaf or the whole plant, depending on the danger posed by the pest or disease. This should be done promptly before the problem gets out of hand. For some pests the leaves should be sprayed with a forceful jet of water in order to wash the insects into the pond and into the mouths of grateful fish. Another technique is to put a piece of sacking over the foliage so that it is weighed down until the insects are drowned.

One common complaint involves neither pest nor disease — it is purely cultural and is the failure of Water Lilies to flower properly. There are a number of causes of poor or absent flowers — the plant may not have reached flowering size or it may have been planted incorrectly (see page 94). With a mature plant it may be at the wrong depth or it may have been moved too quickly into deep water. Shade can be a problem and so can water currents or the droplets from a fountain. If the plant had bloomed well in previous years then it may need feeding (use special fertilizer pellets or sachets pushed into the soil in the planting basket) or it may require dividing and repotting. See the section on Propagation (page 94).

● BLOODWORM

The bloodworm is the larva of one of the non-biting midges and you will find it in most ponds with an earth floor. The red colour is due to haemoglobin, which allows it to take in oxygen without coming to the surface. In its muddy home it builds a tubular shelter of soil, sand and bits of organic matter. The bloodworm is about 1 in. long and occasionally leaves its home to attack damaged roots of Water Lilies or other aquatics. No control measures are needed — these larvae are readily eaten by fish and so never reach epidemic proportions in a well-stocked pond.

● CADDIS FLY

A similar pest in some ways to the bloodworm, but a much more dangerous one. It is the larva ('stick grub') of a moth-like insect and it builds a tubular shelter of grit, plant fragments etc at the bottom of the pond. When seeking material to construct this protective home it attacks roots, leaves and flower buds of aquatic plants, and when installed in its shelter any plant within reach will be bitten. No control measures are needed — in a well-stocked pond they are readily gobbled up by the fish.

● CHINA MARK MOTH

The china mark moth and brown china mark moth lay their eggs in late summer on Water Lily pads and the leaves of other aquatics. The 1 in. long creamy caterpillars which emerge are brown-headed and bear a brown line along their backs, and have an interesting life style. Oval pieces are bitten out of the leaf and two of these segments are spun together with silk to form a shelter. The caterpillar lives inside and then forms its cocoon in late autumn. It is not usually a serious pest, but these floating leaf cases should be removed and destroyed as the caterpillars inside actively eat foliage throughout the autumn months.

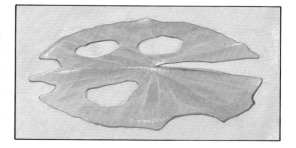

● IRIS SAWFLY

The iris sawfly is a blue-grey grub about ¾ in. long which feeds only on wild and garden Irises. The damage it causes is quite characteristic — during the summer months it eats the edges of the leaves, producing a ragged or saw-toothed effect. A second brood may appear in autumn. Destroy any grubs found on your Irises and remove damaged leaves.

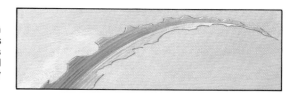

● LEAF-MINING MIDGE

Not a common pest, but it can be very destructive if a severe attack does occur. Eggs are laid on the leaves of a wide range of aquatic plants, including Water Lilies. These eggs hatch and produce small, thin larvae. Unlike the large grubs of the china mark moth and iris sawfly, these larvae are transparent and almost invisible. On soft-leaved plants these insects tunnel into the foliage and rapidly devour the tissue between the veins. The result is that the leaves are partly or wholly skeletonised — it is easy to recognise an attack by the leaf-mining midge. Pick off affected foliage — leave it to the fish to eat the larvae on plants you cannot reach.

● SNAILS

Many types of snails occur in ponds — they are often brought in on the underside of the leaves of newly-purchased aquatic plants. They can be beneficial — they eat both algae and fish waste, but this cleansing activity is often overrated. On the other hand their plant-eating activity is also overrated. Their main plant diet is dead and dying tissues and they will rarely attack a healthy mature leaf. So leave them alone unless they are present in large numbers and young spring growth is being attacked. Reduce the population by floating a cabbage stalk on the surface in the evening and removing it with its cluster of snails in the morning. Never use slug pellets to kill pond snails.

● WATER LILY APHID

This looks like the blackfly which infest Broad Beans and other plants in the vegetable garden. During a hot, dry spell in the summer the leaves, stems and flowers buds may be covered with these aphids — growth is weakened and both flower and foliage may be distorted. In autumn these insects leave the pond and fly to their secondary host — shrubs and trees belonging to the Prunus family where they lay their eggs. Obviously a nearby Plum or Blackthorn makes an attack by water lily aphid more likely, and planting a Weeping Cherry at the pondside is simply asking for trouble. Control this pest by spraying the leaves with water — the dislodged aphids are soon eaten by the fish.

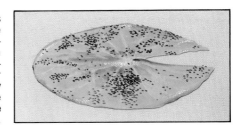

● WATER LILY BEETLE

This can be one of the most destructive of all the pests which attack Water Lilies, but fortunately it prefers large stretches of water rather than garden ponds. The small brown beetle lays its eggs in early summer on the upper surface of the leaves and soon the yellow-bellied black grubs emerge. The leaves are mined and holes appear — eventually the leaf shrivels and rots. The basic treatment is to remove badly affected leaves and to hose down the remaining foliage — you may have to repeat this treatment several times as three or four broods can occur in the season. You should also cut down the dead stalks of Marginals in autumn as this is where the water lily beetle hibernates.

● WATER LILY CROWN ROT

Diseases do not often seriously damage aquatic plants, but this one can be a serious problem. It is related to potato blight and can be just as deadly. The leaves turn yellow and break away from the crown, which eventually becomes black and evil-smelling. There is no cure, so remove and destroy an infected Water Lily immediately. Hopefully the other plants will not have been infected — if the disease is widespread you will have to empty the pond, clean thoroughly and restock with new Water Lilies. Try to stop trouble before it starts — always inspect Water Lily rhizomes carefully before planting and reject any which have a black and soft area.

● WATER LILY LEAF SPOT

This is an occasional problem which affects Water Lily pads — it is most likely to strike during a prolonged spell of warm, damp weather. Spots appear on both the upper and lower surfaces of the leaf — they are usually close to the edge and at first each spot is made up of concentric rings, but these merge and enlarge to form irregular patches. The original red colouration changes to black and the infected patches rot and holes appear. There is little you can do apart from removing diseased leaves immediately so that nearby plants will not be infected.

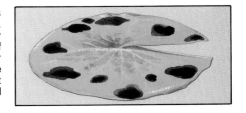

WATER GARDEN TROUBLES — FISH

Fish, like other pets, can be afflicted by a host of problems. A list of potential troubles and ailments makes depressing reading, and so it is useful to begin with two assurances. Most diseases and attacks by parasites only occur when a fish has been injured in some way or is under stress due to unfavourable conditions in the pond. Secondly, you are unlikely to encounter more than just a few of the problems listed in this section.

So as long as you follow the basic rules of fish care there is no point in being unduly worried about the well-being of your fish. Begin by making sure that the fish you buy are healthy — choose a reputable supplier, inspect them carefully, ask advice if necessary and keep them in quarantine for a little while if in doubt. Next, make sure that the environment you have created for them in your pond is satisfactory — simply follow the instructions in this book.

Keep watch for unusual behaviour as you would with any pet. The danger sign is either sluggishness when other fish are active or increased activity. This includes sudden darting to the surface, frenzied swimming to and fro plus rubbing against the side of the pond. There may be a problem, and fish problems are of three types. There may be internal or external parasites or disease on the body of the fish, there may be injury from pests within the pond or there may be injury from pests (cats, birds etc) from outside the pond.

If a problem is suspected it may be necessary to lift the fish into a holding tank (see Inspecting Fish on page 123) for closer scrutiny. Remedial action may be necessary — these days all sorts of chemicals and medicines are available, but do make sure that anything you use is right for the problem and also right for the fish involved. Follow the instructions carefully — the recommended use may be 'topical' (treating the affected area on the fish), 'in-tank' (keeping the fish for the prescribed time in an aquarium or other container filled with the diluted chemical) or 'in-pond' (adding the chemical to the water in the pond). Unfortunately not everything can be cured, and there may be a time when a badly diseased or injured fish has to be destroyed. Not a pleasant job, so do it as humanely as possible by following the technique on page 124.

● ANCHOR WORM

This skin parasite is one of the causes of obvious distress with the fish swimming rapidly round in circles. When the scales are examined a raised bump can be seen — the site of the embedded barbed head of this pest. From this affected area hangs the body of the worm — about ½ in. long, greyish-white and tubular. At the end of the worm there are usually a couple of egg-sacs. Proprietary remedies are available, but the standard treatment is to touch the worm with a paint brush which has been dipped in paraffin. Pull out the parasite with tweezers and dab the wound with a fish antiseptic.

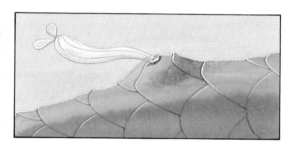

● BIRDS & CATS

Cats often sit at the pondside and stare at the fish below. It is therefore not surprising that they are often blamed for the disappearance of Goldfish, Rudd etc but they are not usually the culprits. A cat does not like water, and a healthy fish can easily avoid its probing paw. It seems that only sluggish and sickly fish get caught.

Birds are a bigger problem. The gull may take a fish or two from a pond and the attractive kingfisher will dive for small fish, but it is the heron which is the chief pond robber. A tall bird about 3 ft high — it stands motionless in shallow water and then with a rapid thrust of the head catches its prey. You may never see this as the heron hunts at daybreak. Netting is one answer, but a less unsightly one is to insert a series of 6 in. high canes around the edge of the pond. Join the tops with fishing line or strong thread. The heron is a wader and will not step over this obstruction.

● DEAD FISH

When a number of dead fish appears on the surface, the most likely cause is a serious fault in the environment — see Environmental Problems on the next page. A single dead fish may be due to an attack by a pond insect or a fatal parasite or disease which can be seen on its body. But deaths do occur when there is nothing wrong with the environment and no external blemishes are present — death may be due to old age or internal problems such as cancer or fish tuberculosis.

DROPSY

An uncommon problem, but a very serious one. The body of the fish becomes bloated and the eyes protrude, but the most distinctive symptom is that the scales are raised to give the 'pine cone' effect associated with this disease. The experts cannot decide just what causes dropsy — there may well be several forms and it is known that one type of dropsy is caused by bacteria. You will sometimes see dropsy cures listed in the catalogues and the condition sometimes corrects itself, but the best course of action is to kill the fish humanely.

ENVIRONMENTAL PROBLEMS

Healthy fish have a protective mucous film on the surface of their bodies, but this immune system breaks down if there is something wrong with the environment. The fish is then susceptible to attack by a disease or surface parasite — in addition the environmental defect may directly harm the fish. **Alkaline water** (page 119) is a good example — if there is just a little lime in the water then some of the mucous coat is removed, but if the water is extremely alkaline then the fish are killed. **Chlorine** is another environmental problem — putting fish in fresh tap water will render them sluggish and the gills will be bleached. **Oxygen shortage** can be a serious problem, especially at night in hot summer weather or during a thunderstorm. The fish come to the surface to gasp for air — the problem is poisoning by excess carbon dioxide in the water and not just oxygen shortage. The answer is to turn on the fountain or waterfall if present — if not spray the surface with a hose and stir the water with a stick. Other environmental problems are a **sudden temperature change** (never move fish from cold to tepid water or vice versa) and **ice** (never leave an unbroken ice film to cover the surface for a long period). The worst environmental problem is **pollution** (see page 119). Overfeeding and overstocking can lead to mildly toxic water which needs a partial water change. But weedkiller leaking into the pond or the presence of poisonous leaves calls for a complete water change as described on page 119.

Inspecting Fish

For many of the problems listed in this section it is necessary to remove the fish from the pond for close inspection and treatment. Use a fish net sold for this purpose — place a little food in one corner of the pond and gently slip the net into the water. Slide it slowly across until you are close to the fish and then quickly raise the net. Place it in a holding tank containing water from the pond — make sure there is little or no difference in temperature. It is essential that your hands are wet before handling a fish — any dry surface will remove the protective mucous layer.

FIN ROT

The soft tissue between the bony rays of the caudal fin (tail) is destroyed by this bacterial disease — it is progressive and death results if it is allowed to reach the flesh of the fish. It can be readily cured if treated promptly — cut away the frayed area of the tail and place the fish in a recommended bactericide solution. The fin will grow again once the infection has been cleared.

FISH LEECH

This 1 in. long worm-like parasite attaches itself to the side of a fish by means of suckers. It draws blood from its host and then leaves, hiding amongst the pond vegetation to digest its fill before seeking another host. The wound caused on the body of the fish is likely to become infected if untreated. Fish leech is an uncommon pest which can be controlled in the same way as anchor worm.

FISH LOUSE

An unpleasant parasite which causes a great deal of distress to the fish which will rub itself against the sides of the pond and will swim in a rapid and erratic manner. The louse is a ¼ in. wide jelly-like disc which uses two suckers to attach itself to the body of the fish, usually close to the base of a fin. It pierces the skin and draws blood from its host. Dislodge it by dabbing with paraffin using a small paint brush — treat the affected area with a fish antiseptic. Alternatively use an in-tank treatment with an organophosphate product.

FROG

The frog is included here for interest rather than as a warning, as it is extremely unlikely that this amphibian will ever cause any harm in your pond. But during the breeding season a male frog will cling very tightly to anything which moves, and very occasionally a fish is damaged or even killed by having its head tightly clasped by the legs of a well-meaning but over-amorous frog.

● FUNGUS

This is the commonest disease of pond fish. The spores of Achyla and Saprolegnia are in the water of your pond, but will not attack the fish if the protective mucus layer on the surface is intact and the immune system of the fish is working. This immunity breaks down when the skin has been damaged or the fish is under stress due to rapid temperature change, spawning, etc. Fungus is easily recognised as cotton-wool like growths anywhere on the fish. If caught early it is quite easy to treat — you will find several fungicides on the shelves of your aquatic supplier for an in-tank treatment.

● GILL FLUKE

You will not be able to see the cause of this complaint as it is a microscopic flatworm which attaches itself to the gills of the fish. You will have to look for the symptoms — the fins twitch constantly and the gills flap in an abnormal manner. This pest is often ignored, but it can be fatal and some experts believe that it is much more widespread than generally supposed. Anti-fluke products are available — it will be necessary to treat the pond as well as the affected fish.

● MOUTH FUNGUS

The name is deceptive as this disease is caused by a bacterium and not a fungus. White growths appear on the jaws and tissue decay occurs. Pollution is the usual reason for the breakdown of the immune system of the affected fish — consider a partial water change. In-tank treatment with a bactericide should check the problem if it has not gone too far.

● POND INSECTS

The predatory insects below the surface are the hidden villains of the water garden — eggs, fry and small fish are damaged and larger fish are wounded. The nymph (larva) of the attractive and harmless **dragonfly** is an example. For a few years this 2 in. long insect lies on the pond bottom or clings to underwater plant stems, occasionally stalking its prey which it catches in its pincer-like jaws. The **great diving beetle** is an even worse menace, as both the 1½ in. long adult beetle and its larvae attack fish as well as other pond fauna. Other insect predators include the **water boatman** or **backswimmer** which is easily recognised by its oar-like legs, the **water scorpion**, which sucks its victim dry and is recognised by its rear-mounted 'snorkel' and the underwater larva of the surface-swimming **whirligig beetle**. There is little you can do to control these pests other than trawling a pond net through the water and disposing of any predators you find.

● PROTOZOAN SKIN PARASITE

Fish affected by these microscopic parasites are in obvious distress. They will be seen rubbing themselves against the side of the pond and their bodies are covered with a blue-grey slimy coating. A badly infected fish will have to be destroyed, so treat this problem as soon as it is seen, using a proprietary pond salt product.

● ULCER

This disease is caused by the entry of bacteria (Aeromonas species) into an area where the skin is broken. The infection causes swelling and then a large open lesion. Some proprietary remedies are available, but there is generally little you can do for a badly ulcerated fish other than humanely dispose of it. For valuable specimens your local vet can prescribe an antibiotic treatment.

● WHITE SPOT

Next to fungus, white spot ('ich') is the commonest disease of pond fish. The symptom you are most likely to see is the unusual frenzy and awkwardness of the fish when swimming. On closer inspection you will find numerous white spots like grains of salt on the surface — do not confuse these with the white spots which appear on the gills of male fish in the mating season. Treat white spot promptly — there are several products which will cure it if used at the early stages, but a badly infected fish may be incurable. To rid a pond of the causative organism no chemical treatment is necessary — simply move the fish for a couple of weeks into a holding pool.

Killing Fish

There will come a time when a badly diseased or injured fish has to be put out of its misery. There is no point in trying to be gentle about this — the most humane way of killing a fish is to throw it vigorously on to a stone path. You will find this less distasteful if you first wrap it in a piece of dry cloth.

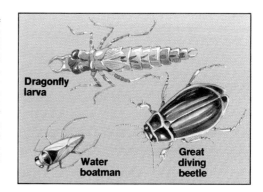

Dragonfly larva

Water boatman

Great diving beetle

CHAPTER 11

PLANT INDEX

Acknowledgements

The author wishes to acknowledge the painstaking work of Gill Jackson, Paul Norris, Linda Fensom, Angelina Gibbs and Constance Barry. Grateful acknowledgement is also made for the help or photographs received from Anglo Aquarium Plant Co Ltd, Pat Brindley, Carleton Photographic, C G Edwards (Goffs Oak) Ltd, Harry Smith Horticultural Photographic Collection, Joan Hessayon, Her Grace The Duchess of Devonshire, Heather Angel, Lotus Water Garden Products Ltd, Michael Warren, Stapeley Water Gardens Ltd, Wildwoods Water Gardens Ltd, John Glover/The Garden Picture Library, Steven Wooster/The Garden Picture Library and Ron Sutherland/The Garden Picture Library.

John Woodbridge provided both artistry and design work. The artists who contributed were John Dye, Evelyn Binns, Deborah Mansfield, Roger Shipp and Debra Woodward.